THE PHILOSOPHY OF STANLEY KUBRICK

The Philosophy of Popular Culture

The books published in the Philosophy of Popular Culture series will illuminate and explore philosophical themes and ideas that occur in popular culture. The goal of this series is to demonstrate how philosophical inquiry has been reinvigorated by increased scholarly interest in the intersection of popular culture and philosophy, as well as to explore through philosophical analysis beloved modes of entertainment, such as movies, TV shows, and music. Philosophical concepts will be made accessible to the general reader through examples in popular culture. This series seeks to publish both established and emerging scholars who will engage a major area of popular culture for philosophical interpretation and examine the philosophical underpinnings of its themes. Eschewing ephemeral trends of philosophical and cultural theory, authors will establish and elaborate on connections between traditional philosophical ideas from important thinkers and the ever-expanding world of popular culture.

Series Editor

Mark T. Conard, Marymount Manhattan College, NY

Books in the Series

The Philosophy of Stanley Kubrick, edited by Jerold J. Abrams
The Philosophy of Martin Scorsese, edited by Mark T. Conard
The Philosophy of Neo-Noir, edited by Mark T. Conard
Basketball and Philosophy, edited by Jerry L. Walls and Gregory Bassham

THE PHILOSOPHY OF
STANLEY KUBRICK

Edited by Jerold J. Abrams

THE UNIVERSITY PRESS OF KENTUCKY

Publication of this volume was made possible in part by a grant
from the National Endowment for the Humanities.

Scholarly publisher for the Commonwealth,
serving Bellarmine University, Berea College, Centre College of Kentucky, Eastern
Kentucky University, The Filson Historical Society, Georgetown College, Kentucky
Historical Society, Kentucky State University, Morehead State University, Murray State
University, Northern Kentucky University, Transylvania University, University
of Kentucky, University of Louisville, and Western Kentucky University.
All rights reserved.

Editorial and Sales Offices: The University Press of Kentucky
663 South Limestone Street, Lexington, Kentucky 40508-4008
www.kentuckypress.com

11 10 09 08 07   5 4 3 2 1

Library of Congress Cataloging-in-Publication Data

The philosophy of Stanley Kubrick / edited by Jerold J. Abrams.
    p. cm. — (The philosophy of popular culture)
    Includes bibliographical references and index.
    ISBN 978-0-8131-2445-2 (hardcover : alk. paper)
    1. Kubrick, Stanley—Criticism and interpretation. I. Abrams, Jerold J., 1971-
PN1998.3.K83P55 2007
791.4302'33092—dc22   2007003153

This book is printed on acid-free recycled paper meeting
the requirements of the American National Standard
for Permanence in Paper for Printed Library Materials.

Manufactured in the United States of America.

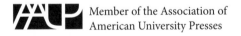 Member of the Association of
American University Presses

Man stands face to face with the irrational. He feels within him his longing for happiness and for reason. The absurd is born of this confrontation between the human need and the unreasonable silence of the world.

—Albert Camus,
The Myth of Sisyphus and Other Essays

Contents

Part Five: The Subject of the Future

Acknowledgments

First, I would like to thank all the contributors for their hard work and excellent essays. I would like to give special thanks to Mark Conard for his incredible editorial support and his continued philosophical dialogue. For editorial guidance and wisdom at every stage of the process, I am grateful to Steve Wrinn and Anne Dean Watkins at the University Press of Kentucky. Ron Mandelbaum at Photofest provided an excellent cover shot of Kubrick. Christopher Erisson provided valuable technical support. ElusiveDVD.com cleaned up and made available Kubrick's once-lost first film *Fear and Desire*. I am also extremely grateful to Elizabeth F. Cooke and Chris Pliatska for many rich conversations on Kubrick, cinema, and philosophy in general.

INTRODUCTION

Stanley Kubrick is one of the greatest American film directors. He is the undisputed master of the tracking shot, the reverse zoom, and the painting technique. Kubrick's images are indelibly imprinted on the pop-cultural unconscious: the creepy mannequin warehouse of *Killer's Kiss;* the stash of money blown all over the airstrip in *The Killing;* Kirk Douglas crucified in *Spartacus;* pedophile Humbert Humbert painting a little girl's toes in *Lolita;* the "cowboy" pilot joyously riding the atom bomb as it falls through the sky at the end of *Dr. Strangelove;* the ape throwing a femur into the sky at the beginning of *2001: A Space Odyssey;* Alex and droogs drinking Milk Plus at the Korova Milk Bar, preparing for a night of "ultra-violence," in *A Clockwork Orange;* Barry Lyndon bravely standing off in a pistol duel; Jack Nicholson's famous "Heeeeeere's Johnny" in *The Shining;* Sergeant Hartman's cruel training of the "maggots" in *Full Metal Jacket;* and the haunting orgy in *Eyes Wide Shut.*

Looking back on this remarkable filmography, it is clear that it has the distinctly architectonic quality of any great philosophical system: it says something about everything. All the facets of human nature are revealed in their wide-ranging diversity: high and low culture, love and sex, history, war, crime, madness, space travel, social conditioning, and technology. Yet, as internally diverse as Kubrick's filmography is, taken as a whole, it is also quite coherent. It takes all the differentiated sides of reality and unifies them into one rich, complex philosophical vision that happens to be very close to existentialism. Existentialism emerged with the works of Søren Kierkegaard, who rejected the nineteenth-century view of the world as a massive mechanical system working out its own logic through history. According to Kierkegaard, this view failed to do justice to the most basic fact about human nature: that each person is ultimately alone and free, and philosophical truth has meaning only if it is *chosen* by the individual. This philosophical movement underwent several variations throughout the nineteenth and twentieth centuries. One can find versions of it in the works of Friedrich

Nietzsche, Martin Heidegger, Albert Camus, Jean-Paul Sartre, and Simone de Beauvoir, though not all would accept the label *existentialist*.

These philosophies, perhaps more than any other philosophical world-view, have succeeded in making their way out of the ivory tower and seeping into popular culture at large. And certainly they had a great effect on Kubrick, who created his own unique brand of cinematic existentialism, while synthesizing it with elements of Stoicism and pragmatism as well (as several of the essays show). In virtually all of Kubrick's films, in one form or another, one finds the subject (the self) existing in opposition to a hard and uncaring external world, whether the natural world or a world of man-made institutions. For this reason, it should come as no surprise that many of the essays in this volume deal directly with some aspect of this existentialist worldview in Kubrick's work.

Kubrick made four war films in all: *Fear and Desire, Paths of Glory, Dr. Strangelove,* and *Full Metal Jacket.* Part 1 of the volume, "The Subject at War," explores this obsession in three essays. In "Understanding the Enemy: The Dialogue of Fear in *Fear and Desire* and *Dr. Strangelove*," Elizabeth F. Cooke discusses the existential themes in Kubrick's first feature-length film and his 1964 cold war comedy-tragedy. This marks a significant contribution to the Kubrick literature, because *Fear and Desire* has rarely been seen. Kubrick was unhappy with the finished product and never had it copyrighted, but recently this film was discovered and rereleased by ElusiveDVD.com. Cooke analyzes this early work in relation to *Dr. Strangelove* and examines Kubrick's unique philosophy of war. Specifically, Cooke focuses on how humans deal with their worst fears when facing the absurdity (in Camus' sense) of war. *Fear and Desire* approaches this theme through isolated individuals and their various monologues; in contrast, *Dr. Strangelove* handles it through constant and ridiculous dialogue between individuals trapped in insane institutions. But, according to Cooke, the war in *Fear and Desire* is not tragic, because each soldier faces his fears as an individual and chooses his fate, whereas in *Dr. Strangelove,* the loss of the existentially conscious individual leads irrevocably to disaster.

In "Chaos, Order, and Morality: Nietzsche's Influence on *Full Metal Jacket*," Mark T. Conard argues that Kubrick's last war film is a Nietzschean study of the world of physical and moral flux. Nothing stays, everything continually changes, and attempting to impose order can be dangerous. But this is precisely what marine boot camp at Parris Island aims to do, under the guidance of Sergeant Hartman. The new recruits receive the same haircut, the same uniform, the same rifle; they stand in rows, walk in lines, shout identically on command—everything is leveled and ordered. This new moral code, however, stands in opposition to the basic flux of the world, which manifests itself in the form of the massive beating of Private Pyle—and then in Pyle's tragic suicide.

Jason Holt, in "Existential Ethics: Where the Paths of Glory Lead," discusses Kubrick's early war film, *Paths of Glory*, as a cinematic analysis of existentialist ethics. According to Heidegger, each of us is "thrown" into the world; we find ourselves thrust into being and immediately facing death, as "beings-toward-death." In war, this is especially salient, and in *Paths of Glory*, the soldiers feel this experience deeply. For the existentialist, there is no moral blueprint or set of rules to guide us in this "thrownness." All we have is our freedom in the face of death, which is also what defines us. And we can respond to that freedom in one of two ways, each of which is depicted in *Paths of Glory*. We can accept our freedom in the face of death and live "authentically" (the existentialist virtue, as Holt calls it), or we can live "inauthentically" by denying that freedom and who we truly are.

Part 2, "The Subject in Love," is devoted to Kubrick's three love stories: *Killer's Kiss, Lolita,* and *Eyes Wide Shut.* In the first essay in this part, "Where the Rainbow Ends: *Eyes Wide Shut,*" Karen D. Hoffman discusses Kubrick's last film. Typically, Kubrick is considered to be a rather dark filmmaker, and most of the pieces in this volume subscribe to that view as well. But Hoffman argues persuasively that *Eyes Wide Shut* holds out a glimmer of hope for love, for sex, and for marriage. In her view, Bill and Alice Harford's marriage reaches a turning point when each realizes that the Kantian moral principle embodied in marriage may never be sufficient to control one's deepest sexual urges. Sexuality is darker and less controllable than we typically care to admit, let alone seek to understand. But Kubrick's hopeful message is that a penetrating examination of this darkness and of our animal sexual natures can lead to a richer and more comprehensive understanding of sex, love, and marriage.

In "Knockout! *Killer's Kiss,* the Somatic, and Kubrick," Kevin S. Decker takes up the philosophical theme of the body in Kubrick's early film about boxing, crime, and romance. Decker reconstructs the history of the body in philosophy, beginning with the ancient Greek philosophers Socrates and Plato, who relegated it to second-class status. Since then, Decker shows that a gradual movement has taken place to recover the all-too-often dismissed philosophy of the body. This shift took place largely in the late nineteenth and twentieth centuries, especially with the work of philosophers such as Maurice Merleau-Ponty, the American pragmatists, Michel Foucault, and Richard Shusterman. All these thinkers placed the somatic form front and center, precisely where it belongs, and Decker persuasively includes Kubrick among this new class of thinkers. *A Clockwork Orange, 2001: A Space Odyssey, Eyes Wide Shut,* and especially *Killer's Kiss* raise rich questions about the importance of the contingent, spatial, somatic form for the thinking subject.

In "The Logic of *Lolita:* Kubrick, Nabokov, and Poe," I discuss the philosophy of detective work in Kubrick's film adaptation of Vladimir Nabokov's novel *Lolita* (Nabokov also wrote the screenplay). The detective Humbert Humbert is modeled on Edgar Allan Poe's master sleuth C. Auguste Dupin in "The Murders in the Rue Morgue." Dupin solves crimes by tapping into two parts of his mad mind: one part is obsessively focused, and the other is creative and hallucinatory. In *Lolita,* however, Humbert is given only one of these sides—namely, obsession. The other side is personified in Humbert's doppelganger, Clare Quilty. By drawing on philosopher Charles S. Peirce's logic of abduction and Umberto Eco's further advances in that logic, I detail why Humbert's obsession—and lack of creativity—causes him to be such a remarkable failure as a detective.

Part 3 turns to "The Subject and the Meaning of Life," with two essays on Kubrick's view of the meaningfulness—and meaninglessness—of life. In "Rebel without a Cause: Kubrick and the Banality of the Good," Patrick Murray and Jeanne Schuler provide a rich analysis of Kubrick's oeuvre, finding in it a unified philosophy characterized by skepticism, irony, existentialism, and the unfettered pursuit of pleasure. Kubrick's fundamental vision is found, in some form, in virtually every film he made: Each individual is fated to die alone, without any basic sense of meaning in a cold and heartless world. No great answers are forthcoming, and there is no good reason to hope. The best one can do is to add one's own meaning to an empty world, always maintaining an ironic stance about the status of that meaning. According to Murray and Schuler, however, this view is an essentially false philosophy because it dogmatically asserts a fatefully limited view of the human creature as purely subjectivistic and atomistic—never plumbing our deeper ontologically intersubjective nature.

In "The Big Score: Fate, Morality, and Meaningful Life in *The Killing,*" Steven M. Sanders reveals the Stoic philosophy at the center of Kubrick's early noir. The Stoic philosophy, which emerged in the ancient world, is a practice-oriented and individualistic view of the world whereby on the difficulties of life and does what one can to live virtuously. The character of Johnny Clay in *The Killing* is, in many ways, a Stoic who accepts his fate in a harsh world. But ultimately, according to Sanders, the heist at the center of the film's plot does not sufficiently capture the idea of fate, which determines Clay's failure. Sanders provides a philosophical account of the inadequacies of those aspects of plot and character in *The Killing* that turn on the notions of fate, morality, and meaningful life.

Part 4, "The Subject in History," is devoted to three of Kubrick's films: *Spartacus, Barry Lyndon,* and *The Shining.* Gordon Braden's essay, "*Spartacus* and the Second Part of the Soul," discusses the Greek idea of the divided soul. In the *Republic,* Plato divided the soul into three parts: the appetitive, represented by the craft class; the spirited, represented by the military class; and the rational, represented by the ruling class (ideally, philosophers). Braden examines the film *Spartacus* as a struggle within the second part of the soul. This part is unruly, violent, and angry; it is also the part that most wants justice and recognition—precisely what the ancient Roman slaves seek. Of course, Spartacus is crucified in the end, but Crassus knows that the battle is not over. The movement of the second part of the soul has only just begun.

In "The Shape of Man: The Absurd and *Barry Lyndon,*" Chris Pliatska discusses the philosophical theme of the absurd, drawing primarily on the work of contemporary philosopher Thomas Nagel. In the film, Barry Lyndon faces the absurd in the form of eighteenth-century upper-class rituals, which ultimately destroy him. This essay is unique in that, rather than finding the absurd in the characters or the plot of the story, Pliatska focuses on how Kubrick generates the theme of absurdity through cinematic techniques. Of particular interest here are Kubrick's use of the unidentified narrator, the regular use of the reverse zoom, and what Pliatska refers to (following Robert Kolker) as Kubrick's "painterly aesthetic."

In "*The Shining* and Anti-Nostalgia: Postmodern Notions of History," R. Barton Palmer highlights the richness of the time dimension in Kubrick's only horror film, providing a unique perspective on the subject in history. Whereas *Spartacus* and *Barry Lyndon* provide views of specific periods of the past, *The Shining* actually provides a view of the nature of historical time itself. Palmer begins by developing Frederic Jameson's theory of the postmodern condition, in which the individual feels detached from the movement of history. Everything appears present, without organization in space and time, much like the mind of Jack Torrance, who is trapped in a continuous and mad present, having spent only one summer at the Overlook Hotel, yet having lived there for generations as the caretaker.

In part 5, "The Subject of the Future," Daniel Shaw's "Nihilism and Freedom in the Films of Stanley Kubrick" provides an in-depth analysis of Kubrick's cinematic adaptation of Anthony Burgess's novel *A Clockwork Orange*. Kubrick is often characterized as a nihilistic and excessively pessimistic filmmaker, but Shaw argues against this interpretation, claiming that his work as a whole, and especially *A Clockwork Orange*, is actually quite hopeful and positive. It is true that Kubrick's films depict a dark and nihilistic world, but this nihilism must be understood primarily as an active form rather than a passive one. Passive nihilism recognizes the emptiness of the world and gives in to it, whereas active nihilism reveals that emptiness for the purpose of pushing beyond it to something greater—namely, a new realization of humanity as fundamentally free and creative.

In "'Please Make Me a Real Boy': The Prayer of the Artificially Intelligent," Jason T. Eberl provides a rich philosophical analysis of *2001: A Space Odyssey* and *A.I.: Artificial Intelligence* (which Kubrick planned and produced but was directed by Steven Spielberg). Eberl brings the philosophy of artificial intelligence, the philosophy of mind, and the Turing test to bear in a detailed analysis of *A.I.*'s robots and the computer HAL in *2001* to show what makes them seem human and what does not. In the process, Eberl also demonstrates what the project of artificial intelligence, as it is presented in Kubrick's films, actually says about us as humans—namely, that we find ourselves struggling against the very creations of our imagination, no longer fully in control of our ideas.

In "Nietzsche's Overman as Posthuman Star Child in *2001: A Space Odyssey*," I discuss the importance of Nietzsche's *Thus Spoke Zarathustra* for understanding Kubrick's science fiction masterpiece. Just as Nietzsche describes human evolution as proceeding from animals to humans to a superintelligent being he calls the Overman, Kubrick's *2001* chronicles the ascent from apes to humans to a final planet-sized fetus, the Star Child. This evolution is directed by an unseen alien race, guiding us toward higher consciousness by way of technology. I end by noting that Kubrick's Nietzschean vision may not be far wrong, considering recent advances in artificial intelligence. But the question of who and what may be directing our evolution and, more importantly, who and what *should* be directing it, ultimately remains open.

PART ONE

THE SUBJECT AT WAR

Understanding the Enemy

The Dialogue of Fear in *Fear and Desire* and *Dr. Strangelove*

Elizabeth F. Cooke

> What is absurd is the confrontation of this irrational and the wild longing
> for clarity whose call echoes in the human heart. The absurd depends as
> much on man as on the world.
>> —Albert Camus, *The Myth of Sisyphus*

According to French philosopher Albert Camus, our most important task is
not to discover the meaning of life but to recognize that it is, in fact, meaningless. Camus calls this human condition the absurd, the fact that although we
long for clarity and meaning in our lives, none is given. Stanley Kubrick was
quite taken with existentialism in general, but it is Camus' philosophy that
we see most prominently in two of his war films that are studies in how we
face the absurd. These are Kubrick's first feature-length film, *Fear and Desire*
(1953), which he removed from the public sphere but has recently been made
available by ElusiveDVD.com, and the much better known *Dr. Strangelove,
or: How I Learned to Stop Worrying and Love the Bomb* (1964).

Fear and Desire is a study in how individuals face fear. Four soldiers are
trapped behind enemy lines and must plan their escape without weapons,
food, or transportation. These four men cooperate with one another, yet each
must also deal with his own personal enemies. Although the setting appears
to be central Europe during World War II, the narrator (David Allen) tells
us that this is not a story about a particular war in history but one about *any*
war in *any* time, and the soldiers "have no other country but the mind." We
learn about this "war of the mind" *through* the mind—through voice-over
monologues (heard as private thoughts) rather than intersubjective public

dialogues. These monologues reveal how differently each character confronts his fears as he questions the purpose of his life and death. Yet, as different as they are, ultimately there is only one message in the film: Each soldier must face his own internal enemy. He must face his own fear, his own mortality, and the meaninglessness of his own life alone.

We see the flip side of this existential view in Kubrick's later film *Dr. Strangelove*. This film is also a study in fear, but rather than the individual's fear of his own death, it is a study of how institutions, or collective minds, face the annihilation of the entire human race. To do this, Kubrick uses the reverse approach of *Fear and Desire*: rather than private monologues, he uses public and, indeed, ludicrous dialogues with insane participants. As an attempt to communicate, understand, or reach an agreement for the sake of cooperation, each dialogue is an utter failure. Each one fails to achieve any real level of understanding, fails to undo the mistakes of past dialogues, and, ultimately, fails to prevent World War III. But the reason for these failures seems to be that institutional procedures exclude the individual (who otherwise might be the only source of sanity and reason). Of course, in the end, two individuals decide the world's fate: General Jack D. Ripper (Sterling Hayden), an insane general whose fear has become his reality, and Dr. Strangelove (Peter Sellers), an out-of-control scientist whose fear of *not controlling* cannot be contained. But these men are not really individuals, because they do not face the absurd as individuals. They are merely products of their institutions, and this is ultimately the cause of their insanity and the war. This is also the underlying existential message: when the individual is lost, we are all lost. Kubrick's criticism—illustrated through one ridiculous scene after the next of the sane talking with the insane (or the drunk)—is that all procedures of institutional deliberation and communication ignore individual freedom. Individuals dissolve into a machine of bureaucracy and a mindless chain of command. In the end, a rational individual can do nothing to make a bit of difference; humans have become slaves to a larger machine that we no longer control. And this might just mean that everyone involved is insane.

So, in a sense, the message in both films is the same: the enemy is always within us, and the absurd can only be faced alone. But in *Dr. Strangelove*, Kubrick leaves us with little to work toward; with certain institutions in place, there is simply no appropriate response to the absurd, because the individual has been lost.

How Do We Face the World?

Philosophy has, from the beginning, attempted to get at the core of what it is to be human. Throughout the ages—from the Greeks through the Middle Ages to the modern period and today—a long and rich tradition has evolved, marked by many attempts to define human nature. Here, it is helpful to provide a brief survey of some of those attempts so that we can understand what is going on in Kubrick's films. One of the earliest methods of philosophy was dialogue, developed in ancient Greece most prominently by Socrates and Plato. The idea here is that humans are rational and that we reason best through conversation, essentially through questions and answers. With this method we can, with a great deal of effort, get to the ultimate and eternal truths of the universe. Plato called these the Forms, the essences of reality, which remain constant despite the flux of matter.

Implicit in this method is the view that our common beliefs about philosophical issues such as reality, knowledge, justice, and the purpose of human life have something *right* about them, but also, inevitably, something wrong. Through critical dialogue we can unveil our mistakes, and a positive theory will emerge. The point is to start from current beliefs and engage critically with others, as well as with oneself, to improve one's ideas. In this way, dialogue entails a commitment to openness, to conceptual change, but also to working toward these static universal truths.

This method, which survived in some form throughout the Middle Ages, was called into question in the modern world. Most famously, René Descartes, the father of modern philosophy, found the traditional methods problematic partly because they could easily leave some false beliefs unques-tioned. So, Descartes set out to overhaul the method. His new method, meant to be more thorough, was one of pure intuitive introspection. Rather than engaging in dialogue with others and improving on our existing opinions, pruning and repruning them, Descartes retreated into isolation to find an absolute foundation for all beliefs in his own mind, or, more specifically, in his own pure self-consciousness. From this one absolute truth—namely, "I think, therefore I am"—he would derive all other truths deductively (and with certainty). The truths achieved through this method could be gained by any individual who engaged in this same examination. But most importantly, the absolute, certain truth could be found only by taking this subjective standpoint.

Although Plato and Descartes had virtually opposite methods—social dialectic and private intuition, respectively—they shared the goal of estab-lishing absolute truths. Existentialism, however, is different. Coming several centuries after Descartes, it still shares the modern Cartesian emphasis on the subject's consciousness as the starting point for philosophy, but existentialism rejects much of both the ancient and the modern philosophical traditions. For example, it rejects the modern emphasis on knowledge over action, and it rejects the traditional philosophical view, both ancient and modern, that there are universal answers to questions regarding what it means to be human. For existentialists, there are no *given* answers to this question. Therefore, the old answers, in the form of philosophical conceptions of a static human nature—human beings as rational or knowing subjects, as creatures of God, or as complex lumps of protein—all miss the point. For existentialists, to be human is to be a conscious and free individual, a point that no third-person perspective, whether scientific or philosophical, can grasp in the form of a definition.

What traditional approaches to human nature forget is that these static definitions are useless unless the individual decides to accept them. At-tempting to provide a one-size-fits-all answer to fundamental questions of human existence ignores the individual's responsibility to *decide* what his or her particular life is about. The individual cannot rely on prefabricated definitions or explanations of what it is to be human and then simply follow them. Only the individual can impose a self-definition, choosing his or her own distinct answer.

That said, the existentialists have quite distinct ideas about how the indi-vidual ought to face and answer these questions, but they all share the view that the individual must ultimately face his or her own freedom. In fact, no truth about humans can have significance unless the individual gives them significance by making choices. It is not a question of knowing the truth but of *choosing* a truth. For example, German philosopher Friedrich Nietzsche reminds us that we have the freedom to reject a belief in God and morality; we have the freedom to choose our own values and live by them. Danish philosopher Søren Kierkegaard emphasizes our freedom to commit ourselves to a universal ethical cause that is greater than the sum of our individual choices (the ethical stage) or to go even further and commit ourselves to something beyond a universal ethical cause and thus enter into a personal relationship with God (the religious stage). French philosopher Jean-Paul Sartre describes our freedom to reject all notions of value beyond the ones we choose, as long as we accept responsibility for the fact that our chosen actions make us who we are. We cannot hide behind anything, nor can we pretend that we are not utterly responsible for who we are. There can be no blaming our upbringing, our genetics, our social roles, or authorities of any kind, because we choose every action and attitude that make up our lives.

Once one becomes more conscious of one's own freedom, the next step is to use it honestly, authentically, and lucidly. Of course, this is not an easy task in a world with so many opportunities to hide from freedom. We lie to ourselves all the time; we tell ourselves that we were forced to do something because we find it so difficult to bear the responsibility of being free. Yet no one, not even the existentialist, can teach another to live freely. Living freely and authentically must ultimately come from the self.

Here, the problem of method arises. Although existentialism embraces individualism, it does not hold out the Cartesian hope of gaining certainty through intuition, nor does it use Platonic dialogue. Existentialism stands opposed to both these methods, in that it does not assume the power of reason or dialogue to compel the individual to do (or believe) the right thing. Rather, existentialists tend to use literature to uncover what consciousness is like, with the goal of making the reader explicitly aware of something that he or she already knows deep down. Perhaps this is why the genre of film lends itself so readily to existentialist themes.

Camus and the Absurd

Kubrick easily falls into the existentialist camp. And while there is much in his view that resembles Sartre's existentialism, I think his view most closely resembles Camus' existentialism (a label that Camus rejected, preferring absurdism instead—although the two are very similar). This worldview of absurdism comes out most prominently in Camus' great work *The Myth of Sisyphus,* in which he claims that the most profound philosophical problem is neither the essence of reality (à la Plato) or the foundation of knowledge (à la Descartes) but rather the problem of suicide. Faced with the human condition, one asks, Why should I not kill myself?

Recognition of the absurd results from the awareness of two things: first, that we have an incredible longing for things to make sense, for the world to have meaning; and second, that the world does not make sense. As Camus puts it: "What is absurd is the confrontation of this irrational and the wild longing for clarity whose call echoes in the human heart. The absurd depends as much on man as on the world."[1] Recognizing this absurdity is half the battle, but once absurdity is recognized, it becomes a passion, and how one lives with this passion is Camus' central concern. Once the passion is admitted, one must choose among three real possibilities: First, one can commit suicide. Second, one can choose to believe in God or a transcendent world, replacing the absurd world with a meaningful one. In other words, one can choose to have hope. Third, one can choose to live in the cold, hard light of the absurd, struggling against meaninglessness by trying to invent one's own meaning.

Neither of the first two options is acceptable for Camus. To commit suicide is to fail to accept the absurdity of the world, to escape, and thus to crumble under the weight of fear and trembling. It is to give up rather than to live authentically. But to have hope in some transcendent meaning amounts to the same thing. To hope is also to escape. To accept a doctrine that explains the absurdity debilitates the individual and relieves the individual of the weight of his or her own life.[2] In fact, the problem with existentialist thought, for Camus, is that it is steeped in vast hope.

A large part of the motivation for hope comes from the idea of original sin. We see ourselves as guilty and seek absolution in another world. But Camus rejects this idea of original sin in all its forms. It is fundamental to the human condition that we feel innocent, and original sin is something imposed on this original innocence. Camus writes: "An attempt is made to get him to admit his guilt. He feels innocent. To tell the truth, that is all he feels—his irreparable innocence."[3] Without any feeling of guilt, an individual has no real need to be saved from guilt and thus has no reason to make an appeal to God.

This, ultimately, is man's question about the absurd, as Camus sees it: "he wants to find out if it is possible to live *without appeal.*" That is what Camus means when he asks, "What other truth can I admit without lying, without bringing in a hope I lack and which means nothing within the limits of my condition?" All one can do, if one is to live without lying, is to accept that "it is essential to die unreconciled and not of one's own free will." One must live lucidly, honestly in the face of the absurd. One must face, rather than try to escape, the absurdity, and then revolt against it. As Camus says of the individual, "The absurd is his extreme tension, which he maintains constantly by solitary effort, for he knows that in that consciousness and in that day-to-day revolt he gives proof of his only truth, which is defiance."[4]

Neither committing suicide nor taking a leap of faith to believe in some doctrine about the meaning of life is a solution for Camus, because neither is honest. So, the absurd man refuses to hope. He is indifferent to the future. He does not believe in the meaning of life (for this implies a scale of values).[5] This is Camus' ideal man, a man who lives honestly. He refuses to lie to himself because he refuses to believe or hope in what he cannot understand. Camus calls this man "the stranger." He is a stranger *in* the world and *to* the world, and he lives in defiance of all the lies about a meaningful world.[6]

Kubrick sought to express this worldview in many of his films, but particularly in *Fear and Desire* and *Dr. Strangelove*. Both present us with perspectives on the experience of the absurd, with individuals constantly failing to face the absurd lucidly, lying to themselves and living dishonestly in the process. And in both films, fear is precisely the issue: fear of the absurd or, more specifically, fear of the self in the face of the absurd. It is a fear of what we will be, fear of what we have become, and, often, fear of having no identity at all. And, of course, these fears are shared by all of us.

Facing the Absurd Alone: *Fear and Desire*

In *Fear and Desire* the narrator tells us that this is not a story of an actual war: "the enemies who struggle here do not exist *unless we call them into being*. . . . Only the unchanging shapes of fear and doubt and death are from our world. These soldiers that you see keep our language and our time but *have no other country but the mind*." Four soldiers have gone down in a plane and are now regrouping behind enemy lines. They are Sergeant Mac (Frank Silvera), Lieutenant Corby (Kenneth Harp), Private Sidney (Paul Mazursky), and Private Fletcher (Stephen Coit). We learn about their distinct characters through voice-over monologues as they march off toward the river. The lieutenant, who leads the group, seems unemotional and steady as he makes prudent decisions and plans for their escape. Fletcher represents the average soldier, with a common, Everyman morality. Mac blames the lieutenant for their predicament and expresses his anger from the beginning. Sidney is clearly the most fearful, giving voice to every doubt he has about their situation.

SIDNEY'S INSANITY

Early in the film, the four characters decide to attack and kill several enemy soldiers and take their supplies so that they can build a raft to get back to their unit. After the attack, on their way back to the river, they spot a woman (Virginia Leith) who is about to discover their presence. Mac, a man of action, captures her before she is able to scream and give them away. They tie her to a tree and gag her mouth, and Sidney is appointed to stand guard while the others continue working on the raft.

But something has changed in Sidney after killing the enemy soldiers, and he starts to lose his sense of reality. While he is watching over the woman, he starts talking aloud to her, even though she cannot respond. In fact, it appears that she does not even speak his language. Still, he forces her to hear him, to recognize him, and even tries desperately to get her to like him. He tells her how he feels about her, although this cannot be based on anything other than physical attraction or the need for her to recognize him and whatever other reality he is conjuring up. He tries to make her laugh with juvenile impressions and gestures. He tells her stories about magicians and pretends to be the general, who is stationed across the river. He pleads with her, begs her to like him, and finally unties her so that they can be together. In doing this, he gives her the opportunity to run away, and she takes it. Sidney, now overcome with *new* fears, shoots and kills her. He is afraid, we learn, that she will tell the general that Sidney was making fun of him—as if that would be a concern of the general, and as if that would be the woman's objective. Even his fears have become nonsensical. If it was not clear that he was mad before, it is certainly clear now.

Already concerned with Sidney's behavior, the lieutenant urges Mac to check on him. When Mac sees the woman lying on the ground and asks Sidney what happened, Sidney makes up a story about how his prisoner was tired and wanted to lie down. When Mac discovers that she is dead, Sidney insists that it was not his fault: "The magician did it. Honest! . . . First we're a bird, then we're an island. Before I was a general. And now I am a fish. Hurray for the magicians." Sidney pretends to be the characters in his own stories, and it is clear that his identity is gone. He tells Mac that he is going to the river for a swim and runs off laughing.

Sidney's fear leads him to do more than lie to himself. It leads him to create an alternative reality. Sidney's insanity lies in his inability to handle his fear alone and to keep the voices inside his own head. He is compelled to share his thoughts with someone, so he forces the woman to listen. He demands from his captive the recognition that he cannot get from his peers. He needs that recognition so that he can stop his fear from getting the best of him. But in the end, it *does* get the best of him. He kills what, only moments before, he thought could save him. He is his own worst enemy, in the deepest sense of the phrase. When he kills the woman, he departs hopelessly from reality—alive, but lost. In the end, Sidney is the most tragic figure because he cannot handle his fate alone.

MAC'S ANGER

Mac, by contrast, is a man of passion and action. At first, he is angry at the lieutenant for making decisions that Mac does not support and for being "all talk" instead of action. But later, Mac redirects his anger toward an enemy general he spots on the other side of the river. He complains to himself that the general is privileged and that this privilege and power force soldiers like himself, on the other side, to follow orders to which they do not consent. So he comes up with a plan to assassinate the general that involves the co-operation of the lieutenant and Fletcher and guarantees Mac's own death. Mac claims that this is what he needs to do to keep from going nuts like Sidney, "nuts in his own way." But later, we learn Mac's deeper motivation: he wants to kill the general because it is his one chance to do something important, a chance to really matter for once. It is an opportunity that is unlikely to present itself again—certainly not after he returns home to his job as a repairman—so he is going to take it.

The plan is this: Mac will paddle down the river to create a distraction while the others slip into the enemy camp and kill the general. As we see Mac heading downriver, he appears to be brave, even fearless, as he faces his own death. But Mac may be the most fearful of all the characters. The difference between Mac and Sidney is that Mac's fear has a focus, an objective. Mac's real fear is that of not mattering, of losing (or never having achieved) his individuality, and this becomes his most important battle. As Mac approaches his chosen death, we hear his thoughts: "It's better. It's better to roll up your life into one night and one man and one gun. It hurts too much. To keep hurting everyone else in every direction and to be hurt, with all the separate hates exploding day after day. You can't help it. A curse buzzes out of your mouth with every word you say. And nobody alive can tell which is which or what you mean. Yeah. You try door after door when you hear voices you like behind them but the knobs come off in your hand." Is Mac choosing death to escape what he has become? Does he choose a purpose to die for, so that he can avoid living in a world he cannot control or understand? He seems to want to escape the responsibility of his past actions, which have consequences beyond his control. Later we hear Mac's thoughts again as he approaches his end point: "Nobody is going to cry for me later or cheer for me now. Nobody else is me. I know that. . . . It was all wrong. Ah, good riddance! Oh, what a trade—him for me! What a thing to come to at the end? Like building a bridge or stealing the crown jewels. Thanks, general [he laughs], thanks! I'll take the tombstone if it's really mine." Mac is alone and unhappy with who he has become, so he is grateful for this opportunity to become something he would otherwise never have been. Through this chosen death, he can claim an identity. And as he continues down the river, he is exuberant. He seems utterly fulfilled and happy to meet his fate.

It is not clear, however, whether Mac is Camus' stranger, fighting against meaninglessness, or whether he is just as deluded as Sidney because he thinks he can make his life (and death) meaningful by killing the general. Perhaps from Camus' point of view, Mac's death is not entirely tragic. At least Mac will die fighting a battle of his own choosing. But we are led to ask of Mac, why *this* battle? Fletcher, a comparatively minor character, goes along with Mac's plan because he seems to think that assassinating the general will matter to the war effort. But Mac does not see killing the general as good for humankind or for some larger cause; he sees it *only* as fulfilling his own desire to matter.

THE LIEUTENANT AS CAMUS' STRANGER

A contrasting approach is found in the character of the lieutenant. The lieutenant is a good leader, but he is not bent on being a hero. He is unafraid in each new situation, even when risking his life. He always acts skillfully, prudently, and cautiously, but he is always detached. His actions are never part of some larger purpose. Among the four men, the lieutenant seems most lucid, in Camus' sense. As we learn through his monologues, he never lies to himself. When they must kill several enemy soldiers to get their food and weapons, the lieutenant does not try to justify the action or give it a larger meaning. He reflects on the dead bodies and says to himself: "We spend our lives running our fingers down the lists and directories, looking for our real names, our permanent addresses. 'No man is an island?' Perhaps that was true a long time ago, before the ice age. The glaciers have melted away and now we're all islands, parts of a world made of islands only." The lieutenant does not try to console himself with any fiction about the meaning of life. He is "aware," or lucid, in Camus' sense. He is aware that there is no point to death and that a man's identity is not a real or permanent thing. So, when Mac presents his plan to assassinate the general, the lieutenant hesitates at first because he does not want to risk his life needlessly, and the cause is not important to him. In response, Mac challenges him, asking him why he thinks his life is so precious. The lieutenant responds only to himself: "Why? The only reason is to hunt for the reason." For the lieutenant, there is simply no hidden meaning. This fits Camus' ideal of lucidly facing the fact that meaning is invented. But the lieutenant, being detached, agrees to Mac's plan, saying (again to himself), "how can I stand in the way of a man with a reason to die?"

The lieutenant has reflected and, in Camus' sense, has recognized the absurdity; being lucid, he does not pretend to understand more than he does. He knows there is no clear meaning to either life or death, and he knows the future is uncertain. He is, in effect, Camus' stranger—entirely indifferent to the future, unafraid and detached, but not exactly eager to throw his life away either. He exists right in the tension that Camus describes for us all: he is neither suicidal nor hopeful—he just is.

After the lieutenant and Fletcher kill the general and steal a plane to fly back to their unit, they ask permission from base camp to await Mac's return by the river. Here they reflect on their journey:

FLETCHER: Do you think he [Mac] will come back?
LIEUTENANT: Not sure yet whether even we've come back. I think
     we've gone too far from our own private boundaries to be certain
     about these things anymore—to come back to ourselves.
FLETCHER: I wish I could want what I wanted before.

Meanwhile, drifting down the river toward base camp, a wounded Mac finds and rescues Sidney. But by the time they reach the lieutenant and Fletcher, Mac has died. With Mac's body stretched across the raft, Sidney mumbles incoherently. These two men cannot return to their old selves either: one is dead, and the other is mad. They have all been changed by facing their fears. But each has faced death as an individual and met his chosen fate.

FLETCHER: I'm not sure I'm built for this.
LIEUTENANT: Nobody ever was. It's all a trick we perform because
     we'd rather not die immediately.

In Camus' sense, and perhaps as the lieutenant sees it, Mac's death is tragic if he is, in fact, escaping—that is, choosing suicide—rather than living with defiant indifference. If the lieutenant is right, there is no larger purpose than Mac's own. But at the same time, the lieutenant respects Mac's need to choose his own death. Is Mac living (and dying) authentically? Is he revolting against the meaninglessness in Camus' sense? Or is he deluded in thinking that he can find an identity in his death? Is he escaping rather than choosing to live with the absurdity and alienation? The lieutenant does not see such meaning or purpose in death; he does not choose these escapes.

So, how should one face freedom and death? With utter and uncontrollable fear, like Sidney, who is so empty that his escape is a complete split with reality? With escape, like Mac, who thinks that death will make him matter (and thereby seems to choose both hope and suicide)? With an Everyman's hope, like Fletcher, who thinks that killing the general might do some good? Or with indifference, like the lieutenant, who faces both life and death with acceptance? Camus' sympathies would be with the lieutenant, who does not try to change what he cannot, but simply lives in the moment and faces each situation with pure lucidity. Although he is not devoid of fear and desire in the mystic sense (since it is clear that he too desires the captive woman), the lieutenant is not *driven* by fear and desire, as the others are. In any other (nonexistential) film, the lieutenant might be a tragic character, but in Kubrick's first film, he is the hero.

THE CONTINGENCY AND ABSURDITY OF WHAT SIDE ONE IS ON

For absurdists and existentialists, the sheer contingency of one's physical and historical context is part of the human condition. One might just as easily have been born at one point in history as another, born a man or a woman, a general or a private. The most important way Kubrick sets up the theme of the absurd in *Fear and Desire* is to establish that which side one is on in this war is entirely arbitrary. We may wish to believe that our side is right, that there is an order to things, that there are right and wrong sides, but there are not. Everything is contingent and therefore meaningless.

Similarly, in *Fear and Desire,* it is clear that the sides are contingent and outside the characters' control. After all, we are told explicitly by the narrator that this could be any war and that each character's "country" is his mind. But not everyone sees the matter as contingent. For example, Fletcher goes along with Mac's plan, but not for Mac's reasons. Fletcher responds to Mac, "Well, [it's] not that I want to seem important. Half the trouble in the world happens because some people do; but I think half the good things happen that way too." Fletcher sees that trying to be important, wanting to matter, can be good or bad; it is a somewhat relative notion. For Fletcher, doing what is truly good is what should be valued. Yet, despite Fletcher's *thinking* that they are doing good, the viewer is given no such sense. We are told nothing about the war, nothing about the cause of it, the morality of it, or even whether these men are committed to it. What is made clear is the sheer contingency of their situation, the fact that they happen to be in enemy territory and want to get back to their own side. Their survival is a common concern, but every other cause or concern is purely individual rather than shared. And although Mac's biggest fear turns out to be not mattering—that is, being contingent—for him and for all of them, this is unavoidable.

To illustrate this point about contingent sides, Kubrick makes the enemy general a sympathetic doppelganger to the lieutenant and even has him played by the same actor (Kenneth Harp); likewise, the captain, the general's assistant, is played by the same actor who plays Fletcher (Stephen Coit). Kubrick was probably low on funds, making versatile actors a practical resource. But there are other key elements in the film that suggest we are to view the general and the captain as mirror images of the lieutenant and Fletcher. For example, in the beginning of the film, the four soldiers come across a friendly dog, but they end up chasing it off for the sake of keeping their presence a secret. We learn later that this is the general's dog, and when the dog returns, the general talks to the dog, asking where it has been and what it has seen. The captain insists that the dog is loyal to the general, but we know that the dog does not care which master it serves. We have seen that it could just as easily have been the lieutenant's dog. Toward the end of the film, the general speaks to his captain, reflecting on his position in life and in the war. Like Sidney, he does not talk to himself but speaks aloud to the officer, who does not say much in response. The general expresses his discomfort at being responsible for the planned slaughter of the four soldiers, whose presence is now known. He expresses his own feeling of being trapped and wonders whether his death is being planned. Indeed, the viewer knows that it is, because at that moment, Mac is pushing down the river toward the general's death and, of course, his own.

The general recognizes and faces the fact that he is a pawn in a game, that he is not in control of his destiny and never was. This might seem tragic, but perhaps he is not much different from the lieutenant. The lieutenant lives and the general dies, but this too is contingent. Each faces his fate with indifference, and each has nothing else to live or die for. Neither man lies to himself, and neither is afraid. The general's death will one day be the lieutenant's death. It will not be chosen, and it will have no larger meaning, but he will be lucid about that, too. He will not pretend to have lived or died for anything more.

For Camus, to live and die with honesty is the central challenge of being human. The task of being human involves asking oneself what one's life is about and being honest about the answer, even if there is no answer at all. But regardless of how one answers this question (whether in the hope of something one does not understand, or with the acceptance of life's meaninglessness), Kubrick's *Fear and Desire* shows us the importance of facing these issues alone. I cannot die for someone else's cause. I *can*, however, choose to accept a reason for my own life, or choose to live without meaning altogether. But above all, I must not try to escape from making this decision for myself. And this, ultimately, is why *Fear and Desire* is not a tragedy. Although not everyone in the film lives with lucidity or with revolt, almost everyone is able to recognize this condition and face it in his own way. With the exception of Sidney, each character faces these questions alone. The other three men are able to cooperate in order to assassinate the general, yet each retains his individuality because each has different motivations for participating.

In *Dr. Strangelove*, we see just the opposite. Here, Kubrick addresses the question of what happens when men try to handle the most important human issues as collectives rather than as individuals—when they pretend to share motivations. Kubrick's answer is anything but optimistic. In scene after scene of ridiculous dialogues—in contrast to *Fear and Desire*'s monologues—thinking, if it is happening at all, is always irrelevant. Indeed, the madness of Sidney in *Fear and Desire* becomes the norm in *Dr. Strangelove*—madness disguised as procedure, protocol, and diplomacy.

Facing the Absurd as a Collective: *Dr. Strangelove*

Dr. Strangelove takes place at the height of the cold war, which, by definition, is not a real war in the sense of combat and bombs. It is, rather, a war like the one depicted in Kubrick's *Fear and Desire*. It is a war of pure fear, located almost entirely in the mind. The difference is that here, it is a war between collective minds, groups of generals plotting against each other. The story begins just as General Jack D. Ripper (an obvious play on the name of murderer Jack the Ripper) has executed Plan R, which calls for a U.S. Air Force wing to fly over Russia and initiate full-scale nuclear combat. The president calls back the wing, but one bomber cannot be recalled. Once it is out of range, and Plan R has been initiated, all communications are cut off, even to the president. This makes the plan irreversible, provided the bomber is not shot down by either side. As General Ripper puts it, we are now forced to accept the only rational option remaining: "total commitment." Ripper does this because he believes that the politicians lack the stomach for it. As Ripper claims, "war is too important to be left to the politicians."

But what Dr. Strangelove knows, and the Americans do not, is that Plan R is also linked to the Doomsday Machine—effectively, the Russians' Plan R. The Doomsday Machine is designed to automatically initiate a counterattack if the Americans ever launch a nuclear strike, just in case there are no Russians left to do so. Like Plan R, the Doomsday Machine cannot be stopped for any reason once it is set into motion, so both represent irreversible courses to total nuclear war. The Russian Doomsday Machine, moreover, has a built-in absolute holocaust mechanism: it will continue to launch the entirety of the Russian nuclear arsenal until every living thing on earth is dead. As Russian Ambassador Alexei de Sadesky (Peter Bull) puts it, the Doomsday Machine is "a device which will destroy all human and animal life on earth." And it appears that this absolute nuclear holocaust is about to take place.

U.S. President Merkin Muffley (Peter Sellers) and the Russian ambassador realize that the matter is out of their hands, so they turn to Dr. Strangelove for help. Dr. Strangelove is an ex-Nazi scientist who once served Adolf Hitler but now works for the United States, presumably obtained through Project Paper Clip, which gave immunity and asylum to German scientists in exchange for their intelligence and services. We do not see Strangelove until near the end of the film, but when we do, the symbolism is apparent. Dr. Strangelove is confined to a wheelchair, which represents Germany's crippled state, but his mind works fine, and he is quite capable of controlling the remainder of the war from the behind the scenes, in a dark corner of the U.S. War Room. The problem is that Dr. Strangelove is completely mad. Having watched Germany's conquerors come begging to him on their knees, Dr. Strangelove is only too happy to offer his own cold war version of the Nazis' "final solution." But instead of just the Jews, as the Germans had planned, virtually everyone will be exterminated. Only a select few—beautiful women and American military men—will be moved underground to wait out the nuclear holocaust, when they will once again take up the Nazi agenda of building a master race.

MANDRAKE AND GENERAL RIPPER

Dr. Strangelove begins with Ripper's execution of Plan R and ends with World War III, but in between, the film tells the story of how those in power attempt to prevent this one little accident from having disastrous consequences. The film is a story of their failure. The first effort to open up a dialogue is led by Group Captain Lionel Mandrake (Peter Sellers again), a British officer who grasps the gravity of the situation and decides to meet with the mad General Ripper. But Mandrake is unable to get through to Ripper and becomes a captive in Ripper's office. Mandrake is horrified, sitting with his face buried in his hands, as Ripper tries to console him. Ripper even puts his arm around Mandrake, adding to the horror, and proceeds to tell Mandrake exactly why he started World War III:

RIPPER: Have you ever seen a Commie drink a glass of water?
MANDRAKE: Well, no, I, I can't say I have, Jack.
RIPPER: Vodka. That's what they drink, isn't it? Never water.
MANDRAKE: Well I, I believe that's what they drink, Jack, yes.
RIPPER: On no account will a Commie ever drink water . . . and not without good reason.
MANDRAKE: Hmm . . . ah, yes. I um, I can't quite see what you're getting at, Jack.
RIPPER: Water. That's what I'm getting at, water. Mandrake, water is the source of all life. Seven-tenths of this earth's surface is water. Why, do you realize that 70 percent of *you* is water?
MANDRAKE [whimpering]: Good lord.
RIPPER: And as human beings, you and I need fresh, pure water to replenish our precious bodily fluids. You beginning to understand?
MANDRAKE: Oh, ah, yes [giggles nervously, scared].
RIPPER: Mandrake . . . Mandrake, have you never wondered why I drink only distilled water, or rainwater, and only pure grain alcohol?
MANDRAKE: Well, it did occur to me, Jack, yes.
RIPPER: Have you ever heard of a thing called fluoridation, fluoridation of water?
MANDRAKE: Yes, I have heard of that, Jack, yes. Yes.
RIPPER: Well, do you know what it is?

MANDRAKE: No. No, I don't know what it is, no.

RIPPER: Do you realize that fluoridation is the most monstrously conceived and dangerous Communist plot we have ever had to face?

[Gunfire comes through the window]

Mandrake is facing a madman. He desperately wants to believe that there is some meaning to it all—some reason why Ripper started a nuclear holocaust. But no rational explanation is given. It is clear to Mandrake that Ripper, by this point, has gone off the deep end, going on and on about water and "our precious bodily fluids."

In a sense, we can understand the causality at work in Ripper's beliefs about fluoridated water. For too long the Russians and Americans have been lying and scheming, and perhaps no conspiracy is too far-fetched at this point. If the aim of nuclear war is the massive destruction of life, then perhaps Ripper's suspicions are not completely out of the question. But his fear has escalated out of control, and now he simply imagines a terrorist plot in every glass of water he drinks.

So, Ripper sees a first strike as the only solution, thus escaping into the false hope that there is actually a way for the United States to win this war. Once he has chosen this escape into hope, however, he realizes that he will likely be captured and tortured. But as he tells Mandrake, he is terrified at the prospect of torture and knows that he will never be able to withstand it. So, after choosing one prong of Camus' "trilemma"—namely, hope—Ripper turns to another one. He casually walks into the bathroom, as though he is going to clean up, and shoots himself, leaving Mandrake alone.

MANDRAKE AND COLONEL BAT GUANO

Now Mandrake is faced with even more insanity and must work furiously to find the secret code to call off the attack, which only Ripper knew. The one man who could have prevented the end of the world is gone, and the only one left who may still have a shot in the dark is Mandrake. He knows that the three letters of the code must be some combination of the first letters of the phrases "Peace On Earth" or "Purity Of Essence" (phrases Ripper kept uttering). Mandrake, however, is taken into custody by a new officer, Colonel Bat Guano (Keenan Wynn). Mandrake demands a rational explanation from Bat Guano but instead gets nonsense:

> MANDRAKE: Colonel! Colonel, I must know what you think has been
> going on here.
> BAT GUANO: You want to know what I think?
> MANDRAKE: Yes.
> BAT GUANO: I think you're some kind of deviated "prevert." I think
> General Ripper found out about your "preversion." And that you
> were organizing some kind of mutiny of "preverts." Now move!
> On top of that I don't know anything about any planes attacking
> Russia. All I was told to do was to get General Ripper on the
> phone with the president of the United States.

Mandrake tells the colonel that the fate of the world depends on his calling the president and that if he does not allow Mandrake to do this, Bat Guano will be lucky if he ends up wearing the uniform of a "toilet attendant." The colonel allows him: "All right, go ahead. But if you try any preversions in there, I'll blow your head off." Mandrake, however, is unable to make the most important phone call in the history of humankind because he does not have any change. So, he tries to make a collect call, but that will not work either. Bat Guano does not have any change either, asking, "You think I'd go into combat with loose change in my pocket?" Desperate, Mandrake insists that the colonel put a bullet in the soda machine to get some quarters to make the call:

> MANDRAKE: Colonel. That Coca Cola machine. I want you to shoot
> the lock off it. There may be some change in it.
> BAT GUANO: That's private property.
> MANDRAKE: Colonel, can you possibly imagine what is going to
> happen to you, your frame, outlook, way of life and everything,
> when they learn you have obstructed a telephone call to the
> president of the United States? Can you imagine? Shoot it off!
> Shoot with the gun! That's what the bullets are for, you twit!
> BAT GUANO: Okay. I'm gonna get your money for you. But if you
> don't get the president of the United States on the phone, you
> know what's gonna happen to you?
> MANDRAKE: What?!
> BAT GUANO: You're going to have to answer to the Coca Cola
> Company.

This scene encapsulates the entire film. This totally ridiculous conversation, in which there is no real communication, reveals Kubrick's pessimism about any chance of reason stopping madness. And the problem at the center of it all is that the individual has been completely lost. Whether the individual has been absorbed by the military, by nationalism, or even by corporations, persons no longer truly exist. The individual is simply the tool of massive institutions and the fears they instill.

CONTINGENCY: THE FATEFUL TRIANGLE OF MANDRAKE, MUFFLEY, AND STRANGELOVE

The three characters of President Muffley, Mandrake, and Dr. Strangelove each represent a different notch in the hierarchy. The president is at the highest level, and Dr. Strangelove is his adviser. Mandrake is a low-ranking group captain. But in fact, the individualities are not real in any significant sense. Dr. Strangelove may stand out as a rich and complicated character, but his designs are no more complicated than General Ripper's: both simply want to strike first in order to trigger a nuclear holocaust winnable by the Americans. Indeed, the German mind is exchangeable with the American mind, and perhaps the same is true of the Russian mind. The Russian ambassador, upon hearing that the probable outcome is the end of the world, barely blinks an eye. It does not matter. He is, however, entirely impressed with Dr. Strangelove's plan to finish the cold war standoff and build a new master race based on Hitler's model. In fact, anyone in the film could be anyone else, which is why Kubrick so artfully has the great actor Peter Sellers play Dr. Strangelove, Colonel Mandrake, and President Muffley. One man could just as easily be the mad scientist or the inept president or the lowly group captain. And all of them are absorbed into the massive collective mind of the American military. They represent their institutions, not themselves. They have become their institutions.

THE GIANT DIALOGICAL ROUND TABLE

In his book *Cinema 2: The Time Image,* Gilles Deleuze discusses this round table in the War Room as the centerpiece of the film and notes that it is precisely what connects *Dr. Strangelove* with the rest of Kubrick's filmography: "If we look at Kubrick's work, we see the degree to which it is the brain which is *mise-en-scène*. Attitudes of body achieve a maximum level of violence, but they depend on the brain. For, in Kubrick, the world itself is a brain, there is identity of brain and world, as in the great circular and luminous table in *Doctor Strangelove*, the giant computer in *2001: A Space Odyssey*, the Overlook Hotel in *The Shining*."[7] Although Deleuze may not intend it, he is also making my point about the eclipse of the individual inside a gigantic collective mind. And, much like the computer in *2001* or the Overlook Hotel in *The Shining*, this mind goes mad and absorbs all its contained and surrounding individuals into that madness. Indeed, this is a constant theme in Kubrick's films. In *Dr. Strangelove* the madness at the round table results from a failure to recognize the individual, who is always welded into the massive mind and its lies.

The very idea that people with such different interests and agendas could come to the same table is the worst lie of all, because each player knows that everyone else at the table is, or could be, lying. And, in a sense, they all *know* that they are lying; while they are deliberating so politely, they all know that there is nothing any one of them or any group of them can do to stop what has already begun. They are not facing the truth that deliberation has already failed. The lie at the round table is the pretense that they *can* deliberate. In actuality, they are completely powerless to stop what one madman has started. And for these reasons, all the men in *Dr. Strangelove* are just as insane as Ripper. Of course, the same problem exists on the other side. The Russian Doomsday Machine also functions to exclude dialogue and exclude the individual entirely. It is built to launch a return nuclear strike *without any individual consent*. The Doomsday Machine was built by men to take men out of the equation, because of the fear of individual choices.

Part of the problem with these deliberations between nations and among branches of the same government is that the participants, rather than being individuals discussing a problem, are representatives of those larger entities. In all cases, these men are not individuals; they are their respective institutions, and they let those institutions determine their actions. Sartre refers to this pretending to be determined rather than free as "bad faith." A person acts in bad faith when, for example, he allows his social role, such as his job, to dictate his actions, as if he were not free to quit that social role, and as if that social role were something other than what he decided to make of it. In *Dr. Strangelove*, the procedures of international diplomacy are set up so that individuals represent their institutions, and those institutions are designed to engineer bad faith. Individuals are no longer free but are merely representations of their institutions. And the more an individual represents an institution, the less of an individual he is. This is exactly Camus' own fear (for philosophy): that ideas take on a life of their own (as in Hegel), and people follow them as if they, as individuals, were not in control. Here Camus reminds us of the complexity of his view and that there are other ways to commit suicide—namely, forgetfulness of self.[8] This is also Kubrick's point: that institutions actually plan on forgetting the self and are, in fact, structured for exactly that purpose.

MAJOR T. J. KING KONG (THE COWBOY)

As a consequence of this institutional eclipse of the individual, *Dr. Strangelove*'s characters do not have private selves. More than that, individuals are lost in the machine, their inner lives gone. Only once in the film do we see an inner soul, in the form of Major T. J. King Kong (Slim Pickens), who prepares his men to carry out Plan R and drop the bomb on Russia, which will mean certain death for the flight crew. The cowboy tells his crew:

> Well, boys, I reckon this is it. Nuclear combat toe-to-toe with the Russkies. Now, look, boys, I ain't much of a hand in making speeches. But I got a pretty fair idea that something doggone important is going on back there. And I got a fair idea of the kind of personal emotions that some of you fellas may be thinking. Heck, I reckon you wouldn't even be human beings if you didn't have some pretty strong personal feelings about nuclear combat. But I want you to remember one thing. That folks back home is, uh, counting on you, and by golly we ain't about to let 'em down. Tell you something else. If this thing turns out to be half as important as I figure it just might be, I'd say that you're all in line for some important promotions and personal citations when this thing's over with. And that goes for every last one of you, regardless of your race, color, or your creed. Now let's get this thing on the hump. We got some flying to do.

But ultimately, the cowboy's inner soul is a false one, because the entire event is nothing but a grave mistake. The death of the crew members will have no meaning, and the folks back home are *not* counting on them to do this—rather, they are hoping desperately that they will not. In fact, the folks back home are trying to shoot them down. The cowboy's sincere speech has no basis in reality; he has been duped. But again, his social role is to take orders without knowing the details and without ever knowing why; his social role is to be in the dark. So, there was never any chance for his speech to have meaning. His speech is based on his hope, in Camus' sense, that if they have been told to initiate Plan R, there *must* be some reason, there *must* be some noble cause, and the folks back home *must* be counting on them. This hope, however, is just as blind as everyone else's hope in these institutions.

Kubrick's Absurdism

Kubrick is a unique kind of absurdist. He studies how we face the absurd in war and, in particular, how we face death and meaninglessness. In Kubrick's *Fear and Desire*, we learn that fear is the real enemy in war and that we lose this battle when we do not face our fear—when we decide that we *cannot* (or *will not*) live with it. If we do not know how to live with our fear, we may try to succumb to it or hide from it, but for Kubrick, this is not the answer; this is just man's failure. The ideal, rather, is to live in the face of fear, and only the lieutenant approaches this ideal in *Fear and Desire*. Every other character is self-destructive, from either insanity or excessive hope—or both. Still, except for Sidney, they all succeed in facing their fear as individuals, in facing Camus' choice between suicide, hope in a transcendent meaning, and living honestly.

In *Dr. Strangelove*, however, it is just the opposite. In terms of Camus' trilemma, there is no hero of the story who is able to live lucidly. Camus describes the absurd as a confrontation with the irrational, the longing for clarity, and the possibility of reconciling these two. But this is exactly what is lacking in *Dr. Strangelove*. There is no clarity; nor is there any recognition of just how irrational this approach to deliberation is. Camus tells us that living honestly and lucidly is to refuse to hope, to be indifferent to the future.[9] We see just the opposite in *Dr. Strangelove*. The participants in each dialogue are too hopeful. And in their optimism, their screwups could not be more abundant. Even Mandrake—perhaps especially Mandrake—is tragic because he is still committed to the hope of escaping the madness, lying to himself completely.

Still, as different as they are, both *Fear and Desire* and *Dr. Strangelove* have the same basic message: failure to live with one's fear, to face it authentically alone, leads to insanity, the most tragic ending of all. Facing the human condition—our freedom, our mortality, and the meaninglessness of our lives—is a one-person job. Kubrick shares the absurdist and existential philosophers' view that we are ultimately alone, and we alone bear ultimate responsibility for our own lives. No universal truth can spare us this burden. And no shared cause or collective can offer a place to hide. Perhaps this is the contribution that Kubrick's films have made to absurdist thought. Kubrick gives us nothing to hope for and nothing to escape into, but he helps us to recognize our condition and pushes us to be lucid about it. Whether we are up to the task is, of course, up to each of us alone.

Notes

I would like to thank Jerold J. Abrams for reading and commenting on an earlier draft of this essay.

1. Albert Camus, *The Myth of Sisyphus and Other Essays*, trans. Justin O'Brien (New York: Vintage Books, 1991), 21.

2. Ibid., 52–55.

3. Ibid., 53.

4. Ibid., 53, 51, 55, 55.

5. Ibid., 60–61.

6. See also Chris Pliatska's essay in this volume, "The Shape of Man: The Absurd and *Barry Lyndon*."

7. Gilles Deleuze, *Cinema 2: The Time Image*, trans. Hugh Tomlinson and Robert Galeta (original French, 1985; Minneapolis: University of Minnesota Press, 2003), 205.

8. Camus, *The Myth of Sisyphus*, 73.

9. Ibid., 56–60.

CHAOS, ORDER, AND MORALITY

Nietzsche's Influence on *Full Metal Jacket*

Mark T. Conard

Full Metal Jacket (1987) is clearly divided into two very different parts—the first dealing with basic training at Parris Island, and the second concerning the war in Vietnam—and each part ends with a killing. At Parris Island, the drill instructor, Sergeant Hartman (Lee Ermey), berates and debases his new recruits in a most inhuman way, attempting to strip them of their individuality in order to turn them into effective killing machines. One of the recruits, Leonard Lawrence (Vincent D'Onofrio), nicknamed Private Pyle, is overweight and of questionable mental ability and so has difficulty following the sergeant's orders and meeting the demands of Marine Corps training. After the sergeant begins to punish the other recruits for Leonard's mistakes, in order to motivate him (or, perhaps better, to take revenge), they beat him savagely. After the beating, Leonard goes insane; he shoots and kills the sergeant and then kills himself on the last night of training.

Private Joker (Matthew Modine) provides a robot-like voice-over during the first half of the film, and he becomes the protagonist of the second half, which is composed of a series of vignettes of chaotic events in Vietnam. Joker is a combat correspondent for *Stars and Stripes* magazine and is ultimately attached to a fighting unit that includes one of his friends from Parris Island, Cowboy (Arliss Howard). The unit comes under fire from a sniper as the men—including Cowboy—are killed one by one. They finally track down the sniper—a young woman—who is seriously wounded in the confrontation. As she lies dying, she begs to be put out of her misery. The other marines are content to let her suffer, but Joker objects and finally shoots her to death.

One of the important themes of the film, which underlies the stark difference between the two halves, is that of chaos and order. For example, in stripping the men of their differences and individuality, by dressing them the same and shaving their heads, the Marine Corps is attempting to impose order and authority on the recruits. This order is reflected in the perfect files of soldiers and the neat rows of cots and toilets in the barracks. In his inability to adapt to that order, Leonard reflects the folly of the entire enterprise, and his murder of the sergeant and subsequent suicide are the shocking consequences of that enterprise. The murder-suicide then unleashes the savagery and chaos of the second half of the film.

I argue in this essay that Kubrick is showing us the chaotic nature of the world—one that resists the imposition of order—and the ambiguous nature of morality in such a world. That is to say, in the chaotic flux that is reality, morality is not nearly as black and white, or as absolute, as "thou shalt not kill." Not all killings are alike. These concerns about morality, and the metaphysical assumptions about the chaotic nature of reality underpinning them, are main currents in Nietzsche's thought. It is not surprising, then, that these themes run through the film, given the strong influence Nietzsche had on Kubrick's work. Consequently, I begin with a discussion of Nietzsche's flux metaphysics and its role in *Full Metal Jacket*.

Nietzsche's Flux Metaphysics

To hold a flux metaphysics is to claim that everything, the entire universe, is continually changing, that nothing endures, is stable, or remains the same. This notion goes back at least to the pre-Socratic philosopher Heraclitus, of whose work only fragments remain. He is known to have said, for example, that "everything flows and nothing abides; everything gives way and nothing stays fixed." More famously, Heraclitus said, "You cannot step twice into the same river."[1] Why not? Well, as the water rushes by, in what sense is it the *same* river? If its constituent parts are continually changing, then it cannot be the same thing. Further, since *your* constituent parts are likewise continually changing, in what sense is it even the same *you* the second time? That is to say, and this is radical enough, Heraclitus seems to believe that in a continually changing world, there is no such thing as identity, meaning some essential properties that remain constant and by which we understand an object as the thing that it is. That is, in such a world, there is no such thing as a "thing."

If Heraclitus implies such a view, Nietzsche comes right out and states it: "Heraclitus too did the senses an injustice. They lie neither in the way the Eleatics believed, nor as he believed—they do not lie at all. What we *make* of their testimony, that alone introduces lies; for example, the lie of unity, the lie of thinghood, of substance, of permanence. 'Reason' is the cause of our falsification of the testimony of the senses. Insofar as the senses show becoming, passing away, and change, they do not lie. But Heraclitus will remain eternally right with his assertion that being is an empty fiction."[2] "Being" is something that remains the same throughout change, something that endures. It might refer to something quite basic, like a thing. We take a chair to be a thing, an object, that can undergo change. That is to say, you can paint the chair, scratch it, dent it, and so forth; it can go through numerous changes, but we assume that it is still the same thing, the same object. Whatever the chair thing is, it remains the same—retains its identity—throughout these alterations (so long as we do not alter it essentially, such as by burning it to ashes or chopping it to bits). In claiming that the world is continually changing, like the waters of a river rushing by, Nietzsche is saying that there really is no such thing as a thing standing outside the change (the only reality is the change, the flux). There is no sameness or identity, only difference.

Where does the idea of a thing, or "thinghood" come from, then? Nietzsche says that our senses show us an ever-changing world, but it is thought, or reason, that falsifies that experience, and this out of necessity. We simply could not survive if we saw and experienced the world as it truly is, if we did not experience the commonality between things that we supposedly find in the world. For example, on the most basic level, if early humans did not see or experience predators as the same, or food sources as the same, they would not have survived.

Further, our conscious, rational thought is inseparable from language, and consequently, our understanding of the world is only possible through language. We use words to designate what we see and experience in the world. But, says Nietzsche: "A word becomes a concept insofar as it simultaneously has to fit countless more or less similar cases—which means, purely and simply, cases which are never equal and thus altogether unequal. Every concept arises from the equation of unequal things. Just as it is certain that one leaf is never totally the same as another, so it is certain that the concept 'leaf' is formed by arbitrarily discarding these individual differences and by forgetting the distinguishing aspects."[3] Our understanding and grasp of the world are achieved through language and concepts. But thought cannot grasp the difference and uniqueness of each individual thing. Rather, it ignores the myriad differences among things and groups them under abstract concepts.

Does "leaf" designate or signify any one unique, individual thing? No, of course not; no word does. It covers or describes countless different things. That is how language functions, and again, our thinking is inseparable from language, such that our understanding of the world is based on this falsification of experience.

So, on a very basic level, reality is a fluid, ever-changing flux consisting of unique, individual complexes that are more like what we call events rather than what we call things, since there is nothing stable and unchanging about them (some events, such as hurricanes, are short-lived, while other events, such as chairs and people, are relatively long lasting, but they are still continuously changing). And again, in order to make our way in such a world, we must see the dissimilar as similar, the unique as falling into a recognizable class. Nietzsche says: "We have arranged for ourselves a world in which we can live—by positing bodies, lines, planes, causes and effects, motion and rest, form and content; without these articles of faith nobody now could endure life. But that does not prove them. Life is no argument. The conditions of life might include error."[4] The order and stability, the sameness of "bodies, lines, planes, causes and effects, motion and rest, form and content," Nietzsche suggests, are not real features of the world but are elements we have imposed on our own experience in order to be able to live.

Suppressing Individuality

As mentioned earlier, this sort of flux metaphysics is implied in *Full Metal Jacket*'s theme of order and chaos. In the first part of the film, at Parris Island, Sergeant Hartman attempts to form his recruits into marines, into killing machines. Part of this process involves suppressing or erasing all individuality and all differences among the men. The very first images of the film are of the various recruits having their heads shaved; then, after the title sequence, we find them in uniform, looking exactly alike and standing in neat rows, as Hartman circles the room and prepares them, in the most vulgar and psychologically abusive way, for what they are to expect in boot camp. In his *Narrative and Stylistic Patterns in the Films of Stanley Kubrick*, Luis M. García Mainar says, "The credit-title sequence includes the shaving of the soldiers' heads, suggesting the power of the military and of war to wipe out all traces of individuality and difference among the men."[5] Indeed, Hartman already views the recruits as the same. As "maggots" (new recruits), he tells them, "you are all equally worthless."

In order to further erase their individuality, Hartman next proceeds to give them nicknames: Joker, Cowboy, Snowball.[6] Note that these are not individual, personal names but rather more like archetypes or classes of things. That is, instead of referring to them by their given names, which would reflect their individuality—names designate our families, our unique lineage or history—and thus their differences from one another, Hartman assigns to them and refers to them by nicknames that are like broad, abstract categories. "Joker" receives his nickname because he foolishly tells a joke on the first day of training when the recruits are at attention and are supposed to be silent. "Cowboy" is so named because he is from Texas. "Snowball" is ironically so designated because he is black. And, just like the concept of a "leaf," these names do not refer to any unique individual; they could designate countless people or things. The important exception among the nicknames is, of course, "Private Pyle," which does name a distinct (albeit fictional) individual, and more about this below.

But why attempt to erase their differences? Why attempt to make them all the same? For exactly the same reason that Nietzsche claims we falsify our experience of the world. Hartman is attempting to impose order on chaos, to introduce sameness or identity into the flux (here, I mean identity in the philosophical sense, the idea that things have some fixed essence standing outside the flux). Again, if the world is in flux, there is *only* difference. Sameness or identity, and the commonality among things we group together, are all fictions, a falsification of experience. But such fictions are necessary for us to grasp and understand reality.

Resolution of Opposites

Kubrick's adherence to a Nietzschean flux metaphysics can also be seen in the way oppositions collapse in *Full Metal Jacket*. That is to say, in a world in chaotic flux, in which there is no such thing as identity, where there are no stable, enduring things, there can be no real oppositions. Nothing is ever the same as itself, so nothing can have an opposite. Like our belief in things, bodies, cause and effect, and so forth, Nietzsche says, our belief in oppositions—heaven and hell, good and evil, reason and desire, altruism and egoism—is also in error. In an early work, he writes:

Almost all the problems of philosophy once again pose the same form of question as they did two thousand years ago: how can

something originate in its opposite . . . ? Metaphysical philosophy
has hitherto surmounted this difficulty by denying that the one
originates in the other and assuming for the more highly valued
thing a miraculous source in the very kernel and being of the
"thing in itself." Historical philosophy, on the other hand . . . has
discovered in individual cases (and this will probably be the result
in every case) that there are no opposites, except in the customary
exaggeration of popular metaphysical interpretations, and that a
mistake in reasoning lies at the bottom of this antithesis.[7]

Previously, thinkers concerned themselves with these oppositions in which
one element was of great positive value (heaven, goodness, reason, altruism)
and the other element was to be shunned, avoided, exterminated if possible
(hell, evil, desire, egoism). Their problem was explaining the origin of the
opposites, and the traditional solution of philosophers and theologians, says
Nietzsche, has always been to assume some "miraculous source" for the
positive element, typically some realm of being outside the nasty, changing,
corrupt everyday world we inhabit.

So, which opposites are resolved or erased in the film? One of the
most important oppositions in the actual war in Vietnam—not just in the
movie—was the opposition between soldiers and civilians, or, perhaps more
accurately, between combatants and noncombatants. Modern just-war
theory is based entirely on this distinction. Noncombatants have inalienable
rights of the sort that Thomas Jefferson enumerated in the Declaration of
Independence—specifically, the right to life. Combatants have suspended
their right to life in favor of war rights, which include the right to wear a
uniform, the right to bear arms in the name of the country, and the right
to kill enemy combatants.[8] One of the reasons that Vietnam was such a
difficult (and, in the end, unwinnable) war was that this opposition or distinction was blurred or erased. The North Vietnamese who fought the U.S.
occupation oftentimes disguised themselves as civilians or noncombatants,
making it very difficult for American troops to distinguish friend from foe.
This resulted, of course, in American deaths at the hands of unsuspected
enemy "soldiers" in civilian dress, but it also resulted in a high death rate
among actual civilians, once many American GIs ceased to worry or care
about clearly identifying enemy soldiers or combatants.[9]

So, when Joker and Rafterman are aboard a helicopter en route to their
assignment, the machine gunner fires indiscriminately at men, women,

children, and livestock. When Joker asks the man how he can shoot women and children, the gunner quips, "Easy—Ya just don't lead 'em so much!" And more importantly, at the end of the film the enemy sniper turns out to be a young woman dressed in civilian clothes. It is only the rifle she is holding that distinguishes her from someone going to the market, doing the laundry, or working in an office.

Another opposition that is played with, if not erased, is that between male and female, or between masculinity and femininity. At Parris Island, Hartman refers to his male recruits as "ladies" throughout. What is more, the gun, a traditional phallic symbol, is here feminized. Hartman orders the recruits to give their rifles girls' names and to sleep with them. He barks at the soldiers, "This is the only pussy you people are going to get!" And again, the fact that the sniper turns out to be a woman clearly plays with our understanding of war as a male-exclusive, testosterone-driven activity.

However, the opposition with which Kubrick seems most concerned is that between the sacred and the profane. In the film, the holy and religious are intertwined with the vulgar, the sexual, the secular. During basic training, Hartman tells the soldiers that if they survive boot camp, they will each become "a minister of death, praying for war," and in fact, they do have a prayer about their guns, which begins: "This is my rifle. There are many like it, but this one is mine." Further, Hartman informs the recruits that "God has a hard-on for marines, because we kill everything we see."[10] Again, my main argument here is that in a chaotic Nietzschean world, morality becomes problematic to the point that killing is not only not necessarily wrong but may be required for the sake of decency or moral order (if there is any such thing any longer). But Hartman's exclamation takes this up a notch or two: God apparently *so* approves of the fact that marines not only kill but kill *everything* they see that he gets a divine erection. This points not only to the ambiguity of morality but also, as I said, to this erasure of the opposition of the sacred and the profane.

More shockingly, at one point Hartman orders Joker and Cowboy to clean the head (lavatory), instructing them to make it so "sanitary and squared away that the Virgin Mary herself would be proud to go in there and take a dump." Interestingly, when Hartman asks Joker whether he believes in the Virgin Mary, Joker responds in the negative, and Hartman is so offended by Joker's impiety that he slaps him, threatening Joker that he had better admit his belief, or else. Hartman does not seem bothered by the tension in believing at the same time that the Virgin Mary conceived immaculately and that she needs to take a crap once in a while (and note the interesting juxtaposition of references to the Virgin and to God's hard-on—though the latter is inspired by the marines, apparently, and not by the one he supposedly impregnated). Last, when Joker is dressed down in Vietnam for simultaneously wearing a peace symbol button and having ".Born to Kill" written on his helmet, the colonel who is chastising him (after describing their mission in the war as if it were a football game) says that what he expects from his men is quite simple: that they obey his commands as they would "the word of God."

To repeat, the resolution of these oppositions points to a world in chaotic flux. In such a world, there is no identity, no sameness; consequently, there can be no real oppositions.

Leonard Lawrence, a.k.a. Private Pyle

As I discussed above, at Parris Island, Hartman attempts to stamp order on chaos, to erase all differences among the recruits, to give them identity or sameness. But, given a Nietzschean flux metaphysics, this is an impossibility. There is only chaos; there is only difference. And it is Leonard, or Private Pyle, who represents the folly of Hartman's efforts. Note that throughout the first half of the film, Leonard retains his uniqueness; he resists the order that Hartman is attempting to foist on him. He is the only recruit who has a distinct personality in this part of the film, and he is the only one who is ever referred to by his real name.[11] Further (at least among his group of recruits), he is the only one whose nickname is that of an individual, Private Pyle; the others are merely archetypes (Joker, Cowboy, Snowball). Of course, in giving him that nickname, Hartman is unironically pointing to the fact that Leonard is a screwup like the Jim Nabors character on the television show *Gomer Pyle, USMC*. However, the Gomer Pyle character most definitely stood out and was different, as is Leonard. Thus, Hartman is unknowingly and ironically labeling the different *as* different, the unique *as* unique, and thereby not only failing in his mission to make them all the same but also illustrating the impossibility of that mission (and, perhaps, also sewing the seeds of his own demise).

Further, it is through Leonard that the disastrous consequences of Hartman's mission manifest themselves. On the last night of training, Joker is on watch and finds Leonard in the bathroom with a rifle loaded with live ammunition. Joker tells Leonard that if Hartman catches them, they will be "in a world of shit," and Leonard replies that he already *is* in a world of shit. He then proceeds to perform the drills that Hartman has been running them through, all the while reciting the cadences and "prayers" the recruits have learned. These are the very drills meant to impose order and erase difference, of course, but as Leonard performs them in the bathroom, they now seem absurd. When Hartman finds the two of them, he orders Leonard to surrender the weapon. Leonard shoots (and presumably kills) Hartman, then sits on a toilet, puts the barrel of the gun in his mouth, and blows his bloody brains all over the pristine white wall. The neat orderliness is thus shown to be a sham; Leonard shows us that the world really is all chaos. This then launches us into the second half of the film, the brutal and chaotic war in Vietnam.

Morality and the Flux

As suggested earlier, one of the main lessons of *Full Metal Jacket* is that in a world in flux, morality becomes problematic. This is certainly Nietzsche's position, although it is complex and sometimes seems contradictory. At times, for example, he attacks and condemns morality wholesale, calling it unhealthy, life denying, and degenerate: "All the forces and drives by virtue of which life and growth exist lie under the ban of morality: morality as the instinct to deny life. One must destroy morality if one is to liberate life."[12] Traditional morality condemns our animal drives and instincts as sinful, vicious, evil. But, as I discuss later, these are the very forces and drives at the very heart of life and nature; consequently, morality is unnatural and life denying and must be rejected or destroyed to "liberate" life. At other times, however, Nietzsche talks about different kinds of morality, one of which might actually be life affirming: "Two types of morality must not be confused: the morality with which the healthy instinct defends itself against the incipient decadence—and another morality with which this very decadence defines and justifies itself and leads downward."[13]

So, on the one hand, Nietzsche condemns morality completely; on the other hand, he says that one type of morality might be healthy and, in fact, necessary. I believe that this only seems to be inconsistent or contradictory because he is using the word *morality* in two different senses: when he condemns morality completely, he is referring to Judeo-Christian absolutist morality (which is supposed to be universal and objective and is—he believes—unnatural and life denying); in the other case, he is referring to other ways of evaluating the world and life, ways that are healthier, do not deny the natural, animal aspects of ourselves, and allow us to flourish. He writes, "Every naturalism in morality—that is, every healthy morality—is dominated by an instinct of life; some commandment of life is fulfilled by a determinate canon of 'shalt' and 'shalt not'; some inhibition and hostile element on the path of life is thus removed. *Anti-Natural* morality—that is, almost every morality which has so far been taught, revered, and preached—turns, conversely, *against* the instincts of life: it is *condemnation* of these instincts, now secret, now outspoken and impudent."[14] The natural type of morality is quite possible, and perhaps even necessary, in a world in flux; it is the antinatural, absolutist morality that becomes very problematic in the chaotic, changing world.

But why is this so? What difference does it make to absolutist morality that everything is continually changing? For Judeo-Christian morality—the version of absolutist morality[15] with which we are probably most familiar and Nietzsche's favorite target in his attacks on morality—the answer is pretty clear. In a world in flux, there is no God, no heaven and hell, no commandments handed down in stone. Traditional Judeo-Christian morality is rooted in Judeo-Christian metaphysics, and it stands or falls with that metaphysics. That is to say, the morality depends on the notion of a creator God who has determined and instilled in everything the worth, value, and meaning that it has. Once God is eliminated, Judeo-Christian morality becomes untenable.[16]

This is all the more so, given the flux as Nietzsche sees it. As I discuss above, Nietzsche denies thinghood, identity, substance; nothing remains the same, and there is nothing unchanging, existing somehow outside the flux. Rather, what we call things are complexes of what he sometimes calls "centers of force." We ourselves, as part of the flux, are not stable, monadic subjects or egos. Rather, we too are multiplicities, conglomerations of instincts, drives, wills, and so forth. He says, "In all willing it is absolutely a question of commanding and obeying, on the basis . . . of a social structure composed of many 'souls.'"[17] Just as there is no such thing as a thing, something containing identity and standing outside the flux, there is likewise no such thing as a unitary soul, subject, or ego. Rather, what we call the "self" is a continually changing complex, a multiplicity. Consequently, Nietzsche denies that there is any such thing as free will, not because our actions are determined and necessary, or unfree, but rather because he denies that there is any such thing as a "will" *to be* free. "Willing seems to me to be above all something complicated, something that is a unit only as a word," and the will is a "manifold thing for which the people have only one word."[18] This certainly problematizes the traditional idea of a free subject who makes decisions and performs actions and is therefore morally responsible for those decisions and actions. And this idea is at the center of traditional, absolutist morality.

Further, the character, or essence (if we can still use such a word), of these centers of force, and thus of the world itself, is what Nietzsche calls "will to power": "Suppose, finally, we succeeded in explaining our entire instinctive life as the development and ramification of *one* basic form of the will—namely, of the will to power. . . . The world viewed from inside, the world defined and determined according to its 'intelligible character'—it would be 'will to power' and nothing else."[19] Elsewhere he says, "*This world is will to power—and nothing besides!* And you yourselves are also this will to power—and nothing besides!"[20]

And so what is the character of this will to power? Nietzsche claims that we see it in the natural world around us: "Life itself is *essentially* appropriation, injury, overpowering of what is alien and weaker; suppression, hardness, imposition of one's own forms, incorporation and at least, at its mildest, exploitation. . . . 'Exploitation' . . . belongs to the *essence* of what lives, as a basic organic function; it is a consequence of the will to power, which is after all the will of life."[21] Far from being peaceful, good, wholesome, or divine, nature works by violation. Living things exist by overpowering and eating other living things.[22] They live by exerting and discharging their strength, at the expense of other creatures. "A living thing seeks above all to *discharge* its strength—life itself is *will to power*," Nietzsche says.[23] This violation, this appropriation and injury, is the very heart and essence of the world and, indeed, of human nature as part of that world. And yet, violation and injury are precisely what traditional morality would label as "immoral" or "evil." In other words, traditional, absolutist morality condemns life and nature and is therefore, Nietzsche says, unhealthy and degenerate.

Yet, part of what it means to be a human being in this chaotic world is to evaluate and posit values: "Life itself forces us to posit values; life itself values through us when we posit values."[24] As living beings whose character or essence is will to power, we seek to express that power in whatever way possible; we seek to overcome obstacles, to attain goals, to consume, to overtake. Thus we evaluate things in the world around us as beneficial or harmful to the discharge and expression of our power, things that help or hinder us in achieving our goals. And the rules contained in a (healthy, life-affirming) morality or system of evaluation aid us in reining in our various chaotic drives and instincts, allowing us to give a certain coherence and structure to our lives and thus allowing us to flourish.

Morality as a Problem in *Full Metal Jacket*

There are a number of references to the problem of morality in the film. I have already mentioned Hartman's claim that God has a hard-on for marines because they kill everything they see. Again, that kind of indiscrimination, the failure to distinguish the evil from the innocent, combatants from noncombatants, points to the dissolution of any kind of absolute good or evil in a chaotic world in flux. This is also seen in the machine gunner's response when he is asked how he can kill women and children. He takes it as a practical issue, how he is physically able to shoot them when they are running; he does not concern himself with the moral distinction between enemy soldiers and civilians. Further, during basic training, Hartman asks the recruits if they know who Charles Whitman and Lee Harvey Oswald were. Cowboy identifies Whitman as the man who went on a killing rampage, shooting people from a tower at the University of Austin in 1966, and Snowball identifies Oswald as President Kennedy's assassin. About Oswald, Hartman tells them: "He was two hundred and fifty feet away and shooting at a moving target. Oswald got off three rounds with an old Italian bolt-action rifle in only six seconds and scored two hits, including a head shot!" When asked where these two men learned how to shoot, Joker responds that they learned in the marines. Hartman—admiringly—says, "In the marines! Outstanding! Those individuals showed what one motivated marine and his rifle can do! And before you ladies leave my island, you will be able to do the same thing!" Again, Hartman focuses on the killing abilities of Whitman and Oswald, treating them as if they were model soldiers, with no concern about who their targets were. They are examples of men who killed as indiscriminately as Hartman says marines do, once more pointing to the ambiguity of morality.

Finally, as I have mentioned, this problem of morality is essential to the structure of the film. Each half ends with a killing: Leonard kills Hartman and then himself, and Joker kills the sniper, but the meaning and relevance of each are completely different. Leonard's actions, and his and Hartman's subsequent deaths, are mad, absurd, completely unexpected, and senseless.

And, as I have argued, they are the results of attempting to force order on chaos. Joker's killing of the sniper, however, is humane, compassionate; it is the only thing that makes sense in an insane world. In an insane, chaotic world, morality is not so simple or absolute as "thou shalt not kill." Not all killings are alike. Morality is far more complex than that.

Notes

I would like to thank Jerold J. Abrams for his very helpful comments and suggestions on an earlier draft of this essay.

1. Philip Wheelwright, ed., *The Presocratics* (New York: Macmillan, 1985), 70, 71.

2. Friedrich Nietzsche, "Reason in Philosophy," in *Twilight of the Idols,* from *The Portable Nietzsche,* ed. Walter Kaufmann (New York: Penguin, 1976), 480–81. The concern with essences is an ancient one. In an attempt to explain how some things change while others seem to stay the same, and to explain how we can have real knowledge of the world, Plato, for example, introduced his notion of the Forms: eternal, perfect models of things standing outside space and time. The changing, physical world around us, he said, is a less real appearance of that true reality, something like a shadow on a cave wall (see the *Republic,* especially books V–VII). Aristotle talked about "secondary substances," which are the essences of individual things, or what he called "primary substances." For instance, a primary substance would be an individual man, such as Socrates; the secondary substance would be human being, that which makes Socrates the kind of thing he is. We have real, scientific knowledge only about secondary substances, Aristotle says, since that is knowledge of the universal aspect of things (their essence) and is thus necessary knowledge. Aspects or characteristics of an individual as an individual (for example, the fact that Socrates is fat) are changing, accidental, and contingent properties of the individual (Socrates does not have to be fat in order to be Socrates, but he does have to be a human being in order to be Socrates) and are thus not the object of scientific knowledge (see especially Aristotle's *Categories* for a discussion of substance). Nietzsche is looking to reverse Plato's appearance-reality distinction; for him, being is the artificial construction, whereas becoming is the only reality.

3. Friedrich Nietzsche, "On Truth and Lies in a Nonmoral Sense," in *Philosophy and Truth: Selections from Nietzsche's Notebooks of the Early 1870s,* trans. Daniel Breazeale (Atlantic Highlands, N.J.: Humanities Paperback Library, 1979), 83.

4. Friedrich Nietzsche, *The Gay Science,* trans. Walter Kaufmann (New York: Vintage, 1974), 177.

5. Luis M. García Mainar, *Narrative and Stylistic Patterns in the Films of Stanley Kubrick* (Rochester, N.Y.: Camden House, 1999), 199.

6. Michel Ciment says, "Before being killed off under a hail of bullets, the soldiers

are stripped of their identity. They are called Joker, Animal Mother, Eightball, Cowboy, Rafterman, Pyle." *Kubrick: The Definitive Edition* (New York: Faber and Faber, 2001), 234.

7. Friedrich Nietzsche, *Human, All Too Human*, trans. R. J. Hollingdale (Cambridge: Cambridge University Press, 1986), 12. In a similar passage, Nietzsche says: "For one may doubt, first, whether there are any opposites at all, and secondly whether these popular valuations and opposite values on which the metaphysicians put their seal, are not perhaps merely foreground estimates, only provisional perspectives." *Beyond Good and Evil*, trans. Walter Kaufmann (New York: Vintage, 1966), 10.

8. For an excellent discussion of just-war theory, see Michael Walzer's classic work *Just and Unjust Wars* (New York: Basic Books, 1977), especially chs. 8 and 9.

9. For example, the massacre at My Lai. See Walzer, *Just and Unjust Wars*, 309–16.

10. Just before this line, Hartman says, bizarrely, "Today is Christmas! There will be a magic show at zero-nine-thirty!" It is interesting that he says there will be a magic show, not a mass or a prayer service. This seems to be another mixture of the sacred and the profane, but it might also point to the illusory nature of God and religion. That is, they are having a celebration of illusion rather than of a real God. My thanks to Jerold J. Abrams for pointing this out to me.

11. The one exception to this is Snowball. In the first scene, Hartman asks him what his name is, and he responds, "Sir, the private's name is Private Brown, sir!" Hartman then tells him that from now on, he will be called "Private Snowball."

12. Friedrich Nietzsche, *The Will to Power* (New York: Vintage, 1968), 189.

13. Ibid., 153.

14. Nietzsche, "Morality as Anti-Nature," in *Twilight of the Idols*, 489–90.

15. There are other sorts of absolutist moralities, such as Immanuel Kant's ethics, that Nietzsche would and does attack and that he believes are equally as problematic as Judeo-Christian morality.

16. In *The Gay Science*, Nietzsche infamously proclaimed that "God is dead," meaning that metaphysical systems such as Platonism and Judeo-Christianity, which posit some otherworldly absolute and unchanging being, have been undermined by scientific progress and scientific explanations of the world. Further, the value systems built on those metaphysical systems, such as Platonic or Christian ethics, are now foundationless and thus must be rejected. See "The Madman," in *The Gay Science*, 181–82. For further explanation, see my "Nietzsche and the Meaning and Definition of Noir," in *The Philosophy of Film Noir*, ed. Mark T. Conard (Lexington: University Press of Kentucky, 2005), especially 17–19.

17. Nietzsche, *Beyond Good and Evil*, 21.

18. Ibid., 25, 26. Elsewhere he says: "Freedom of will or no freedom of will?—There is no such thing as 'will'; it is only a simplifying conception of understanding, as is 'matter.'" *The Will to Power*, 354.

19. Nietzsche, *Beyond Good and Evil*, 48.

20. Nietzsche, *The Will to Power*, 550.

21. Nietzsche, *Beyond Good and Evil*, 203.

22. As Arthur Schopenhauer so poetically put it, "This world is the battle-ground of tormented and agonized beings who continue to exist only by each devouring the other. Therefore, every beast of prey in it is the living grave of thousands of others, and its self-maintenance is a chain of torturing deaths." *The World as Will and Representation*, vol. 2, trans. E. F. J. Payne (New York: Dover, 1969), 581.

23. Nietzsche, *Beyond Good and Evil*, 21.

24. Nietzsche, "Morality as Anti-Nature," in *Twilight of the Idols*, 490.

EXISTENTIAL ETHICS

Where the Paths of Glory Lead

Jason Holt

Paths of Glory (1957) is far from Kubrick's best-known film. In fact, it is not even his best-known war film. If one thinks of it at all, it comes well down the list, certainly after *Full Metal Jacket* (1987) and, although they are not strictly war films, *Spartacus* (1960), *Dr. Strangelove* (1964), and *Barry Lyndon* (1975). Still, *Paths of Glory* is a fine entry in Kubrick's numerically modest but aesthetically powerful body of work. It is arguably his most underrated film. Some critics consider it the best antiwar film ever made, but even this positive verdict sells the movie short. *Paths of Glory* is much more than an antiwar film; it is as much about the necessary absurdity of the human condition as about the contingent horror of war. As such, it is a perspicuous, poignant, and truly profound film.

In this essay I explore how *Paths of Glory* illustrates, and even illuminates, certain important facets of existentialism. Rather than focusing on particular existentialist philosophers, my concern is with the existential viewpoint in general, especially as it bears on ethics—that is, moral philosophy and principles of right and wrong.[1] *Paths of Glory* illustrates some of the basic tenets of existential ethics and illuminates certain problems associated with it—especially what might be called the paradox of existentialism (the denial of objective values along with the affirmation of an apparently objective value) and the problem of authenticity (the "existential virtue," which, from one perspective, seems unavoidable and therefore not a virtue)—as well as roads to solving those problems.

Here is a brief rundown of the film: During World War I, the fictional 701st Regiment of the French army, led by Colonel Dax (Kirk Douglas), is ordered by General Mireau (George Macready) to leave the trenches and attack the Ant Hill, a German stronghold. Everyone knows that the stronghold is impregnable. When the attack fails, three men from the regiment are randomly selected to stand court-martial for cowardice. Despite Dax's skilled efforts to defend them, it is a kangaroo court-martial, and the men are found guilty and executed by firing squad. Although Mireau eventually gets his comeuppance, Dax and the surviving members of the 701st are ordered to return to the front immediately.

Mortal Thoughts

The screenplay for *Paths of Glory* was written by Kubrick, Calder Willingham, and Jim Thompson and based on the 1934 novel by Humphrey Cobb. The title comes from Thomas Gray's "Elegy Written in a Country Churchyard." Here is the applicable stanza:

The boast of heraldry, the pomp of power,
And all that beauty, all that wealth e'er gave,
Awaits alike the inevitable hour.
The paths of glory lead but to the grave.

I include this stanza not only because it fleshes out the film's literary background but also because the sentiment it expresses is, in many ways, at the very core of the existential point of view.

The themes of death and, in some sense, the pointlessness of life loom large not only in existential philosophy but also, quite expectedly, in many war films. *Paths of Glory* is no exception. Note the following dialogue between two soldiers in the 701st the night before their suicide mission to attack the Ant Hill:

YOUNGER SOLDIER: Look, just like I'm trying to tell you: If you're really afraid of dying, you'd be living in a funk all the rest of your life, because you know you've got to go some day, any day. And besides, if it's death that you're really afraid of, why should you care about what it is that kills you?

OLDER SOLDIER: You're too smart for me, "Professor." All I know is, nobody wants to die.

That we, as humans, are not only mortal but also *concerned* with our own mortality—that we are beings *toward* death (more or less as Martin Heidegger put it)—though perhaps not terribly insightful, pervades the existential point of view, and it makes sense of the two main ingredients of the existential stance.

The first main ingredient of the existential stance is a view of how the world is; in particular, it is about what it means to be a human being in the world. We are *thrown* into the world. The situations in which we find ourselves are the products of external influences, past decisions, and so on. These situations both present possibilities and constrain opportunities for choice and action. We are free, in such situations, to choose how to act and what to value. Nothing external to us—not nature, morality, social pressure, history, and so on—can determine what we choose, value, or do. "Thrownness" means freedom constrained by situation. Heidegger's term for the kind of being that is peculiar to humans is *dasein,* a situationally constrained being-in-the-world whose existence (defined partly by its inevitable demise) is an *issue* for it. As Jean-Paul Sartre phrases it, a person is *pour-soi* (being-for-itself), condemned to freedom; this freedom causes, and in some sense constitutes, anxiety and anguish.[2] Clearly, the men of the 701st, complete with anxiety and anguish, are *thrown* into their situation, whether in or out of the trenches.

Whereas the first ingredient of the existential stance is a view of how things stand, the second ingredient is a view of how one ought to act, an existential ethics. Although there are, in a sense, no objective values (that is, no binding principles that tell us what, specifically, to do), there are existentially *better* and *worse* ways of making choices and performing actions. Existentially appropriate choices and actions are *authentic,* while inappropriate ones are *inauthentic.* It is not easy to figure out what exactly existentialists mean by "authenticity." Part of what it means is acknowledging the fact that one is thrown into the world, that one is free, and that the burden of choice, value, and action falls squarely on one's own shoulders. Failing to acknowledge this, thinking instead that one's actions are determined by outside forces, is what Sartre calls bad faith. But there seems to be more to it than that. Looking at a few problems with the existential point of view will help us get a better grip on authenticity.

Good Form

Before we try to understand what it means to be authentic, however, we are faced with a problem—the paradox of existentialism. On the one hand, we are positing that there are no objective values, that there is no legitimate moral maxim that tells us how to behave, no way we can determine before the fact, in an abstract way, what we ought to do. On the other hand, we are positing that we ought to behave authentically, that there is at least one legitimate moral maxim expressible as "Be authentic" or "Thou shalt be authentic." Call this the existential imperative. Such a maxim, if legitimate, expresses an objective value—one of the things that we are positing do not exist. So, is existentialism inconsistent? Does the denial of objective values imply that there are objective values? This is the paradox of existentialism.

The very formulation of the paradox suggests the way to resolve it. Perhaps there is no legitimate moral maxim telling us *what* to do. The existential imperative does not tell us what to do but rather *how* to do it. Authenticity is a matter of how one acts, not what one does. It is *form*, not *content*, that matters. Authenticity is a formal virtue in this sense. It is content-nonspecific, rather like sincerity (meaning what you say, no matter what you happen to say), consistency (between whatever values you say you have and the acts you commit), and integrity (acting in accordance with your true values, whatever they happen to be). The connection between authenticity and these other formal virtues is more than a passing one. Sartre, for instance, sometimes uses the term *sincerity* (presumably of a rare, existential kind—sincerity of *action* rather than run-of-the-mill sincerity of speech) to contrast with *bad faith,* his term for inauthenticity. Along with inauthenticity, there are a number of formal vices corresponding to the formal virtues listed above: insincerity (not meaning what you say), hypocrisy (acting contrary to the values you say you have), and inconsistency (acting contrary to your own true values). In fact, inconsistency is a reasonably close approximation of inauthenticity, and integrity comes close to capturing what authenticity means (together with the clear acknowledgment of one's freedom). In other words, genuine existence is not a matter of the particular values one happens to have but rather a matter of how one's actions—and one's life, really—comport with those values. The paradox is resolved by distinguishing objective values (which are denied) from meta-values (values about values, or second-order values), which is the kind of thing authenticity is.

In *Paths of Glory,* two characters in particular illustrate the formal vices and virtues mentioned above. General Mireau is insincere (the lives of his men do not matter to him, even though his rhetoric says otherwise), and he is a hypocrite (for instance, for ordering the artillery to fire on his own divisions and insisting that men of the 701st be court-martialed for cowardice)—an inauthentic soldier. Colonel Dax, by contrast, is sincere (in claiming that he cares about his men), is consistent (in doing his soldierly duty), and has integrity (by defending the men whom he believes are being treated unfairly). Dax is an authentic soldier, paradigmatically, and ultimately to his detriment. Dax is offered Mireau's command by General Broulard (Adolphe Menjou), who presumes that Dax has been angling for the promotion all along and that his motivation in bringing Mireau to account was advancement, not justice. Dax, however, does not take the easy way out (of the trenches, as it happens); he refuses the commission, expresses vehement outrage to Broulard, and returns to his men, knowing full well that they will soon have to return to the front.

Dying Well

In *Manhattan* (1979), Woody Allen's character says, "Talent is luck. The most important thing in life is courage." There is something to that. To see why, let us consider a potential problem with the perspective outlined in the previous section.

What I have called the existential imperative obliges us to be authentic, to exhibit formal virtues, to be true to ourselves. But is it possible to be inauthentic? Can one avoid being true to oneself? Whatever one chooses, for whatever reason, one would seem to be, in that moment, unavoidably true to oneself, unavoidably authentic, because one *has* made the choice. From this point of view, General Mireau is no less authentic, no less true to himself, than Colonel Dax is. Freedom cannot be held hostage to anything—even (maybe especially) one's past choices, values, and actions. Is the call to authenticity, then, an empty requirement?

Seemingly not, because one might make choices and act without acknowledging one's freedom, thinking that one's actions are determined by something outside the self. Such choices and actions would be inauthentic. But is that all there is to it? Presumably not, because then being authentic would merely be a matter of knowing something, of epistemic (knowledge-related) virtue, and authenticity, in a strange way, is the existentialist's version of moral virtue. Authenticity is not mere clear-sightedness. One might acknowledge one's thrownness, one's freedom, without that knowledge entering into one's action at all.

The phenomenon of weakness of will, or *akrasia*, should help clarify this issue. Suppose I have made a certain choice to act in the pursuit of some value, but when I am tested, in the moment of truth, my nerve fails and I turn coward. In *Paths of Glory,* Roget (Wayne Morris) is a prime example. In such a moment of weakness, he ends up killing (by grenade) one of the men under his charge on a mission in no-man's-land. As the Roget case nicely illustrates, in some situations one might not have the courage to act in accordance with one's values, to further the cause on behalf of which one has decided to act. One might fail to be authentic because of a lack of backbone.

This means that even with a stripped-down ethics à la existentialism, with a morality of form rather than content—a "formalist" ethics, if you like—content sneaks in through the back door. The foundation of authenticity, of all formal virtues, is courage. Since Aristotle at least, the virtue of courage has been considered a character trait, a mean (average) state between cowardice (where courage is deficient) and foolhardiness or rashness (where courage is excessive and thus not courage proper). Existential artworks almost invariably depict antiheroes who, though rejecting traditional morality in the name of freedom, exhibit courage. This is especially clear in cases in which characters "die well." In *Paths of Glory,* the three men court-martialed for cowardice are found guilty and sentenced to death. In front of the firing squad, Arnaud (Joe Turkel), who is badly injured, falls unconscious; Ferol (Timothy Carey) melts into a blubbering mess; and Paris (Ralph Meeker), despite his earlier failure of nerve, faces death with a steadfast, open-eyed equanimity and poise. As senseless as his execution is, he dies well. Even though he is not a perfect hero, even by existential standards, Paris's death is a triumph. Wartime provides many opportunities for authenticity, and many temptations away from it.

Music Hath Charms

One of the striking motifs in *Full Metal Jacket* is the duality of human nature suggested by the juxtaposition of a peace symbol and the slogan "Born to Kill." A similar duality is suggested in a crucial scene at the end of *Paths of Glory.* After Mireau's comeuppance and Dax's imprudent, if authentic, refusal to assume Mireau's command, Dax returns to his men and watches them through a café window. The men partake of "entertainment" in the form of forcing an attractive and presumably captive German woman (Susanne Christian, a.k.a. Christiane Kubrick) to sing. They harass her with ugly hooting, hollering, and catcalling; their intentions, whether sublimated or delayed, are as obvious as they are sinister. But then, as they listen to the beautiful singing, their ugliness dissipates, becoming silent attention and, eventually, tearful, chantlike, almost solemn humming along. Their basic human decency has been reclaimed, and Dax gives them a momentary reprieve before following the order to return to the front. Despite the doom that awaits the 701st, this ending provides a note of great poignancy and—uncharacteristic for Kubrick—hope.

The appeal and return to basic human decency might seem inconsistent with the existential point of view. According to this viewpoint, to say that human beings are essentially free is to say that there is no such thing as human nature. If there were such a thing as human nature, then that nature, not a person's free choosing, would determine his or her actions. The basic humanity that redeems the 701st, as well as the initial will to evil that puts them in a position to be redeemed, might be seen as an essential, behavior-determining pair of forces. Add to this the sense that the members of the 701st are pawns in a generals' chess game, and the outcome seems to have nothing to do with free choice and more to do with myriad internal and implacable external forces that they can neither negotiate successfully nor ultimately resist.

The apparent tension here is, however, merely apparent. In this military chess game seemingly doomed to a pointless stalemate, the members of the 701st have limited freedom in deciding their fate but full freedom in how they choose to meet it. More important, even if they are naturally disposed to feel the tension between good and bad impulses (as in the café scene), it is ultimately their choice whether "Born to Kill" or the peace sign is the winning slogan. Although the outlook suggested here involves a much more tightly constrained thrownness than many would like to admit—many existentialists included—it remains consistent with the fundamental premise of human freedom. It may appear that freedom is hamstrung by these limitations, but in reality, it is not. However narrowly circumscribed one's options are, they are always there for the choosing.

Paint It Black

Although the Rolling Stones' "Paint It Black" is played over the closing credits of *Full Metal Jacket*, not *Paths of Glory*, I want to end on a strong if somewhat incongruous note. Kubrick is a master of the cinematic sound track, and his use of "Paint It Black" is a masterstroke.

Using *Paths of Glory* to illustrate, I have argued that some of the apparent problems with existentialism—in particular, what I call the paradox of existentialism and the seeming inevitability of authenticity—can be solved. By distinguishing between formal and "contentful" virtues, the first problem is soluble. By acknowledging that actions can be performed without acknowledging one's own freedom and, more important, that in performing or failing to perform actions one may exhibit a weakness of will, the second is soluble. By the same token, or so I have argued, the more traditional virtue of courage underlies an existential, or similarly "formalist," ethics.

Notes

For helpful comments, I thank Jerold J. Abrams, and for useful discussion, I thank Ami Harbin.

1. For a good general introduction to existentialism, I recommend Robert Solomon, ed., *Existentialism* (New York: McGraw-Hill, 1974), a wide-ranging selection of primary texts, both philosophical and literary.

2. For those interested in such matters, consider the following equation: Sartre = Heidegger + Descartes.

PART TWO

THE SUBJECT IN LOVE

WHERE THE RAINBOW ENDS

Eyes Wide Shut

Karen D. Hoffman

Stanley Kubrick's *Eyes Wide Shut* (1999) is an existential film about human nature, sexuality, marital fidelity, and the nature and significance of choice. It is one of Kubrick's most optimistic films. The rituals and banalities of life that often exercise a deadening, soporific effect on the main characters in Kubrick's other films function here in a positive way, providing opportunities for awareness rather than obfuscation. Even though Bill Harford (Tom Cruise) and Alice Harford (Nicole Kidman) are subject to all the difficulties of the human condition so prevalent in Kubrick's earlier films, *Eyes Wide Shut* awakens its protagonists to the reality of their condition and thereby enables them to make conscious choices that eventually strengthen their bond. During the course of the film, the Harfords remove their literal and metaphorical masks, becoming revealed to each other. Although this unmasking exposes some uncomfortable truths about human desires and how these desires challenge marital fidelity, it also strengthens the Harfords' marriage. By the film's end, Alice and Bill are cognizant of their own and their partner's desires for other people. But rather than destroying their marriage, the couple's honest confession of these desires ultimately reinforces their commitment to stay together. Although human fallibility and frailty may render Bill and Alice incapable of living with their eyes fully opened, Kubrick's final film suggests that their eyes can at least be wide shut.

Clothing as Masks: Introducing Alice and Bill

Eyes Wide Shut opens with a highly erotic image of Alice Harford. With her back turned to the camera, she gracefully removes her dress. Shostakovich's Jazz Suite Waltz no. 2 plays in the background. In an instant, Alice is nude.

But before she can turn around, the camera lens closes, the screen goes black, and the title of the film appears. Alice has been glimpsed fully naked but only partly revealed. Although this opening sequence lasts only a few seconds, it sets the tone for the rather lengthy film that follows: it establishes that the film will provide an intimate, erotic, and sometimes shocking glance into the private lives of its characters.[1]

As the music continues, Kubrick shifts our attention from the private to the public; the camera moves to the world outside the Harfords' cozy New York City apartment. The noise of the bustling traffic contrasts with the ordered waltz inside. In the next shot, the camera returns to the private realm and introduces Bill Harford. He too is seen from behind, framed by drapes colored a deep red that reappears throughout the film. But, in contrast to Alice, who was in the process of removing her clothes, Bill has just finished dressing. Bill is fully and formally clothed and anxious to leave for a Christmas party. Though we might therefore expect the next image of Alice to be one in which she too is fully dressed, Kubrick surprises us once again: Alice is next seen sitting on the toilet in a shot that some might consider even more shocking and intimate than her earlier nudity. Kubrick seems intent on letting his viewers know that Alice's character will be unmasked long before Bill's. Bill will try to keep much more hidden.

Social Masks and Romantic Seductions: Victor's Christmas Party

Shortly after arriving at the party, Bill and Alice are separated. Despite Bill's initial contention that he does not know "a soul" at the party, he encounters several familiar faces. He talks first to his old friend Nick Nightingale (Todd Field), a medical school dropout who has been hired to play the piano at the party. Bill then runs into a flirtatious model, Gayle (Louise Taylor), and her friend, Nuala (Stewart Thorndike), who coyly offer to take Bill "where the rainbow ends." Before he has a chance to accept or reject the proposal, their conversation is interrupted by a request that Bill come to the aid of Victor Ziegler (Sydney Pollack), the party's host, in reviving a prostitute, Mandy (Julienne Davis), who has overdosed in Victor's bathroom.[2] As if to reinforce the fact that he has not decided whether to follow the women to the rainbow's end, Bill turns to the models and says, "To be continued?" with an intonation that suggests a question. Bill is noncommittal: he does not appear to know whether the journey to the rainbow's end is one he wants to make.

His wife also shows signs of being somewhat noncommittal in her refusal of Sandor Szavost (Sky Dumont), a suave Hungarian who propositions her at the party. When he suggests that she join him for a private dance in the sculpture gallery, Alice replies, "Maybe . . . not just . . . now." Like her husband, she is initially reluctant to completely reject the possibility of an adulterous encounter. Unlike her husband, though, she does not require an external interruption to end the attempted seduction. Instead, she decides that she must find her husband and ultimately tells Sandor that the fact that she is married precludes their scheduling a later rendezvous. Although she seems momentarily tempted by Sandor's offer—an offer no doubt facilitated by champagne—Alice's ultimate refusal of him is unequivocal.

These scenes at the party are significant because of the insight they give into each of the film's main characters and because they depict an attempted seduction of each. The scenes at Victor's house are also interesting because of what is said about marriage, particularly about the role of sex in marriage. Representing the consummate aesthete, Sandor begins his conversation with Alice by making a reference to Ovid's poetic treatment of love. Alice counters by suggesting that the pursuit of romantic love might destroy true intimacy, not create it: Ovid died painfully alone. Undeterred, Sandor notes that Ovid might have died alone, but he "had a good time first—a very good time." Although this exchange might seem to be mere cocktail party banter, it establishes one of the crucial themes of the film: the contrast between the good time of romantic love and the true intimacy of marital love.

Sandor seems to deny that there is much value to marital love and suggests that one of the few charms of marriage is that it adds excitement to extramarital affairs by making "deception a necessity." He explains that one of the reasons women used to get married was so that they could become sexually active with men who were not their husbands—"the ones they really wanted." Sandor appreciates the value of marriage in furthering the aesthetic possibilities for love, either by introducing the exciting elements of danger and deception or by expanding one's range of potential partners. But this is the only value he finds in marriage. In a culture that does not chastise unmarried women for being sexually active, Sandor has difficulty understanding the rationale for marriage and asks Alice, "Why does a beautiful woman, who could have any man in the room, want to be married?"

Philosophically, Sandor introduces an important challenge to Alice's view of marriage. Taken together with her refusal to pursue the possibility of an extramarital sexual encounter, Alice's position seems to be that marriage requires fidelity to one's spouse and that, despite occasional temptations that must be denied, the good of marriage is clearly preferable to the alternative—so much so that marriage needs no external justification.

Deception and Desire: Alice's Search for a Straight Answer

In case viewers needed to be reminded of the sexuality inherent in marriage, Kubrick moves directly from Alice's affirmation of the value of marriage and the assertion that she must go find her husband to a shot of her at home—once again nude, slowly removing her earrings. The camera angles are particularly interesting here. As before, Alice is shown from behind. But now, more of her character has been revealed, so more of her body is shown. As she stands in front of a mirror, both sides of her body are seen.

Chris Isaak's song "Baby Did a Bad, Bad Thing" establishes a sexually charged atmosphere that intensifies with the appearance of Bill in the mirror. We have already seen Alice naked on two occasions by the time Bill finally appears without his clothes. And even then, we do not initially see him; we see a *reflection* of him. As the camera slowly zooms in to capture the couple's passionate kiss, it tracks toward the reflection in the mirror. Only as Alice removes her glasses does the camera finally switch from the mirror to the couple standing in front of it. But Alice seems reluctant to let the image go and continues to focus on their conjoined image rather than on her husband. She appears to be thinking not only of him but also of the two of them together. Her conversation with Sandor has forced her to reflect on the relationship between sex and marriage, which she now does literally as well as figuratively.

A few scenes later, after a sequence interspersing shots of Bill's and Alice's daily routines in their roles of doctor and mother (including yet another view of Alice nude), Alice discusses her reflections about sex and marriage with Bill. Fueled by the marijuana they are sharing, Alice initiates a conversation about fidelity, asking Bill if he "fucked" the two models with whom she thinks he disappeared at the party. As her voice takes on an accusatory tone, she physically rises to Bill's level, trading her supine position for a seated one. With her husband now seated beside her, she listens to his denial and laughingly answers his questions about the man with whom he saw her dancing. All seems to be well until Bill identifies Sandor's lust for Alice as "understandable," since she is a beautiful woman. At this point in the conversation, Alice disentangles herself from her husband's arms, leaves the warm tones of the bed, and goes to stand in the doorway. Her cooled passion is reflected in the deep blue tones behind her. Alice is particularly troubled by Bill's passive acceptance of Sandor's attempted seduction because, she claims, it implies that Sandor's interest in her is purely physical and that men are expected to desire physically attractive women. Pursuing the latter point, she notes that if all men want to sleep with beautiful women, then Bill wants to sleep with Gayle and Nuala, because both models are beautiful.

Struggling to head off a possible argument, Bill replies that he would want to sleep with Gayle and Nuala if not for the fact that he loves Alice, and his love makes him an exception to the rule. To be safe, Bill adds that he does not desire other women because, as he tells Alice, "we are married and because I would never lie to you or hurt you." Unfortunately, Bill's claim only fuels his wife's anger, because Alice interprets it to mean that Bill's only reason for not sleeping with the models is out of "consideration" for her, not because he does not desire them. At last, viewers start to understand why Alice is upset: she has asked her husband a question about his desire for other women, and he has answered by claiming that he would not act on his desire—failing to answer the question he has been asked. Alice thus becomes frustrated with her husband's inability to give her "a straight fucking answer."

Perhaps she is also frustrated because of her own desire for Sandor and because she is not certain that she could explain this desire to her husband. If so, her frustration would explain why Alice takes particular offense at Bill's claim that his female patients do not fantasize about having sex with him. Bill claims that women "basically just don't think like that." This statement reveals that Bill does not know much about women in general, and he does not know much about his wife. He compounds this error by noting that he does not get jealous when other men are drawn to Alice because he knows that she would never be unfaithful to him. He has "complete confidence" in her.

Bill's confidence is too much for Alice to bear, because she knows that it is misplaced. Breaking down in a paroxysm of laughter that leaves her in a fetal position on the floor, Alice makes an important confession: the previous summer, during a trip to Cape Cod, she found herself inexplicably and irresistibly drawn to a naval officer (Gary Goba) who was staying at their hotel. Although the man did no more than glance at her, she was so filled with desire for him that she would have been willing to trade her "whole future life" as a wife and mother to spend just one night with him. Her desire was complicated by a coexisting recognition of her love for her husband—a love both "tender and sad." Even now, months later, Alice is plagued by the reality of her desire for the naval officer, particularly when she juxtaposes her desire for another man with her unwavering love for her husband.

In this pivotal scene, Alice's confession raises some of the central philosophical questions of the film: How is sexual desire related to love and to marriage? Are erotic attractions always subject to our control? Might we experience a desire so overwhelming as to be irresistible? What are the implications for marriage if such desires exist? Can spouses realistically choose to remain faithful? To the extent that fidelity is possible, is it merely the accidental result of the failure to experience desire for other people?

Duty and Desire: Alice's First Confession

Questions about the extent to which fidelity is possible and whether it can be chosen only in the absence of contrary desires are at the root of the conversation between Alice and her husband. She has expressed concern not only about Bill's fidelity but also about *why* he has been faithful. When pressed to reveal whether he *wanted* to sleep with the models, Bill evades Alice's question and maintains that he would not *act* on any such desire. Notice what Bill does here: while he skirts the question about his desires, he reassures his wife that he will be faithful to her regardless of any desires he might have. In philosophical terms, he makes a moral claim that might have come straight from the writings of German philosopher Immanuel Kant.[3] Believing that we cannot be morally responsible for that which lies outside our control, Kant requires individuals to act according to rational moral principles and to act from the motive of duty. Because he does not believe that desires and inclinations are fully subject to rational control, Kant does not include these in his discussions of what duty requires. Kantian morality obligates people to do the right thing, irrespective of their particular inclinations and desires. Bill makes a Kantian appeal: his commitment to his wife is a rational moral principle that trumps any temptation he might feel to be unfaithful. Bill implies that a person who loves his or her spouse and who has a principled commitment to him or her will not experience an inexorable sexual desire for someone else. Bill also seems to think that even if a person of principles *does* experience a strong sexual desire for another person, a person of principle will be able to control his or her response to the desire and resist the temptation.

Alice's experience with the naval officer forces her to question both these claims. In her confession, she lets her husband know that she experienced an overwhelming desire for another man that she believed herself incapable of controlling. Alice's experience thus challenges both of her husband's assumptions. Alice calls into question the Kantian contention that one's moral obligations can be followed no matter what conflicting inclinations exist.

Kantian ethics suggests that although we cannot will desires into or out of existence, we *can* will ourselves to act according to something other than our desires: we can do what duty requires and act according to moral principles. So, our desires are subject to our control inasmuch as we have the ability to ignore them. But Alice believes that she was incapable of ignoring her desire for the officer. Even though circumstances intervened to remove the temptation—the officer received a telegram that prompted his immediate departure—the possibility of her betrayal has left Alice concerned that her fidelity to Bill is accidental. She may have remained faithful to him only because a more attractive and readily available alternative failed to present itself. And when such an opportunity did present itself, it was mere chance that prevented her infidelity.

Her awareness that her own fidelity might be accidental leads Alice to question whether Bill's fidelity might be accidental too. Alice might reasonably wonder whether her husband's moral luck is similar to her own. She is curious about whether the circumstances of Bill's life, particularly his profession, have created opportunities for infidelity, prompting her to inquire about his relationships with his female patients. Bill denies that his profession grants him any opportunities for sex; however, the next scene of the film, in which Marion (Marie Richardson), the daughter of an elderly patient, confesses her love for Bill and kisses him, reveals that Bill is either lying or deluded.[4]

Understandably, Bill is struck dumb by Alice's confession. The complete confidence he had in her moments earlier has been replaced by jealousy and suspicion. Perhaps more important, the most basic assumptions about his marriage, about women, about his wife, and about the power of sexual desire—the assumptions by which he has organized his life—have been called into question. His eyes have been opened to the knowledge that the love one has for one's spouse does not preclude the existence of an unremitting desire for another person. Marital vows provide no guarantees of fidelity. Love—even love fortified by the institution of marriage—might not always emerge the victor over dark, inexorable sexual desire.

Throughout the remainder of the film, Bill tries to come to terms with the implications of what he has just been told. He embarks on his own sexual journey, attempting to clarify his own sexual desires and fantasies. He seeks to experience the phenomenon of overwhelming sexual desire that was so central to his wife's confession. Finally, he tries to come to terms with the jealousy that has been awakened in him as, for the first time, he contemplates his wife's sexual interest in another man. During the course of the film, Bill's eyes are opened to the wide range of possibilities for sexual desire and for marital transgression. And he veers dangerously—almost fatally—close to choosing infidelity.

Awakening Desire: Bill's Journey Begins

Bill's journey begins immediately after his wife's confession. He has not even had time to formulate a response when a telephone call takes him away from his bedroom and out into the night. Before arriving at his destination, he is confronted by his first jealous visions of Alice acting out her fantasy with the naval officer. Imagining his wife reclining on a bed, Bill envisions her revealing herself to another man. The bright colors so ubiquitous in the rest of the film are absent in this black-and-white sequence.[5]

Once he arrives at his first house call of the evening, Bill encounters the aforementioned Marion, who proclaims her love for him. With death quite literally residing in the bed beside them in the form of her deceased father, Marion voices a confession that echoes the one Bill has just heard from his wife: despite the fact that she is engaged to another man, Marion claims to be strongly attracted to Bill and recklessly takes advantage of what might be her last opportunity to passionately kiss him, ignoring her father's dead body and her fiancé's imminent arrival. If Bill had any doubts about the veracity of his wife's overwhelming desire for a man she barely knew, these are quickly removed by Marion's advances. Although Bill believes that Marion's grief has left her emotionally confused, Bill cannot deny that Marion appears to harbor a passionate desire for him—about which her fiancé, Carl (Thomas Gibson), is ignorant. As a result, Bill's initial beliefs about women's desires, including his statement that women "just don't think like that," are undermined.

Walking the streets of New York, pondering the strange confessions of the evening, Bill encounters a prostitute, Domino (Vinessa Shaw). Like the other women Bill has encountered, Domino propositions him. Leaving the busy street to enter the fourth domestic setting of the film, Bill follows his companion through the red door of her building, into the perilous territory of her apartment. Now Bill's moral luck appears to be changing. Despite the fact that he shows no great desire for Domino, he allows himself to be led to a place where adultery becomes a real possibility. But he is passively following, not actively choosing. When Domino asks Bill what he would like to do, he has no idea and has to ask her what she recommends. His response reinforces what we have begun to suspect about him: he has no strong sexual fantasies or desires that he would like to fulfill.

Domino has barely begun her seduction of Bill when they are interrupted by a call from Alice. Although Domino does not "keep track of the time," Alice does. She has been waiting up for Bill but is now going to bed, giving Bill the opportunity to spend as much time as he wants with Domino. But instead, Bill says that he must leave. The phone call from Alice has interrupted the flow of events and reminded Bill of his wife. To commit adultery now, Bill would have to actively choose it, with a conscious awareness of his infidelity, rather than passively allow it to happen to him. So he decides to leave.

Bill does not return home, however. Instead, he walks the streets again and finds himself at the Sonata Café, where his friend Nick Nightingale is playing piano. Bill is intrigued when Nick mentions that later in the evening he will be playing at a party where he will be required to wear a blindfold. Bill, who is in the process of having his eyes opened, is drawn by the possibility of something forbidden to sight. After another of the film's many phone calls interrupts their conversation, Bill sees Nick write down the password to the mysterious party. Realizing that he could use the password to gain entry, Bill presses Nick for the party's address. Once he has it, the only thing Bill needs to gain entry is the proper attire, for it is a masquerade party. He cannot attend as himself but must don a mask and costume and take on another persona. The figurative mask that Bill has worn until now will be replaced by a literal one.

Bill's quest for a costume takes him nearer the rainbow's end; his cab stops at Rainbow Fashions, a rental shop that he believes is owned by a patient of his. In his attempt to gain admittance to the shop, Bill not only invokes his identity and profession but also produces documentation to substantiate his claims. Interestingly, Bill must prove his identity as part of his attempt to lose it.

In a surprising departure from the Arthur Schnitzler novella on which the film is based, Bill requests that the owner of Rainbow Fashions (Rade

Sherbedgia) rent him a tuxedo, a black cloak with a hood, and a mask.[6] In the process of selecting a cloak for Bill, the owner of the store catches his daughter (Leelee Sobieski) in a ménage à trois. In a room directly under the brightly lit rainbow that beams the store's icon, the young girl and her male companions introduce another level of sexual transgression at the rainbow's end: both men are wearing makeup and wigs, and they are engaging in sexual activity involving multiple partners, one of whom is underage.

An Orgy of Masks: Bill's Journey Continues

During the cab ride to Somerton, the location of the masquerade, Bill is again plagued by images of his wife and the naval officer. This time, his imagination takes him further into his wife's fantasy; Bill pictures Alice naked in the arms of her Lothario.

Upon arriving at Somerton, Bill gives the cab driver a monetary incentive to wait for him, strolls up to the gentlemen guarding the main gate, and says the password, "fidelio." Once inside, Bill walks past the scarlet drapes tied to the sides of the doorway and steps onto the bright red carpet that runs the length of the main entry. The warning signs are everywhere: Bill is entering dangerous territory. After donning his mask, Bill steps into a room where a religious ceremony is in progress. In a fascinating mix of aesthetic images and religious ritual, black-robed figures encircle another cloaked in red.[7] Those participating in the ritual stand on a prominent red carpet, while other robed figures observe the proceedings. The sense of sight is not the only one aroused: the high priest carries incense, and ominous music and rhythmic chanting echo in the background. As the high priest moves his scepter, the figures in the circle alternately kneel and prostrate themselves. Then, at a prearranged signal, they unexpectedly throw off their robes to reveal that they are all attractive women. But even without their robes, they are practically indistinguishable. The masked women share nearly identical physical proportions; each woman represents any woman, not any individual woman. These women are nearly naked, but not revealed. If anything, their nudity is almost like a costume donned for the evening. Moreover, the intimacy they purport to offer is a false one: just as the kisses at this party are merely masks touching masks, the sexual acts Bill will soon witness will be merely bodies touching bodies. No deeper connections will be formed. Although the participants might, as Sandor would note, "have a very good time," no true intimacy will be had.

The scene of reckless abandon that might be expected at an orgy is no-where to be found. The proceedings are meticulously ritualized and aim to maximize anonymity. As Bill travels through the only house in the entire film that has no Christmas lights—and, indeed, shows no sign that it is the holiday season—he sees a great deal of graphic but highly impersonal sex. No erotic desire of any kind is evident. This orgy is not a bacchanalian celebration of debauchery. It is nothing like the highly erotic encounter Bill imagines his wife sharing with the naval officer. At Somerton, the participants appear to be actors, imitating eroticism rather than experiencing it. Even the audi-ence for whom they perform seems artificial and unmoved; the bystanders, posed as mannequins would be, are unnaturally still and do not appear to be aroused by what they see. Bill may be spending his evening searching for desire, trying to awaken his own desires and to re-create the phenomenon Alice experienced, but what he continues to find is merely sex.

Ultimately, Bill's quest is a quixotic one. His attempt to experience inexo-rable desire will almost certainly fail. As C. S. Lewis argues in *The Four Loves,* a truly erotic desire cannot be voluntarily constructed but must be passively discovered.[8] Lewis maintains that an erotic desire is not, strictly speaking, a desire for sex so much as a desire for another person—a particular person with whom one is smitten. An individual might very well desire sex—that is, desire the physical act itself—but such a desire is not truly erotic. Bill can experience a desire for the physical act of sex, and this desire can be pursued for its own sake, but this is not what Bill seeks. He already desires Alice and desires sex with her. Whether Bill realizes it or not, the aim of his quest is not sexual conquest; rather, it is to experience the same kind of overwhelm-ing desire for another woman that his wife had for another man. Bill seeks physical attraction but discovers only physical acts. He seeks Eros but finds only artificial imitations and approximations of it.

Only Bill, along with the camera that represents his perspective, moves somewhat naturally through the various rooms at Somerton. Bill is not artificial enough to be completely at home in this masked world, and he cannot pass as one of the invited guests. The party's suspicious hosts have Bill escorted back to the great hall, where he finds himself facing three im-posing figures, one of whom is the high priest from the earlier ceremony. Ominous notes once again reverberate as the priest requests that Bill give the password. After uttering the password that allowed him to enter the gate, Bill is surprised to be asked for a second password, the one for the house. When Bill claims that he has forgotten it, he is asked to remove his mask.

Bill complies, and he is then told that he must get undressed. It seems that he will be forced to fully expose himself to those present; nothing will be allowed to remain hidden. This time, Bill hesitates. Although he will permit himself to be unmasked, he will not agree to be revealed.

As the high priest threatens to forcibly remove Bill's clothes, a woman who had earlier warned Bill to leave the party appears on the balcony above the proceedings. She shouts that she is ready to "redeem" Bill, even though she knows what she is taking upon herself in doing this.[9] Bill is immediately freed, and the mysterious woman is led away, seemingly to be sacrificed on his behalf. The religious imagery introduced by the initial ceremony is completed by the appearance of a savior ready to pay for the sins of another. When Bill inquires what price the woman will have to pay to redeem him, he does not receive a satisfactory answer. He is told only that she has made the conscious choice to save him, with full knowledge of the consequences of doing so, and that her fate is therefore sealed. The high priest explains, "when a promise has been made here, there is no turning back."

Interestingly, this orgy at Somerton, a gathering that seems to represent the ultimate marital transgression, contains important echoes of marriage. "Fidelity" is required for entrance. The sexual encounter one experiences after entry—into the marital institution or into the masked party—is publicly sanctioned. Individuals who have entered are capable of redeeming one another through the willingness to make personal sacrifices. Finally, promises that are made are permanent and cannot be taken back.

Dreams and Desire: Alice's Second Confession

Perhaps to help ensure that viewers will juxtapose Bill's experiences at Somerton with those of his marital bed, Kubrick takes us directly from the orgy to Bill's arrival back home. After carefully hiding his costume, Bill enters his bedroom and encounters his sleeping wife. Moments later, we hear the sound that preceded Alice's earlier confession: her laughter. As before, her laughter is indicative not of joy but of despair; she has been having some of her own nocturnal adventures in the form of a nightmare.

At Bill's request, Alice begins to relate the contents of her dream and thus enters into her second confession of the evening. This time, the story she relates is not something she actually experienced, but the dream nevertheless reveals a great deal about her unconscious desires. What she has to tell Bill about her dream is so offensive that Alice cannot even remain by his side while she tells him. She sits up in bed, enacting a physical separation that will be echoed in the dream she tells. The bedroom that was earlier filled with warm tones of yellow and red is flooded in cold blue light as Alice explains that she dreamed that she and her husband were naked in a deserted city. She was angry with him because she thought he was responsible for their plight. In her dream, Bill left her to search for clothes. Instantly cheered by his departure, she lay down in a beautiful garden and watched as the naval officer approached. She was shamed as the officer looked at her and laughed.

Here, Alice pauses, pained by the memory of her dream. She once again reclines beside her husband. But perhaps because he feels the need to maintain their physical separation, he elevates himself to a seated position. Encouraged by Bill to relate the entire narrative, which is, as he says, "only a dream," Alice sits up, tightly embraces her husband, and continues her tale. As she speaks, the camera transitions back and forth between a shot of the intertwined couple shown from the side and a frontal shot of Bill's face. Although Alice is visibly upset, Bill's face registers utter despair, all the more troubling because of his silence. The camera lingers on his face and shows the viewer something that Bill's wife does not see. Despite his own claim that her nightmare was only a dream, he seems to be taking the content of the dream to heart. The earlier jealousy he experienced upon hearing of his wife's desire for another man is exacerbated as Alice admits that she had sex with the officer in her dream. In fact, she admits that she slept with many men in her dream. To add insult to injury, Alice tells her husband that when she realized in her dream that Bill could see her "just fucking all these men," it encouraged her to make fun of him and to laugh in his face. That was why she was laughing when Bill awakened her.

In her dream, then, Alice has experienced the shame of being laughed at by the naval officer and the shame of being the one laughing at her own husband. Her dream suggests that there is something simultaneously ridiculous and empowering about erotic desire. Alice imagines herself to be ridiculous in the eyes of the naval officer; thus he laughs at her. But when she sleeps with him and with the other men, she seems to gain possession of her sexuality in a way that shifts her from victim to perpetrator. When she sleeps with other men, no one is laughing at her. Now the laughter emanates from her; it is her husband, not she, who plays the fool.

Her dream, of course, parallels the events of the evening. Alice exposed herself through her confession and admitted the foolishness of her desire. But her sexual desire and her recent confession have also given her the last laugh. Because of her confession, Bill has been subjected to sexually explicit visions of his wife with the other man. Moreover, he might have imagined Alice as the female participant at Somerton as he was wandering through the rooms watching anonymous women having sex with various men.

The mental landscapes that Bill and Alice have been occupying are not so far apart. He has observed a supposedly real orgy that had many elements of a dream; she has dreamed that she was a participant in an orgy that seemed quite real. It is not clear which constitutes the greater transgression: to have actually cheated on one's spouse in a dream, or to have merely considered cheating while awake. Kubrick seems to be asking his viewers to contemplate this question. The camera lens closes, and the screen goes black.

Death and Desire: The Danger Intensifies

The camera lens opens again the next morning and follows Bill as he returns his costume and tries to find Nick. He gets bad news on both scores: the mask Bill wore to the party is missing, and Nick has been forced to leave town under mysterious and potentially threatening circumstances. Bill decides to ignore the warning he received the previous evening about making further inquiries and arranges to drive to Somerton. Once he arrives at the gate, portentous music echoes the danger indicated in the note Bill receives—a note that constitutes a second warning to cease his investigations.

Bill tries to resume his daily routine but finds himself haunted by his wife's dream and by the images of Alice having sex with the officer. His visions of her sharing a passionate encounter with another man have become more explicit. Unlike the impersonal and detached sex he witnessed at the orgy, Bill sees Alice in a graphic scene of true eroticism. In fact, these scenes are the most erotic moments in the film.[10] But these scenes depict Alice's fantasy, not Bill's; they just happen to play in Bill's mind.

Bill has not yet succeeded in developing any fantasies of his own; he has not been overcome by desire. Continuing his quest, in a sequence that seems even more dreamlike than the events of the previous evening, Bill begins to retrace his steps from the night before. He first tries to call Marion but is forced to hang up when Carl answers the phone. He next takes a pizza to Domino's apartment, only to find that she is not home. Her roommate, Sally (Fay Masterson), lets Bill in anyway. It is immediately apparent that Bill is much more forward than he was the night before. By visiting Domino, he seems to have made the decision to take advantage of the opportunity she proffered. Even so, he still has no particularly strong desire for Domino; Sally will do just as well. Whereas Bill earlier sought desire, he now seeks sex, perhaps in the hope that it will create erotic desire—at least enough to fill his mind with his own fantasies rather than his wife's. Bill soon discovers, however, that sex with Sally is not to be. She rejects his advances and then relates the devastating news that Domino's blood tests have revealed her to be HIV positive. Bill's moral luck has improved; it has intervened to help him avoid the twin perils of sex with Domino and sex with Sally. Both possibilities are ended by Domino's test results.

Bill leaves the apartment and continues to retrace his steps from the night before. This time, as he walks the streets, it appears that he is being followed. The music that has heretofore warned the audience that Bill is in danger begins again. Having narrowly avoided an indirect encounter with death in the form of HIV, Bill apparently faces the threat of a more direct encounter in the form of the dark figure (Phil Davies) that trails him. At this point in the film, the taxis do not heed Bill's call; there is no ready escape from the danger that pursues him. It is only after Bill stops at a newsstand and turns to confront the stalker that the stranger walks away. Metaphorically, the stalker represents aspects of Bill's life, sexuality, and marriage that are dangerous precisely because Bill refuses to confront them.

Once the dark figure is gone, Bill stops at a café to read the newspaper he has just purchased. He is stunned to find the headline "EX-BEAUTY QUEEN IN HOTEL DRUGS OVERDOSE." Viewers of the film share not only Bill's surprise but, given the strange wording of the headline, also his bewilderment. The camera lingers on the text, but no verb reveals *what* has happened to the ex-beauty queen; we are left wondering, as Bill is, whether the woman in question is still alive—and whether she is the woman from the previous night's party.

Our confusion about whether the woman has survived is answered in the next scene, when Bill arrives at the hospital where the ex-beauty queen was taken.[11] He is horrified to learn that the woman, Amanda Curran (Julienne Davis), died that afternoon. As with all his travels on this, the final evening of the film, the woman he seeks is not to be found. Having just missed an indirect brush with death by failing to find Domino, Bill encounters death directly through Amanda's corpse in the hospital morgue. Devoid of all sexuality, Amanda's nude body is fully exposed. In case we have missed the significance of her death, Amanda's voice reminds us what she told Bill the night before: his mistakes might cost Amanda her life, and they might cost Bill his.

Like Bill, we do not yet know that Amanda is also the same Mandy that Bill treated for an overdose in Victor's bathroom during the Christmas party. We do not yet know that this is the same woman who was warned by Bill that her mistakes, particularly her abuse of drugs, might cost her her life.

Decisions and Desire: Taking Responsibility

Amanda's identity is revealed in the next scene, in which Bill once again makes a house call at Victor's residence, at the latter's request. Kubrick shows us Bill walking the corridor at Victor's, retracing his steps from one of the early scenes of the film. This time, instead of entering the ballroom, Bill enters Victor's study and finds his host "knocking a few balls around" on the bright red pool table that serves as the focal point for the room. Not in the mood for games, Bill declines an invitation to play. Moments later, Bill is told by Victor not to play games. Victor knows about Bill's presence at the orgy and about his actions since then. Victor was at the orgy and saw everything. Moreover, he has been watching Bill—and has had him followed.

Interestingly, Victor claims that Bill is not to blame for attending the party; he holds Nick responsible. Nick erred in making Bill aware of a possibility that he could not reasonably be expected to refuse. In a move that signals his moral superiority to Victor, Bill accepts responsibility for his own actions and choices, claiming that he is the only one to blame for his presence at the orgy. It was not Nick's fault at all.

The question of Victor's culpability is raised momentarily when he admits that he owes Bill an apology for having him followed, but no apology comes. Instead, Victor proceeds to justify his actions, claiming that he was acting in Bill's best interests. If anything, Victor seems to believe that Bill is indebted to him: Bill was in danger the previous evening. Although the identities of the people at the party cannot be revealed, they are not "ordinary people," and Bill "wouldn't sleep so well" if he knew who they were.

Bill does not ask about the identities of the partygoers but instead inquires how his own identity was discovered: "Was it the second password" that gave him away? Bill is surprised to hear that there was no second password; the first password, "fidelio," was all that was needed. But as Victor notes, suspicions were immediately raised about Bill when he arrived in a taxi rather than the usual limousine and when the receipt for the rental costume—a receipt that contained Bill's real name—was found in his coat pocket. Although it is difficult to know how much to make of the circumstances surrounding Bill's discovery, two things are interesting: first, Bill erred when he failed to realize that "fidelity" was sufficient for participation in the events, and second, he failed to become an anonymous participant in the orgy largely because he used his identity (his real name) in order to lose it (rent the costume). To become a fully anonymous masked man would have required a more thorough and calculated loss of Bill's identity.

Next, Bill turns the conversation to questions about the consequences of his presence at the party, specifically for the woman who volunteered to redeem him. Here, the camera, which had been alternating between tracking shots following Victor's agitated motions and close-ups of a motionless Bill, shifts to a wide-angle shot from a different part of the room—a shot that encompasses both men. Bill sits, assuming another static position, as he shows Victor the headline about Amanda and asks whether she was the woman from the previous night's party. Upon hearing that she was, Bill launches into motion, rising out of his seat. Angrily he asks how the events of the evening could have been the "charade," the "fake" that Victor claimed they were if a woman had lost her life as a result. This outburst constitutes the strongest emotional response we have seen from Bill.

Victor answers that Bill's concerns are misplaced, that the woman's warnings and her "whole play-acted 'take me' phony sacrifice" were designed to scare Bill into silence; nothing happened to Mandy that had not happened to her many times before: she had sex with several people and returned safely home. Her door had been locked from the inside, and the police did not suspect foul play. So, Victor argues, Bill should not trouble himself over the death of one drug-addicted "hooker" for whom it was only a matter of time until the next overdose. As Victor glibly remarks, "Nobody killed anybody. Someone died. It happens all the time. Life goes on. It always does, until it doesn't. But you know that, don't you?"

This important scene ultimately leaves viewers where it leaves Bill: puzzling over which of the two radically different and irreconcilable explanations best accounts for Amanda's death. One explanation makes her a mere sexual pawn who died an accidental, unchosen, and ultimately meaningless death. The other makes her a sacrificial lamb who died as a result of her deliberate choice to redeem Bill. Both are deeply disturbing.

We are not given enough information to know which of the two accounts is correct. Although Victor urges the former, he shows no concern for Amanda's life or death and appears to be most interested in telling Bill a story that he will believe. Moreover, even though Bill does not mention it, the fact that the headline about Amanda's death refers to a *hotel* (while Victor claims that Amanda was found inside her locked *home*) gives viewers reason to doubt Victor's story. Ultimately, the truth about how and why Amanda lost her life remains hidden.

Loss of the Mask: Bill's Journey Ends

The true circumstances surrounding Amanda's death remain obscure, but Bill is ready to become revealed. His nocturnal wanderings come to an end, and Kubrick shows us Bill arriving home. As Bill enters his home, he turns off the Christmas lights that have been so prominently displayed throughout the film, as if to signal that the fantasy is over.[12] It is time for Bill to face his wife. The terrifying musical notes from the orgy accompany Bill's entry into the bedroom and intensify as he sees his missing mask resting on the pillow where his own face should be. For the first time in the film, he completely loses his composure and, sobbing uncontrollably, collapses on the bed next to Alice. Literally as well as figuratively unmasked, Bill exclaims that he will tell his wife everything. For perhaps the first time, nothing will be held back.

What he has to say is not easy to hear, and Kubrick next shows us Alice in the early-morning light, her face red and her eyes filled with tears. When the camera cuts to Bill's face, viewers see that he, too, has been crying. Neither seems to know what to say. Alice breaks the silence by reminding her husband that their daughter will be awake soon, and they have promised to take her Christmas shopping. Whatever else may have deteriorated in their relationship, they still share parental duties and familial obligations. These shared duties provide a structure to sustain them through the difficult day ahead.

Perhaps Kubrick means to suggest that the banalities of daily life, which can be inimical to marital bliss, can also buttress a struggling marriage. As Danish philosopher Søren Kierkegaard puts it, marriage has "its enemy in time, its victory in time, its eternity in time."[13] In contrast to romantic love, which gives lovers a false sense of escaping the world and existing outside of time, marital love exists in time. Although time can be the enemy of marital love if unreflective habit settles into the relationship (leading the individuals to take each other for granted), time can also give marital love a history that connects present moments to the past, making both more meaningful. Moreover, the fact that marital love is inseparably tied to daily activities allows those activities to serve as a bulwark against separation: the shared obligations and activities give the couple a common bond that transcends their momentary feelings.

Remaining Awake with Eyes Wide Shut

The final scene of the film follows Bill and Alice as they take Helena (Madison Eginton) shopping. The film that began in the privacy of a bedroom ends in a public department store. The solemnity of the main characters is heightened by the contrast with their surroundings: the store is in the midst of a celebration of the Christmas season, with bubbles in the air and festive music and excited laughter in the background. Excited by the prospect of receiving many toys, Helena flits from one item to the next, telling her parents what she wants and what she might do with various gifts. Focusing on what she hopes Santa might bring her, Helena talks of her wishes and is told that she will have to wait to see what the future brings.

When Helena runs ahead of her parents, leaving them to discuss their future, Alice tells Bill the same thing she has just told her daughter: it is good to have hopes and dreams, but they will have to wait and see what the future brings; there are no guarantees of a "happily ever after." Even so, Alice seems somewhat optimistic about their chances of staying together. Rather than lamenting her husband's recent adventures and attempted infidelities, Alice suggests to Bill that they should be "grateful that we've managed to survive through all of our adventures, whether they were real or only a dream." Alice questions whether "the reality of one night, let alone that of a whole lifetime, can ever be the whole truth." Bill agrees, noting that "no dream is ever just a dream."

Although her infidelity occurred only within the confines of her mind, Alice is not without culpability. Similarly, although Bill has technically refrained from physically cheating on his wife, he is not without blame. There is no need to answer the question whether Bill's nocturnal wanderings actually happened or to ponder whether Alice's fantasies and dreams contain real import.[14] Whether real or imagined, the possibilities for marital infidelity exist, and both characters awaken to the fact that their marriage is not immune to these mysterious and sometimes overwhelming desires. Alice and Bill must be grateful for the awareness they have acquired; their task now is to move forward, not to dwell on the past. As Alice puts it, "The important thing is, we're awake now and, hopefully, for a long time to come."

To Bill's query about whether they will be able to maintain their awareness "forever," Alice suggests that they not use that word. They do not know what the future will bring, but there is reason to be optimistic. Alice does know that she loves her husband. And, in the final line of the film, she suggests that there is something "very important" they "need to do as soon as possible": "fuck." The physical interaction that they have envisioned with other people is something that they need to share with each other.

Some viewers might be surprised not only by the nature of Alice's suggestion but also by her word choice, particularly because she is standing in a crowded department store with her daughter nearby. Kubrick probably intended for the film's last line to be somewhat shocking. But, given that the theme of the film is one of awakening, it seems appropriate that the final line not only call attention to the sexual act (which has been so central) but also do so in a way that delivers a final surprise to the viewer. Additionally, Alice's use of the word "fuck" to describe the sex she needs to have with her husband serves a philosophical purpose: it reminds viewers that the raw sexual expression epitomized by the term can be a part of marriage. Marital sex need not be confined to gentle lovemaking. The kind of physical encounter that either character could have had with any number of other people can be shared with each other. Alice's terminology, then, suggests that marriage is not inimical to full sexual expression.

But one might be left wondering whether *Eyes Wide Shut* problematizes marriage in other ways. Marriage is an institution designed to—and predicated on the belief that individuals are able to—control the expression of sexual desire. Yet Kubrick's film suggests that the darker forces of the personality are whimsical and unpredictable; they cannot be willed into or out of existence (Alice cannot eliminate her desire for the naval officer; Bill cannot create such an attraction at will). The tension created by the instability and unpredictability of desire propels the film. Marital vows require that desires be subject to our control, yet experience makes us believe that desires might not be controllable. Like the other institutions of life that try to help us sublimate our darker impulses, marriage does its best to channel our sexual desires in a constructive way. But even though marriage is the product of choice, we are still subject to desires that we do not choose.

We cannot eliminate these desires, and importantly, the film suggests that we should not want to eliminate them; they are part of what makes us human and part of what makes human life worth living. *Eyes Wide Shut* shows us that the desire spouses have for each other can be strengthened by their attraction to other people. For instance, when Bill and Alice return home from Victor's Christmas party, their flirtations with others fuel their desire for each other. They are scarcely undressed and have not even made it into bed when they begin to make love. Perhaps Kubrick is suggesting that the intensity of the sexual relationship within marriage is partly tied to the possibility of infidelity, and if one wants to retain sexual desire in marriage, one cannot eliminate the possibility of sexual desires that transcend the marriage.

In the end, the film finds a middle ground between the institutional constraints of marriage and the raw desires of sexuality. Although we may, inexplicably, find ourselves in possession of overwhelming desires—like the desire Alice experienced for the naval officer—Kubrick's film suggests that marriage can survive the presence of such desires, so long as their existence is acknowledged. At the film's close, Alice concludes that it is not the *presence* of strong sexual desires for other people that threatens her marriage but rather the *masking* of those desires. As long as Alice and Bill honestly admit the existence of their own desires, and as long as each acknowledges the existence of his or her spouse's desire for other people, their marriage might survive. Alice is grateful for the awakening that she and her husband have undergone. Their commitment to each other will no longer be accidental; it will no longer be the result of the moral luck generated by the absence of live options, by the lack of real possibilities to be unfaithful. Now their fidelity will be consciously chosen, with an awareness of alternatives.

Whether Alice and Bill will succeed in remaining awake and retaining the honesty they have recently attained remains to be seen.[15] The film's title suggests that living with eyes wide open is not a realistic possibility. Yet, in many ways, *Eyes Wide Shut* is an optimistic film, perhaps Kubrick's most optimistic. Even though the characters are subject to desires that are beyond their complete control, they have at least acknowledged this fact and can work together toward mastery.[16] Moreover, the film shows that, even when we fail, the possibility of redemption and reconciliation remains. Alice tells Bill in the final scene that she is *grateful* for what they have endured.[17]

Unlike other critics of Kubrick's final film, who interpret it as suggesting that it is "better to shut one's eyes to what lurks in the mind than to open them and face the truth,"[18] or those who believe that the ending signifies "a return to the routine, boredom, and emotional blindness we observed in the Harfords' lives at the start of the film,"[19] I believe that the nocturnal adventures of Bill and Alice are not meaningless, as a nihilistic interpretation of the film would suggest. Instead, these adventures improve the Harfords' awareness and their intimacy. At the end of the film, Alice wants to be physically intimate with her husband as soon as possible; she does not want distance from him. Admittedly, it is not clear how long the couple's newfound intimacy will last, but this lack of certainty is no cause for despair. A solution need not be permanent to be of value. Even if it will require constant vigilance to maintain the honesty, awareness, and intimacy the Harfords have recently found, Bill and Alice have a better understanding of what they need to do to have a marriage that transcends mere social convention.[20]

Kubrick does not end *Eyes Wide Shut* with an individual who has failed in his attempt to engage in one of the relationships that society most values.[21] Instead, Kubrick ends his film with a couple that has triumphed over adversity and is still together—sustained rather than alienated by the everyday rituals and obligations of family life. The solitary individual of Kubrick's earlier films is no longer left to face life alone.

Although the marital relationship generates its own challenges, it also creates its own rewards. In marriage, the world, and our place in it, can be viewed with more than one pair of eyes. And even if we do not thereby gain the power to see clearly, even if our eyes remain closed to many of the mysteries of human desires, Kubrick's final film offers viewers the hope that our eyes might at least be *wide* shut.

Notes

I am grateful to Alan Hoffman and David Hein for their comments on earlier drafts of this essay. I am especially indebted to Jerold J. Abrams, the editor of this volume, for being such a thoughtful reader and for offering numerous suggestions for improvement.

1. Alexander Walker makes a similar claim: "Exposure and denial, temptation and retreat: such are the recurring motifs of what follows." Alexander Walker, *Stanley Kubrick, Director* (New York: W. W. Norton, 1999), 344.

2. When Bill is called to help Victor, viewers are once again unexpectedly exposed to nudity. It is shocking because nothing has prepared us for this scene and because we have been introduced to Victor and his wife, who is not the naked woman in Victor's bathroom. In the film's first portrayal of Bill in his role as a physician, we see him make a gradually successful attempt to wake Mandy, the unconscious prostitute who has overdosed. In the process, Bill repeatedly asks Mandy to open her eyes. This scene helps establish the theme of awakening—a theme that is literally and figuratively repeated throughout the film.

3. See, for example, Immanuel Kant, *Groundwork of the Metaphysics of Morals,* trans. Mary J. Gregor (Cambridge: Cambridge University Press, 1998).

4. Additionally, viewers might recall that Gayle, one of the models who propositions Bill at the party, met him through his role as a physician. Moreover, at this point in the film, viewers have witnessed two scenes—one in Victor's bathroom and one in Bill's office—in which Bill's profession has led him to interact with beautiful nude women.

5. Kubrick's decision to use black-and-white film here is a bit surprising. Edited in a way that suggests that this scene occurs in Bill's mind, the camera here represents Bill's point of view. Yet surely Bill would imagine the liaison in color. Perhaps Kubrick uses black and white to serve the practical purpose of separating this scene from the strange but supposedly real events that Bill witnesses. Or, because color is used so carefully throughout the film, perhaps Kubrick intends the lack of color here to symbolize Bill's vision of the emotional deadness of the scene. Alternatively, Kubrick might be suggesting that even when Bill experiences a sexual fantasy, he fails to grant it much vibrancy.

6. Arthur Schnitzler, "Dream Story [Traumnovelle]," in *Night Games and Other Stories and Novellas* (New York: Ivan R. Dee, 2001). In Schnitzler's story and in the original draft of the screenplay, Bill requests a priest's cassock. Additionally, both the novella and the original screenplay call for the women at the masked party to be wearing the veils of nuns. It is not clear why Kubrick changed these costumes while retaining other clear elements of religious ritual in the orgy scene that follows. It is worth noting that there are other ways in which Kubrick's film reduces the religious imagery of Schnitzler's novella. For example, in "Traumnovelle," the character of Fridolin/Bill is crucified in his wife's dream. For a fuller discussion of this crucifixion and of other ways that Schnitzler's story differs from Kubrick's screenplay, see Thomas Allen Nelson, *Kubrick: Inside a Film Artist's Maze,* 2nd ed. (Bloomington: Indiana University Press, 2000), 262–68.

7. Nelson (*Kubrick,* 288–89) elaborates: "Bill wanders into this Italian *commedia dell'arte* amalgam of Catholic solemnity, pagan virgin sacrifice, and Saturnalian pornography wearing the colorful, ornamental mask of a feminized male hero. . . . He is the only male in attendance who is not wearing the kind of misshapen or dehumanized mask that projects either the ruthless power and mockery of an aging male order or the unbridled pleasures of Saturnalian lust."

8. C. S. Lewis, *The Four Loves* (New York: Harcourt, 1991), 91–115.

9. It is interesting to note that the language Bill's savior uses here raises a possibility not seen elsewhere in Kubrick's films: that one person may be able to redeem another. If we take this redemption seriously, as I think Kubrick intends, then *Eyes Wide Shut* repudiates Robert Kolker's claim that Kubrick's "characters are never redeemed. They merely die or are diminished, isolated, trapped, and used." Robert Kolker, *A Cinema of Loneliness,* 3rd ed. (New York: Oxford University Press, 2000), 117.

10. Since these are the most erotic moments of the film, and since these scenes represent the desire that haunts Bill, I take them to be central to the film. I therefore disagree with Walker, who maintains that the black-and-white shots of Alice's fantasy

of engaging in an erotic encounter with the naval officer "are hardly necessary—though quite effective in revealing Kidman's anatomy" (Walker, *Stanley Kubrick,* 356). My interpretation of the value of the black-and-white scenes is much closer to Randy Rasmussen's, which argues that the scenes are significant because they "are the film's only examples of unrestrained, unselfconscious sex. Every other sexual encounter, including the Harfords' stand-up affair in front of a mirror, features at least one barrier or counterpoint." Randy Rasmussen, *Stanley Kubrick: Seven Films Analyzed* (Jefferson, N.C.: McFarland, 2001), 342.

11. Before we see Bill exit the cab and enter the hospital, Kubrick shows us the spinning circular doors through which Bill must pass. Like so many of the colorful thresholds that have been crossed in the film, the glass doors of the hospital bear red lines. Here, the scarlet warning that has marked dangerous portals throughout the film launches into motion, producing a visual image reminiscent of a siren.

12. I am grateful to Rasmussen's analysis (*Stanley Kubrick,* 355) for bringing this to my attention.

13. Søren Kierkegaard, *Either/Or,* vol. 2, ed. and trans. Howard Hong and Edna Hong (Princeton, N.J.: Princeton University Press, 1987), 139.

14. In an interview with Michel Ciment, Kubrick summarized the plot of the novella on which his screenplay was based: "It explores the sexual ambivalence of a happy marriage, and tries to equate the importance of sexual dreams and might-have-beens with reality." James Howard, *The Stanley Kubrick Companion* (London: B. T. Batsford, 2000), 185.

15. Nelson (*Kubrick,* 9–10) correctly notes that the director worked "to avoid all pat conclusions and neatly tied up ideas," since Kubrick believed that "there's something in the human personality which resents things that are clear, and conversely, something which is attracted to puzzles, enigmas, and allegories." In an interview, Kubrick elaborated: "When you deal with characters and a sense of life, most endings that appear to be endings are false, and possibly that is what disturbs the audience: they may sense the gratuitousness of the unhappy ending. On the other hand, if you end a story with somebody achieving his aim it always seems to me to have a kind of incompleteness about it because that almost seems to be the beginning of another story." Stanley Kubrick, "Kubrick on Kubrick," in *Perspectives on Stanley Kubrick,* ed. Mario Falsetto (New York: G. K. Hall, 1996), 23.

16. Kolker does not seem inclined to permit this more optimistic interpretation of the film's title and theme. Although he admits that *Eyes Wide Shut* had only recently been released when his book *A Cinema of Loneliness* went to press, Kolker's initial reaction to Kubrick's final film was that it was "somewhat incomplete, . . . weak in subject, and lacking the usual Kubrickian visual and narrative energy." Kolker wrote that it seemed to be the work of a director who was increasingly distant from his material and experiencing a "cooling of his imagination" (*Cinema of Loneliness,* 169–70). I believe that my analysis of the film, which benefited from multiple viewings, shows Kolker to be mistaken.

17. As part of his insightful discussion of *Eyes Wide Shut*, Nelson (*Kubrick*, 296) argues that there is an additional reason to take Alice's final remarks seriously: Alice is the "most psychologically complete character found in any of [Kubrick's] films, one whom he allows to speak in his voice."

18. Walker, *Stanley Kubrick*, 359.

19. Rasmussen, *Stanley Kubrick*, 356.

20. Nelson (*Kubrick*, 261) notes that, as early as 1958, Kubrick worried that many middle-class people "have learned to accept a kind of grey nothingness, to strike an unreal series of poses in order to be considered normal."

21. For this reason, I think Kolker is wrong in interpreting Bill to be Kubrick's Nietzschean "last man." Kolker thinks that Bill fits this description because, for such a character, no redemption and no rebirth are possible: "Bill is a pathetic remnant of what should be an energetic participant in the world" (Kolker, *Cinema of Loneliness*, 173). In an earlier note I suggest that Kolker overlooks the extent to which *Eyes Wide Shut* explicitly embraces the possibility of redemption. I would add here that my interpretation suggests that the character of Bill has at least been awakened, even if he has not been completely reborn. Bill is not the same person at the end of the film that he was at the beginning. The fact that the waltz playing at the end of the film is the same music accompanying the opening sequence does not negate the value of the Harfords' recent adventures. Bill and Alice both value their marriage; the fact that it will continue is a testament to the resourcefulness of human relationships, not a denunciation of the human inability to change.

KNOCKOUT!

Killer's Kiss, the Somatic, and Kubrick

Kevin S. Decker

Through the cinema screen, Stanley Kubrick speaks to us not merely as a writer and director of films but also as a person with philosophical vision. His films serve more than the purposes of entertainment and edification. They also cast a penetrating, sometimes disturbing light on the human condition. In this, Kubrick, qua artist-philosopher contrasts sharply with many contemporary directors who can only be called entertainers, formulaically pressing the emotional buttons of their audience but never putting them at serious emotional or intellectual risk. Kubrick, however, never avoids the gargantuan task of illuminating the human spirit (and, as I will argue, the human body), and he does so in a way that we may find uncomfortable or that we may try to resist. One strategy that Kubrick studiously avoids is the use of larger-than-life characters. Instead, he infuses them with flaws and pathos that solicit personal comparisons with his audience, and he reminds his audience of the contingency that attends every human life, whether that contingency is dramatic or not. Even in his most outré productions, Kubrick's sense of realism plants these characters into situations defined by hard edges and haunting remembrances of our own world, inviting the audience to fall into what is happening on the big screen but not sheltering them from the risks of what it is to be human.

This essay looks at the roles that Kubrick assigns to the human body and how the body functions in terms of its mobility through and alignment in space, its perceptions, and its relations with other bodies. As a filmmaker, Kubrick has an unusually heightened sense of the significance of the bodily (or the somatic dimension of life) in evoking a response from his audience, and this sense has philosophical significance. Only recently has the body come to be seen as important for our understanding of perennial philosophical themes such as truth, experience, and reason. Socrates, Plato, and Christianity inaugurated a long-standing tradition of denigration of the somatic, perhaps beginning with Socrates' argument in Plato's dialogue *Phaedo* that when he wills to act, his body is not in any way accountable for the willing. I propose therapy for this ancient evasion in the form of a look at Kubrick's work through the lenses of two contemporary traditions in Western thought: existentialism and pragmatism. These overlapping schools of thought highlight the underrated and undertheorized place of the body in understanding the human condition. The question that guides this essay is as follows: how does Kubrick's philosophical vision of the human condition unfold through and in his presentation of bodies in space, and why is this vision significant beyond the study of his cinematic storytelling?

Round One: Her Soft Mouth Was the Road to Sin-Smeared Violence

Killer's Kiss (1955) is an unlikely candidate for philosophical consideration, as both professional and amateur critics agree. According to one Internet reviewer, "Kubrick's stylish film-noir plods along for the first half of the film with a never-ceasing narrative that leaves nothing for the viewer's interpretation. The street scenes of New York in the fifties with their quirkiness and strange characters (Shriners, etc.) are the most enjoyable part of the film. The main protagonists never really catch your interest as they seem to walk through the scenes with little investment."[1] Unlike many of Kubrick's later films, his second feature fails to grab the viewer initially. It is blessed with neither the astounding visuals of *Spartacus* (1960) and *2001: A Space Odyssey* (1968) nor the quirky plotlines of *Dr. Strangelove* (1964) and *Eyes Wide Shut* (1999). The locations for *Killer's Kiss* were set around the New York City apartment of its director, who "wanted to film the smell, the feel and the color of the city."[2] Kubrick noted that the film lost half of its $40,000 shooting budget after release and, more importantly, later admitted that the film was "amateurish" and marked by poor performances.[3] Despite all this, *Killer's Kiss* tells its story well with only spare dialogue, and it makes good use of lighting, camera angles, and incidental music (or the lack thereof). Because all these factors are significant to the theme of the somatic in Kubrick, I discuss them in greater detail later.

Adding to this reputation is the film's simple and perhaps simplistic plot. Jamie Smith plays Davy Gordon, the central character and narrator, whose thoughts we hear while he anxiously paces in Grand Central Station as the film begins.[4] Our protagonist is a prizefighter from Seattle who is past his prime and spends his days brooding about his next fight in a minuscule one-room flop in New York City. The pace of the movie escalates when Davy enters the boxing ring, however. This gritty fight scene, bereft of music and illuminated by hot lights that are almost always in scene, was likely to be noticed at the time as more realistically violent than the then-current norm. Today, this scene—one of the highlights of this unevenly lackluster contribution—could be compared to both *The Day of the Fight,* the 1951 boxing documentary that probably inspired it, and the Scorsese-DeNiro classic *Raging Bull* (1980). It ends with Gordon's defeat and an intriguing visual metaphor for his descent into unconsciousness in the form of a negative film image of a high-speed career through towering city blocks.

It is not Davy Gordon's identity as a boxer but rather his identity as a *failed* pugilist that drives the rest of the story. Perhaps because of his disillusionment with the end of his career, perhaps because he is just a nice guy, or perhaps because of both, Davy takes an interest in the life of Gloria (Irene Kane). She lives in the same building as Davy, and her equally small and squalid apartment is directly and conveniently in view of his tiny window. Gloria makes her living as a dancing partner at a sordid, pay-as-you-go dance hall called Pleasureland. Her boss, Vinnie Rapallo (Frank Silvera), takes an unhealthy interest in her, in contradistinction to her complete lack of interest in him. Eventually, Vinnie's emotional dam breaks, and he throws himself at Gloria in her apartment one night after her shift ends. She screams and faints, alerting Davy, who spies Vinnie yanking down the window shade and heads to the stairs and to Gloria's rescue.

Vinnie has beat a quick retreat, and the suddenly chivalrous Davy makes Gloria comfortable, casually looking over her sparse effects while he waits for her to regain consciousness. When she does, she tells him the tragic story of how her father's disappointment scuppered her sister's ballet career and forced her to marry for money, and how these events ended in the deaths of both her father and her sister. Necessity thus led to Gloria's job at the "human zoo" of the dance hall. In the shadow of their mutual defeats and tragedies, Davy declares his love for Gloria and his desire to be with her. Gloria, perhaps more cynical due to her soul-deadening job at Pleasureland, replies, "Love me? That's funny. It's a mistake to confuse pity with love." Undeterred, Davy suggests that they escape to his hometown of Seattle—he, fleeing from his failed career; she, from Vinnie.

As they make their plans to pull together what little money they have and leave town, Vinnie finds out about Gloria's new love interest. Pretending to accept her decision to leave, Vinnie decides in a jealous rage to have Davy killed. However, through a mix-up, Davy's manager, Albert (Jerry Jarret), is chased into an alleyway and killed in the film's most atmospheric and chilling scene. Here, Kubrick balances contemporary standards of film violence against both the audience's salacious need to be present at the murder and the aesthetic considerations of the use of space. A wide shot is maintained for the last ten seconds of the chase as Albert, walking backward and protesting his innocence, grows smaller and smaller, vanishing around a corner. Cast by an actinically bright, offscreen light, the gaunt shadows of the hired killers pursuing him become contrastingly larger, and we hear, rather than see, the crime take place around the corner. Kubrick judges this close enough to satisfy our schadenfreude but far enough away to ensure our visceral comfort.[5]

Davy is not unaffected by the crime. Although it is close to the end of the film when he finds out that Albert has been killed, suspicious police officers come looking for him almost immediately. In addition, Gloria has mysteriously, frustratingly vanished. Davy follows Vinnie to the warehouse where he is holding the object of their mutual attraction, but Davy's rescue attempt goes bad. In one of Kubrick's earliest attempts to sketch the antihero (but certainly not his last), the pugilist falls to Vinnie's goons and is knocked out. To make things worse, Davy wakes later and, feigning unconsciousness, hears Gloria give in to Vinnie's demands. "I don't wanna die," she pleads. "I'll do anything." Whether because of this betrayal or not, Davy bolts through the window and leads Vinnie and his two henchmen on a merry chase through a maze of alleyways, industrial buildings, and grim-looking tenements. The expected showdown between Davy and Vinnie—a climactic fight that, unsurprisingly, the gangster loses in a terminal fashion—has an unexpected twist: it takes place without music in an echoing mannequin warehouse, where the bodies of others—literally—are used by the two combatants against each other. Vinnie wields an axe to smash away the mannequin bodies and limbs that Davy incessantly throws at him. Davy grabs a hooked pole to defend himself. Both men destroy "body" after "body" and, covered with plaster dust, might be deemed indistinguishable from the pallid mannequins that surround them. When Davy kills Vinnie with his improvised weapon, Kubrick quickly superimposes a close-up of a nearly featureless mannequin face, which blurs and fades out to bring us back to the present, to Davy-as-narrator in Grand Central Station and to the reuniting of the two lovers in a lukewarm if nominally happy ending.

One route, albeit an unusual and indirect one, into philosophy from Kubrick's oeuvre is to recognize the opportunities for both mediated and immediate experience of characters and situations through Kubrick's eyes. This warrants an explanation, for to a certain extent, all film (like all art) is a form of mediated perception, the experience of which is invariably tied up with the appropriation of the content of the art via its medium. Simplistically, then, one must find the value of Michelangelo's *David* through, rather than in spite of, the marble of which it is composed. As much contemporary aesthetic theory and art criticism emphasizes, however, we should not be quick to separate form from content in art, if in fact we can do so at all. Indeed, one of the transcendent themes of modernist art has been to dissolve this distinction—for example, in Pablo Picasso's cubist masterpiece *Les Demoiselles d'Avignon* (1906–1907) or Joseph Stella's *Brooklyn Bridge* (1917). In contrast, postmodernist art ironically and playfully exposes and deconstructs this distinction—as evidenced by Duane Hanson's hyperrealistic sculptures symbolizing the failure of the American dream or the heroically sized *Giant Ice Bag* of Claes Oldenburg (1969–1970). Much as these and other works do in terms of form and content, Kubrick's films artistically exploit the tension between the distance required to examine characters and "handle" plots, on the one hand, and the need to "get under the skin" of the players through the portrayal of subjectivity, the use of space, and the focus on the human body, on the other hand.

Killer's Kiss is Kubrick's contribution to film noir, the genre that exploits the prominent modernist tension between the objectification of and distancing from the body and the subjectivity of and obsession with the visceral. Through its artful use of space and shadows, as well as obtuse camera angles (such as the ankle-height perspectives in *Killer's Kiss*), noir accomplishes the former; conversely, its thematization of the visceral is revealed in its compulsion toward dramatic and often wrenching violence, passionate love shading off into (and often indistinguishable from) lust, and first-person subjectivity in the form of voice-over narration and personal flashbacks and flash-forwards. V. Penelope Pelizzon and Nancy M. West, in connecting film noir to the tabloid journalism of the 1920s and 1930s, note that "no other family of films is shaped by the linked concepts of reiteration, duplication, and recycling that are so crucial to the tabloids. . . . Film noir [has a] narrative dependence on recurrence, with voiceovers and flashbacks insisting that we are watching a recapitulation of something that has already occurred. Doppelgangers and cases of mistaken identity abound, suggesting the duplicability of appearances. Moreover, no other film cycle even approaches noir's fixation with that primary technology of visual reproduction, photography."[6] With its anchoring elements of boxing, organized crime, desperate love, a petty dance-hall gangster, and confusion of identity, the noir elements of *Killer's Kiss* could easily have been taken from the popular tabloids of the time, such as *Confidential*.

To tell its story, *Killer's Kiss* evokes visceral responses from its audience, even as it fails to provide any genuine evolution in its characters or its story line. Today we might see this as ironic, but it is unlikely that Kubrick intended the irony. Nonetheless, the presence of the visceral and, by extension, the somatic is important to the film's lasting impact. Sometimes, the somatic is used in ways that are common currency to the film trade in general. As one student of Kubrick's style writes:

> Close-ups are used to reveal the true natures of characters; they use the emphasis on the physicality of the image to approximate the character's nature to the viewer and to make it significant for the development of the plot. Most of the time this importance is marked not through what characters convey but through the mere emphasis on their physicality; therefore, it is a purely textual emphasis, a textual strategy, a stylistic product. In *Killer's Kiss* close-ups are invariably accompanied by distortion: Davy's face is seen in close-up through the fishbowl suggesting his being trapped; starkly lit close-ups convey Rapallo's evil nature.[7]

Other, more Kubrick-specific elements of the film evoke images of the use and misuse of the human body, its relation to other bodies, and its existence in space. In Davy's aforementioned boxing match, for example, the athleticism of the human body and its complementary brute capacity for destructive force are put on display under harsh lights and without the distraction of incidental music. Conversely, Vinnie's fight with Davy at the end of the film may be seen as a sardonic play on the match at the beginning, with the "bodies" in the mannequin factory being used as weapons rather than the hands and muscles of the combatants themselves. Yet Kubrick misses the opportunity to underscore Gloria's stress over her job at Pleasureland by creating that location as a mise-en-scène of smoke and sweaty bodies, evocative of a cattle market. Instead, the sweat, smoke, and immersion in samba music are saved for Vinnie. Ultimately, perhaps this makes sense, because it is Vinnie, more than her work as a dancing partner, that is the undoing of Gloria's tenuous life in the big city. Pleasureland may be only minimally tawdry, but Kubrick makes the conscious decision to interpret the connection among violence, movement, music, and the somatic by illuminating Vinnie's escalating anger over Gloria's lack of interest (and perceived infidelity) through background Afro-Latino jazz that grows louder, and eventually becomes deafening, before he cuts away. Throughout the movie, Kubrick consistently uses prominent, often intrusive incidental music to highlight changes in the interior lives of the main characters, while action scenes are (contrary to today's dominant practice) left bereft of accompaniment.

Consciousness of space and the use of it in Kubrick's oeuvre are marks of his modernism and another manifestation of his concern with the somatic. At first, the significance of space for a philosophical understanding of the body might not seem to make any obvious sense. Prior to the twentieth century, thinkers such as René Descartes and Gottfried Leibniz had treated space as being merely a kind of "container" in which experience and motion take place. Isaac Newton's revision of physics (and Immanuel Kant's philosophical glosses on it) treated every point in the universe as a potential *Nullpunkt*, or "zero point," from which an observer could track motion. In both kinds of theories, space itself had no significance, and bodies (including human bodies) extended in space were better represented as mathematical formulas than as living, breathing flesh. More recently, philosophical endeavors reversed this trend; for example, one philosopher studying the phenomena of our immediate experience as creatures that fill up and move through space claimed that "space is not the setting (real or logical) in which things are arranged, but the means whereby the position of things becomes possible." Western conceptions of spatiality as being a necessary, if null, condition are difficult to transcend, but it may be possible, as this thinker believes, to view space dynamically, as "the universal power enabling [all things] to be connected."[8]

In *Killer's Kiss*, spatiality figures in Davy's dream sequence after he is knocked out in the ring. The rapid advance of city blocks to either side, but in the negative reversal of the film, suggests a mood of danger and menace yet, at the same time, that some progress will be made in Davy's otherwise humdrum life. As several reviewers of the film noted, this scene is a "future echo" of the chase scene through a deserted Manhattan near the end of the film, in which a sense of desperation and hollowness is created by the lack of incidental music and the superimposition of the sound of a ringing telephone. Kubrick "changes spaces" for a few grainy, brief, yet effective scenes of genuine New York nightlife outside Vinnie's office space in the middle of the film. Particularly appealing are the drunken Shriners who are featured in several of these scenes. Undoubtedly some form of comic relief from the danger facing Davy and Gloria in this part of the film, they are both entertaining and troubling at the same time. Certainly, space is key to the effectiveness of the scenes in which Davy's manager, Albert, is murdered. His pursuit down the nondescript but nonetheless threateningly linear alleyway is on camera, but the killing is not, and the hiddenness of the crime reinforces its brutality. It is also a reminder that we innocents (if indeed, we are innocent) are, like Albert, exposed to danger even in familiar places.

Finally, as Thomas Nelson argues in his book *Kubrick: Inside a Film Artist's Maze,* one of the enduring themes in Kubrick's work is the recognition of *contingency,* as opposed to the timeless and universal, in the human condition. In *Killer's Kiss* we are unexpectedly treated to the creation of an antihero in Davy's final boxing match, a fight in which he fails to land any blows at all and that leaves him without a career and without hope. Gloria's sister makes the decision to end her career in the ballet and to marry for money because her father is ill, only to have him die soon after her marriage. Perhaps the most tellingly emotional episode of contingency in the film comes when Gloria apparently betrays Davy to save herself. Of course, examples of this kind of contingency abound in other Kubrick films: the ease with which HAL (voice by Douglas Rain) kills the astronauts in *2001* as a reminder of how contemporary human life is sustained and can be destroyed by the misfiring of a simple electrical circuit; the way the cold weather puts an end to the murderous possession of Jack Torrance (Jack Nicholson) at the end of *The Shining* (1980); and, as Nelson notes in his analysis of Nicole Kidman's character in *Eyes Wide Shut,* the way Kubrick speaks through Alice as she dismisses her husband's (Tom Cruise) use of the word "forever."[9] The philosophical theme of contingency is eminently well suited for ruminations on the nature of the body and how it constitutes us as subjects. In this respect, a critical view of Kubrick's vision can be widened by putting his films into the contexts of body, subjectivity, and contingency explored by French existential phenomenologist Maurice Merleau-Ponty.

Round Two: Philosophy versus the Body in the Match of the Century

Who thinks about the body? In philosophy, does our corporeality matter, and if so, why? Until recently, these questions could be answered easily: virtually no one thinks about the body, and corporeality matters, but not in a good way. Socrates, for all his self-deprecating good humor about his own ugliness and the unkindly effect of time on the human body, initiated a long tradition of separating what was most human about us—whether that be soul, mind, reason, intelligence, or the capacity to deliberate or to use language—from the crude matter that is host to such capacities. In the thought of Socrates, Plato, and many others after them, it may seem that, in the dualism of mind and body or soul and body, philosophers found a hierarchy in which the immaterial mind or soul was held to be of highest value and the body of lesser value. This may very well be the case; however, for most ancient and medieval philosophers (there are notable exceptions), the care of the soul firmly entailed rejecting bodily demands, desires, and concerns. In other words, in terms of the ancient Greek problem of appearances versus reality, our body pulls us constantly into a world of *appearance*—of apparently important desires, pains, lusts, pangs, and aversions—but in *reality*, the demands of reason and the cultivation of the mind should be our central focus. In Plato's dialogue *Phaedo*, for instance (in which Socrates is on the Athenian equivalent of death row yet finds the time to incisively sketch theories of knowledge and virtue), Socrates claims that "when the soul makes use of the body to investigate something, be it through hearing or seeing or some other sense . . . it is dragged by the body to the things that are never the same, and the soul itself strays and is confused and dizzy, as if it were drunk."[10] From this theme of distrust of the senses, coupled with the empirical fact that the body grows, degenerates, and dies and the supposition that the mind or soul, as immaterial, might not be subject to the same erosion and elimination, comes a view of philosophy as the care of the soul *in spite of* the body. Again, according to Socrates: "The lovers of learning know that when philosophy gets hold of their soul, it is imprisoned in and clinging to the body, and that it is forced to examine other things through it as through a cage and not by itself, and that it wallows in every kind of ignorance. Philosophy sees that the worst feature of this imprisonment is that it is due to desires, so that the prisoner himself is contributing to his own incarceration most of all."[11] Although this prejudice against the body makes sense in the context of religious asceticism, such practices were not demanded by the religion of the ancient Greeks and are more properly associated with St. Paul's distaste for all things bodily in the early Christian era. To the Greek man in the street, the antisomatic views of Socrates and Plato would have had less resonance than, say, those of Aristotle, who held that material things, although essentially passive and unintelligible, are important to the metaphysical scheme of things. Even Epicurus, with his "lifestyle" philosophy of simple pleasures, made more of the body than the denigrating Platonic-Christian view. Yet, through theological reinforcement (such as monastic communities and Thomas Aquinas's appropriation of the Aristotelian passivity of matter) and the philosophical boosterism of Descartes—we are both mind and body, but mind first and foremost—the Socratic-Platonic view won out. The views I have mentioned here are thousands or hundreds of years old, and they not only carry the weight of tradition in the academy and the seminary but also interpenetrate culture at a number of levels.

By contrast, when does a philosophical view that takes the body seriously emerge? There are two ways to answer this question, depending on how one interprets it. If we restrict our understanding of what philosophy does to its traditional roles of explaining being (what there is) and knowing (how we know what there is), then our consideration mainly takes the form of looking at the body as a condition of and constraint on our contact with being or knowledge. Baruch Spinoza, for example, in his incredibly hard-to-read *Ethics* (1677), claims that to understand the human mind, we must first understand "its object," the human body. As an example of the importance of this conceptual move, Spinoza warned of the dangers of perceptual multitasking (and he did so 270 years before the invention of the computer): "In proportion as a [human] body is more apt than other bodies to act or be acted upon simultaneously in many ways," he wrote, "so is its mind more apt than other minds to perceive many things simultaneously. . . . From this we can . . . see why we have only a very confused knowledge of our body, and many other facts which I shall deduce from this basis in what follows."[12]

Slightly later in the early modern period's renascence of philosophy, John Locke explicitly reversed the Socratic prejudice against the reliability of the five senses, declaring that humanity's knowledge is gained either through that route or through the mind's reflective understanding of its own operations. Obviously, this basic tenet of empiricism drastically elevates the importance of the body's sensory receptor organs, the systems that support those organs and keep their tissues alive, the neural system, and, of course, the brain. The provisional result of this train of thought, followed through to its empirical implications, is what most cognitive scientists tell us today: that human capacities held to be philosophically significant (such as reason, free will, and judgment) depend on the body and its systems as a condition of their proper and excellent functioning. Thus, George Lakoff and Mark Johnson, summarizing the results of cognitive science as they apply to the traditional problems of philosophy, claim that "the same neural and cognitive mechanisms that allow us to perceive and move around also create our conceptual systems and modes of reason. Thus, to understand reason we must understand the details of our visual system, our motor system, and the general mechanisms of neural binding."[13] The reverse of such claims is that the body and its systems are also a constraint on the kinds of contact (knowledge or otherwise) humans have with being, or what is. So, echoes of Kant's brilliant eighteenth-century insights into how creatures with minds like ours construct the reality we perceive can be found in the contemporary neurological research of figures such as Oliver Sacks, who bases his conclusions on the idea that the "modularity" of the mind corresponds to dedicated function areas of the brain and that damage to one section of the brain or neural system can fundamentally change the way a patient perceives reality and functions within it.

There is yet another way to interpret the question of the body, but this way requires us to abandon the old project of philosophy as one that is revelatory of being or strikes at the heart of certain knowledge. Abandoning one philosophical mantle does not mean throwing the emperor out with his old clothes, however—especially if we are willing to interpret the philosophically weighty (and confusing) term *experience* in a different way. In this view, there are good reasons to believe that two commonsense understandings of *what experience is* should be questioned.[14] The first understanding is that experience is something private, that something impacts me differently from those around me, and that experience cannot be truly communicated to others. The second is that experiences—ideas or images that I have of the world around me—are things that I can compare to the world to verify their accuracy, but they are not things in the world themselves. This representational view of experience makes our minds, our inner lives of imagination and concepts, something alien in a world that is otherwise composed of unproblematic, real things. This has driven thinkers such as Descartes and Spinoza (and many others) to undertake a quest for certainty, to search for foundational ideas—about the soul, God, or even laws of physics or psychology—that represent the world absolutely correctly.

Let us imagine that experience need not be private, even though there are some events and thoughts that are privately experienced and may be difficult, or perhaps impossible, to communicate. In fact, there are many fundamental things about how humans live in community with one another that structure experience to be public—signs and symbols, language, habits, and the commonalities that our bodies, as human, all share. Let us further imagine that experience (now understood as imagination, ideas, and concepts in our mental lives) has its significance not in representing or mirroring the world but in adding to and changing it. After all, ideas are real things, and as someone once said, "ideas have consequences." Richard Shusterman, a pragmatist thinker who is deeply interested in how the body changes our notion of experiencing the world, draws one valid conclusion from our reconceiving of experience in this way: "Philosophy should be transformational instead of foundational. Rather than a metascience for grounding our current cognitive and cultural activities, it should be cultural criticism that aims to reconstruct our practices and institutions so as to improve the experienced quality of our lives. Improved experience, not originary truth, is the ultimate philosophical goal and criterion."[15] Shusterman and other pragmatists, such as Shannon Sullivan,[16] turn to Merleau-Ponty as the first step in a reconsideration of the body as crucial to this kind of philosophy.

Round Three: In the Far Corner, "Mauler" Merleau-Ponty

Although he is not a pragmatist, Merleau-Ponty, as an existential phenomenologist, shares a similar conception of the transformative place of philosophy. Just as we have decided to take the body seriously, phenomenology is the area of philosophy that takes appearances seriously (recall the appearance versus reality problem mentioned earlier). It does not pose questions such as, "This is how I *experience* this apple, but what is the apple *really* like?" Rather, it takes the experience of the apple as significant in its own right and treats a consideration of the phenomenological experience of the apple appearance as key to understanding our later reflective, philosophical, or theoretical understanding of it. Taking appearances seriously allows the phenomenologist to grapple with philosophical problems by asking, "What conditions within experience make the posing of this problem possible?" From Merleau-Ponty's perspective, the answer to such a question often shows that traditional philosophical problems suffer from presuppositions that do not allow them to be answered intelligently at all. More often it shows that the philosophical problem originates in an understanding of experience that is incorrect and misleading because it is nonphenomenological—that is, it ignores appearances to force a preconceived notion or theory on experience. I might, for example, invite a student to consider Descartes' mind-body dualism—that is, the way he divides the mind and body into separate, distinctly comprehensible "substances" in his *Meditations.* To clarify this division, I might ask the student to ignore the mind-boggling complexity of the experience that might be characterized as "being hungry made me think about where I was going to eat lunch" or the one that could be called "being KO'ed in the ring sent me unconscious, but I gradually returned to the world of the living." When I do so, am I really talking philosophically about the *experience* of being where and when mental and physical (or perhaps inseparable mental-physical) states occur? Or am I just drawing attention to Descartes' pretty picture, painted from ideas and submitted for our consideration?

The cornerstone of Merleau-Ponty's existential phenomenology, presented in his book *Phenomenology of Perception,* is how he recapitulates traditional philosophical questions about spirit and matter, body and mind, that bear on the way the somatic has been denigrated in the Western tradition since Socrates. In this project, Merleau-Ponty aims to establish how subjectivity—the complex property of being an interpreter and an agent of the world and yet being *within* that world—depends on corporeality, that is, on being a body. Merleau-Ponty's understanding of what a "subject" is rests on a Hegelian distinction refined by his fellow phenomenologist Jean-Paul Sartre in *Being and Nothingness.* This distinction is between the kind of things in the world that are *en soi* (in itself) and those that are *pour soi* (for itself). Whereas the *pour soi* is a subject of thought and experience, the *en soi* can only be the object of thought and experience. Trees and rocks are paradigmatically *en soi,* but human persons are paradigmatically *pour soi.* Against materialists, Merleau-Ponty holds that as *pour soi,* we are not merely highly complicated physical objects (this seems rather obvious). He also holds, this time against idealists, that we are not best understood as consciousness—mind or soul. But we are not merely a combination of these two elements either, as Descartes argued in the *Meditations.* Rather, the originality of Merleau-Ponty's position is found in the implications of his simple statement, "I am my body." By this, he means that, for *pour soi* beings like us, subjectivity *is* physical; there is no separating body and mind, even at the conceptual level, because we are both, primarily and originally, intertwined and inseparable. For many reasons, Merleau-Ponty believes, one's body is different from other *en soi* objects and is therefore a fundamentally different type of thing from an object. For example, I can turn away from the laptop in front of me or close the window shade on my lovely backyard, but while I am conscious, I constantly perceive my body. My body is "an object which does not leave me. But in that case is it still an object?"[17] Likewise, whereas I can inspect objects such as my laptop or my backyard from a variety of perspectives, my body simply *is* the perspective from which I inspect these things and, by extension, from which it inspects itself.

Merleau-Ponty's arguments in *Phenomenology of Perception* about why we should think of the body in this way, as well as the implications of this view, are too numerous to recount here.[18] For our purposes, it is important to underscore his idea that our primary experience of the mind-body integration that constitutes *us* is immediate and prior to the reflective thought that establishes distinctions and applies concepts. Merleau-Ponty's phenomenology therefore treats each human as "a unity . . . not yet broken," that is, until philosophical judgment imposes a conceptual framework such as mind-body dualism (à la Descartes) on it.[19] Further, as humans, we are a dynamic, not a static, unity: "the phenomenological body is not fixed but continually emerges anew out of an ever changing weave of relations to earth and sky, things, tasks, and other bodies."[20]

In the ancient Greek clarion call to the care of the soul, it is easy to see how the philosophers' sundering of mind and body could obscure the investigation of what role a healthy, normal body plays in constituting and limiting human nature and experience. But Merleau-Ponty's point is deeper than this. According to Shusterman, in fact, "Merleau-Ponty prizes the body's mystery and limitations as essential to its productive functioning."[21] This means that, far beyond the critical point scored by existential phenomenology against the philosophical tradition for ignoring the body, Merleau-Ponty is concerned with how our conscious consideration of our bodies—the tautness of our neck and shoulder muscles when we feel stressed, the way we hold our hands and arms when typing for long periods—can obscure "our recognition of primary unreflective embodied perception and its primary importance."[22] This disturbance to our customary and prereflective orientation to the world is an impediment to our sense of self, understood in Merleau-Ponty's sense of integrated mind and body as a unity.

I will return to the question of whether paying this kind of attention to what many pragmatists and phenomenologists call the "lived body" can actually disrupt our functioning at the primary level of integration that Merleau-Ponty identifies. First, however, I want to show that the roles Kubrick assigns to the human body can motivate audiences to reflect on the nature of the bodily, the inherently spatial and temporal nature of experience, and the contingency raised by the fragility and morality of the lived body. In many cases, Kubrick also aims to make his audiences uncomfortable through visceral responses to subtle and not-so-subtle manipulation of bodies on the screen. These themes extend to films beyond *Killer's Kiss,* so in the next section, I examine three later productions from this perspective: *2001: A Space Odyssey, A Clockwork Orange,* and *Eyes Wide Shut.*

Round Four: The Lived Body, a Dangerous Sophistication

"The camera eye" is a simple phrase that implies a close connection, though one that is difficult to make explicit, between the cinematic arts and the philosophical rehabilitation of the body. At its best, cinema entices, lures, even tricks us into taking new perspectives on the situations and characters it depicts. But it is important to understand that, in this sense, the word *perspective* is used metaphorically. Its original sense is tied to having—or, more properly for Merleau-Ponty, being—a body that provides the point of view from which each of us inhabits and transforms the world. In this section, I apply the thought of Merleau-Ponty—as well as reconstructions of his thought by pragmatist sympathizers such as Shusterman and Sullivan—to three of Kubrick's films that came after *Killer's Kiss.*

In the long era of science fiction films that the flash and speed of the *Star Wars* films brought to a close, *2001: A Space Odyssey* epitomized the awe and grandeur of man's ascent to the stars. In this collaborative effort, writer Arthur C. Clarke and director Kubrick were critically and popularly successful at exploring the depths of both time and space in a story that reached from the human conquest of space back 500,000 years to the origins of human intelligence. In a highly philosophical review of *2001* provocatively titled "Bodies in Space," Annette Michelson labels the film "an instrument of exploration and discovery," designed in terms of a "higher algebra of metaphors."[23] As a film, *2001* is a vehicle of exploration not of space but of the significance of spatiality for the normal functioning of the human body and, by extension, for human experience.

Michelson suggests that *2001*—with its apparent imbalance between grand, sweeping visuals and incremental zero-gravity motion (of human or spacecraft), on the one hand, and its minimal story line and characterization, on the other—is more a "mode and model of cognition" than a space or action film. For the audience, "taking on the perspective" of scientist and space traveler Heywood Floyd (William Sylvester) or astronaut Dave Bowman (Keir Dullea) requires not so much seeing or understanding the universe in a new way but rather feeling it differently. Michelson explains: "Navigation—of a vessel or human body—through space in which gravitational pull is suspended, introduces heightened pleasures and problems, the intensification of erotic liberation and of the difficulty of purposeful activity. In that floating freedom, all directed and purposive movement becomes work, the simplest task an exploit. The new freedom poses for the mind, and through the body, the problematic implications of all freedom, forcing the body's recognition of its suspended coordinates as its necessity."[24] Our role as audience is not cognitive: there is no puzzle to unravel, no mystery villain to unmask. It is, rather, visceral, and it extends past the gut tension we feel when HAL kills Bowman's fellow astronauts and jeopardizes the mission. The role of each person in the audience is to rediscover his or her own body in its own space and to examine the presuppositions that lay behind the normal functioning of our bodies on earth, in standard gravity and in conditions that do little to push the envelope of our sensations (much as the Stargate must have done for Bowman). Such a film alienates us from these experiences at the level of bodily discomfort and reorientation and forces certain cognitive realizations: my perspective, my body is insignificant, given the vastness of space, yet it is the most important constituting condition of my world of experience; more of the universe is characterized by conditions inimical to my bodily existence than by friendly ones; experiences outside my frame of comfort are both horrifying and strangely compelling at the same time—should I seek them out or shun them?

Quoting Merleau-Ponty, Michelson constructs her review around the immediacy of this heightened sense of embodiment that *2001* grants its receptive viewers. The central point of commonality between spatiality in Kubrick's masterpiece and Merleau-Ponty's existential phenomenology is, she agrees, their dissolution of the opposition of body and mind. Space adventurers on the screen are mirrored by the audience, "human organism as adventurer," in a way that "bring[s] home to us the manner in which 'objective spatiality' is but the envelope of that 'primordial spatiality,' the level on which the body itself effects the synthesis of its commitments in the world."[25] We learn about bodies in space through *2001*, but this learning is mediated through a process of self-discovery. Although it is a kind of knowledge that we often take for granted, our understanding of movement and repose is wholly mediated through our own bodily coordination—or the lack thereof. Ultimately, *2001* is a film that suspends that coordination in weightlessness—and perhaps frighteningly illuminates the fragility of the human body, and thus human nature, in such conditions—even as it suspends our final judgments about human nature in its open-ended conclusion about our future development.

A Clockwork Orange also thematizes the human body, but from a distinctly different perspective and for purposes that are more discernibly rooted in questions about human nature. This Kubrick production wears its modernist sensibilities on its sleeve in its concern with extremes and oppositions. Synthesized funeral dirges contrast strongly with romantic favorites from Beethoven, the hero of the main character, Alex (Malcolm McDowell). The ultraviolent activities of the droogs and their leaders level questions regarding whether humans (or perhaps just men) are aggressive by nature, yet it is possible that others in Kubrick's future-of-today society (such as Alex's parents) are victims by nature. (This puts an intriguingly Nietzschean twist on Aristotle's infamous "natural" classes of masters and slaves.) As a forerunner to films such as *The Running Man* (1987, Paul Michael Glaser), *The Truman Show* (1998, Peter Weir), and the current plethora of reality television series, *Clockwork Orange* also throws a sharp, actinic light on how the entertainment of some must be "inscribed on the body" of a victimized and humiliated few. (How far is *Fear Factor* from Christians and lions in the Roman arena?) The audience's shock at Alex's lifestyle soon turns to ironic pleasure as Alex himself is apprehended and "rehabilitated."

Kubrick's forthrightly disturbing method of portraying the Ludovico method of "curing" Alex is yet another example of how this filmmaker succeeds by appealing directly to the somatic. One cannot forget the deeply averse, visceral reaction from the audience at the sight of Alex's eyes propped open by his "anti-droog helmet" while he is made to watch ultraviolent footage. Yet Merleau-Ponty would unquestionably disagree with the Ludovico treatment for a variety of reasons. Ludovico's method is undoubtedly a form of brainwashing, and as such, it disrupts the normal connections between one's cognitive and intellectual behavior and the more basic bodily functions, "rewiring" these connections by a combination of physical and emotional stress and rehabituation. Merleau-Ponty would object to this on at least two different levels. His unsurprising response would be that brainwashing exploits the integrated body-mind in such a way as to use its learning potential against the wishes of the person being brainwashed. Even more fundamentally, however, Merleau-Ponty disagrees with "scientific" method of reflecting on our preconscious somatic experience with the intention of changing it at the fundamental level.[26] If we recall the critical thrust of a phenomenology of the body against philosophical distortions of experience, it is clear that Merleau-Ponty believes that "reflective consciousness and somatic representations are not only unnecessary but inaccurate for explaining our ordinary perception and behavior which are usually unreflective."[27] Any effort to fundamentally reorient the body's functioning through the mind, or vice versa, would be, in this view, to efface or destroy what phenomenology tells us is most fundamental about humanity: its prereflective, bodily experience.

In contrast, pragmatists such as Shusterman and Sullivan, though likely recoiling at the coercive nature of Alex's treatment, would also point out that rehabituating humans to change their perspective on life occurs all the time, and we often initiate or agree to our own rehabituation ourselves. What is the philosophical justification for this? Shusterman, following the classic American philosopher John Dewey, notes that "aesthetic satisfaction takes privilege over science, which is simply a 'handmaiden' providing the conditions for achieving such satisfaction more frequently, stably, and fully."[28] Knowing and acting are, for the pragmatist, key to aesthetic satisfaction (or, quite literally, making our lives more beautiful and rewarding), and somatic experience is key to solidly linking our knowing and acting to the ends we have chosen. For example, in this view, a lifelong smoker who desperately wants to quit but cannot do so on his own is less a victim of strength of will and more a victim of ignorance. He is ignorant of what it has taken biological science, psychology, and the rehabilitative arts to tell nonspecialist individuals: the body can be taught to dispense with an old habit not merely by "breaking" that habit cold turkey but by replacing the undesirable habit with another one. The reason why quitting smoking remains difficult, as well as how a promising treatment can make a nonsmoker out of a lifelong smoker, is the same reason why Alex's "cure" ultimately works in situations in which flaunted nudity demands desire and violence demands violence (but in both cases, only nausea emerges). As Shusterman puts it, again following Dewey, "Proprioceptive discriminations beneath the level of thematized consciousness structure our perceptual field, just as unformulated feelings . . . influence our behavior and orient our thinking."[29] That is, bodily sensations or feelings display certain regularities that we cannot always consciously recognize or change, but they can be changed nonetheless. Pragmatists simply disagree with Merleau-Ponty that there is something essential about what Shusterman calls "nondiscursive somatic experience" that forbids our conscious efforts to change our bodies and their habits. Rather, they are more concerned with coercive changes, whereby hegemonic structures of social power urge or force changes that have little or nothing to do with an individual's own genuine desires. Sullivan, for example, argues that "bodies are not isolated physical objects existing outside or prior to their meanings," so just as there is no privileged set of phenomenological experiences that are to be protected from our conscious reflection on them, there is no "natural body" to reclaim or reconstitute.[30] As I show later, this view is not without an element of danger with regard to our autonomous appropriation of our own bodies, since it leaves us with fewer foundational arguments against those—from doctors to the state to hegemonic social forces—who would change the way we think about our bodies for purposes alien to ours.

Power, desire, and the body are central themes of what was to be the last film Kubrick directed: *Eyes Wide Shut.* This film of deception, betrayal, and secrets turns on the fundamental disconnect in the relationship between the main characters, Bill and Alice Harford, which alienates them both and drives him to seek sexual adventure outside their marriage. In a series of elegant but disturbing scenes, Bill infiltrates a modern-day "Hellfire Club" where masked and robed men enjoy the sexual pleasures of similarly anonymous, attractive, nude women. In this film, as in *2001,* Kubrick displays a flair for depicting space and motion through tableaux that make use of his trademark Rotoscope camera work in steady circles and through the winding halls of the club, combined with the haunting score by Jocelyn Pook. The music and camera work in the club are distinctly different from those used to reveal the "mundane" aspects of Bill's everyday existence, creating another modernist opposition in Kubrick's oeuvre that compels the unfolding of the story: Who are the members of this club, and how long has it existed in the heart of New York City? Who is the woman who attempts to help Bill in the club? Does she know who he really is, and if so, how does she know him? For a fleeting moment, audience members might actually think that

Bill's "guardian angel" is his wife, but questions about her involvement in the club arise as well.

Much of the tension involved in Bill's infiltration of the sex club has to do with the anonymity of its members, both male and female, and the potential for his being found out. The perils and possibilities of anonymity in this setting form an apt metaphor for the phenomenology of the "anonymous body" in Merleau-Ponty's philosophy. That our bodies are fundamentally the same—in terms of morphology, systems, afflictions, and abilities—makes any given body "anonymous" to Merleau-Ponty. Before we are individuated through relationships and practices of culture and society, we are born the same, and this anonymity of the body persists through life, making, for instance, the medical sciences and their treatment of universal human conditions possible. But the anonymity of the body at this basic level is significant to Merleau-Ponty's phenomenological understanding of communication as well, for the anonymous body makes communication possible. In the words of Sullivan: "According to Merleau-Ponty, because my body and your body exist on a level other than that of individuation, we can recognize each other's intentions. Because of the body and the knowledge it provides, we gain an understanding of each other that makes coexistence possible. I am not lost in my own world of meaning, because when I see another body in action, the objects around it take on a significance beyond that which I give them."[31] Beyond the perspective that my body provides me a means for being a part of the world, it allows me to project or "externalize" my intentions in gestures and actions, and the way I interact with my environment establishes commonalities that another human body may seize on to establish communication. In earlier centuries, establishing contact with peoples around the globe who had developed largely outside Western spheres of influence depended almost entirely on this interpretation of gestures and the use of objects, since no common linguistic frame of reference was available. It would be important to observe, for example, that although a number of decorated gourds were on display in a native person's home, only a few were used for fetching water, while others served ceremonial purposes. Without the native host's even intending to communicate, the common bodily need for water can, in this case, establish a common frame of reference that might later lead to linguistic cross-understanding.

The problem of anonymous bodies arises because of the *way* Merleau-Ponty thinks they are used to establish communication, according to Sullivan. She charges that "Merleau-Ponty's phenomenology of projective intentionality fails to explain how corporeal beings can create a genuinely common ground between people that is nondominating."[32] Her concern, shared by other thinkers, is that for this French phenomenologist, meaning is not a kind of *sharing* but rather an *imposition* of one human body on another.

The anonymity of bodies in the men's club of *Eyes Wide Shut* is precisely what makes the attraction of the club—casual, guilt-free sexual exploits—possible. But along the lines of Merleau-Ponty's theory of communication, it is precisely this same anonymity that gives rise to the alienation among the club's members and their exploitation of women. The strict requirement that masks be worn at all times gives the club's members license to experiment sexually in a setting where they are unlikely (by a code of "gentleman's honor," no doubt) to be found out. Perhaps, like pornography, this cathartic experience is not an entirely bad thing, given the "anonymous" lust that most male bodies feel. The seriousness with which the anonymity requirement is taken is cast into bold relief when Bill is finally found out and stripped of his mask. Without it, in a sea of harshly lit, disfigured mask faces, he stands out more starkly than if actor Tom Cruise had been naked himself.

In the secret club, communication is kept to a minimum, consisting of only ritual chanting and the few gestures and words necessary to establish the pairings of men and women. It would seem that the significance of bodily intentionality established by Merleau-Ponty is underscored when facial expressions are obscured behind masks and communication is dampened in this way, and we are left (as is Bill) to guess the true intentions of those around us. In the setting of the club, the anonymity that is key to Merleau-Ponty's projective intentionality funds domination, not liberation, and this is what disturbs us about these scenes. The sole sexual purpose of the club allows its male members to "project" their familiarity with their own bodies onto the club's women, replacing the women's intentions with their own and disregarding the former in the process. Particularities of perspectives and intentions are just as important to our identities as are our anonymous bodies; ignoring this fact is the danger of anonymity. It leaves the door open for potential abuses, as Michel Foucault copiously chronicled, by those who would impose "regimes of biopower" on us in the name of an "essential body" or "universal human conditions."[33] Sullivan writes, "When I impose on another the way that I transact with my world, I dominate her by refusing to recognize all the particularities that constitute her. . . . Avoiding such domination means that common ground between bodily beings must take their differences into account. A common ground is something for which we must strive, not a starting point from which we depart."[34]

Round Five: A Cinematic Knockout

Throughout this essay, I have had many opportunities to compliment Kubrick's cinematic genius, but much of the focus has been on his contributions to our understanding of the human spirit and, in particular, the significance of our philosophical contemplation of the body to human experience. Kubrick's influence in this respect extends from *Killer's Kiss,* which I have portrayed as a half-successful, early, experimental work that delves into themes of spatiality, contingency, and the somatic, to deeper reflections on cognition and spatial experience in *2001,* changing the mind through the body in *A Clockwork Orange,* and anonymity and the body in *Eyes Wide Shut.* My brief foray into an analysis of Kubrick and the somatic has not been exhaustive, and there are undoubtedly many more episodes in his oeuvre that could further illuminate these themes. By leaving this essential query into somatic humanity open to the reader's further interest and judgment, I attempt to do, in some small way, what Kubrick did by inviting us into his vision through worlds that often disturb and unsettle us, putting us both mentally and viscerally off balance. Does Alex's experience in *A Clockwork Orange* show us that humans are redeemable, despite our primal aggression? Are human bodies evolutionarily distinctive through infinite adaptability, as *2001* intimates? Is a happy ending for mind and body possible, as *Killer's Kiss* and *Eyes Wide Shut* pronounce, both indifferently and with little fanfare? Stanley Kubrick made films as if his role were to pose these questions but, like a good existential or pragmatist philosopher, not to give the final answers to them. Instead, he left that task to us and to future generations of audiences to determine after the curtains have fallen and the camera eye has grown dim.

Notes

Insofar as this essay expresses its points clearly and coherently, credit is due to the skill and persuasive powers of editor Jerold J. Abrams. I owe him many thanks.

1. zeke-14, Review of *Killer's Kiss,* Internet Movie Database, February 25, 1999, http://www.imdb.com/title/tt0048254 (accessed November 3, 2005).

2. Stanley Kubrick quoted in review for *Killer's Kiss, Rotten Tomatoes,* http://www.rottentomatoes.com/m/killers_kiss/ (accessed November 26, 2005).

3. Joseph Gelmis, "An Interview with Stanley Kubrick," *The Kubrick Site*, http://www.visual memory.co.uk/amk/doc/0069.html (accessed November 3, 2005). Excerpted from Joseph Gelmis, *The Film Director as Superstar* (New York: Doubleday, 1970).

4. *Killer's Kiss* is among the overwhelming majority of Kubrick films to feature voice-over narration. Only *Dr. Strangelove, The Shining,* and *Eyes Wide Shut* do not feature voice-over.

5. Nietzsche writes: "*Schadenfreude* originates in the fact that, in certain respects of which he is well aware, everyone feels unwell, is oppressed by care or envy or sorrow: the harm that befalls another makes him our *equal,* it appeases our envy.—If, on the other hand, he happens to feel perfectly well, he nonetheless gathers up his neighbour's misfortune in his consciousness as a capital upon which to draw when he himself faces misfortune: thus he too experiences '*Schadenfreude.*'" Friedrich Nietzsche, *Human, All Too Human: A Book for Free Spirits,* trans. R. J. Hollingdale (Cambridge: Cambridge University Press, 1996), 314.

6. V. Penelope Pelizzon and Nancy M. West, "Multiple Indemnity: Film Noir, James M. Cain, and Adaptations of a Tabloid Case," *Narrative* 13, no. 3 (October 2005): 233.

7. Luis M. Garcia Mainar, *Narrative and Stylistic Patterns in the Films of Stanley Kubrick* (Rochester, N.Y.: Camden House, 1999), 38.

8. Maurice Merleau-Ponty, *The Phenomenology of Perception,* trans. Colin Smith (London: Routledge, 1989), 243.

9. Thomas Allen Nelson, *Kubrick: Inside a Film Artist's Maze,* 2nd ed. (Bloomington: Indiana University Press, 2000).

10. Plato, *Phaedo,* trans. G. M. A. Grube, in *Plato: Complete Works,* ed. John M. Cooper (Indianapolis: Hackett, 1997), 69–70 (79c3–8).

11. Ibid., 72 (82d8–83a1).

12. Baruch Spinoza, *Ethics,* trans. Samuel Shirley, excerpted in *Modern Philosophy,* ed. Roger Ariew and Eric Watkins (Indianapolis: Hackett, 1998), 155.

13. George Lakoff and Mark Johnson, *Philosophy in the Flesh: The Embodied Mind and Its Challenge to Western Thought* (New York: Basic Books, 1999), 4.

14. Why should these understandings be questioned? Primarily because they are less grounded on what happens to us on a daily basis than holdovers from Locke's rather limited view of experience being all about what the five senses tell us. Historically, this "sensational" empiricism has penetrated theories in science, education, psychology, economics, and many other areas. Because it runs so deep, it seems like common sense, but it is not.

15. Richard Shusterman, "Somatic Experience: Foundation or Reconstruction?" in *Practicing Philosophy: Pragmatism and the Philosophical Life* (New York: Routledge, 1997), 157.

16. Shannon Sullivan, *Living across and through Skins: Transactional Bodies, Pragmatism, and Feminism* (Bloomington: Indiana University Press, 2001).

17. Merleau-Ponty, *Phenomenology of Perception,* 90.

18. Merleau-Ponty's prose is somewhat difficult to read in the original, so the interested reader should consult Stephen Priest's analysis in *Merleau-Ponty* (New York: Routledge, 1998).

19. Maurice Merleau-Ponty, *The Structure of Behavior,* trans. A. L. Fisher (London: Methuen, 1965), 188.

20. Carol Bigwood, "Renaturalizing the Body (with the help of Merleau-Ponty)," *Hypatia* 6, no. 3 (Spring 1991): 62.

21. Richard Shusterman, "The Silent, Limping Body of Philosophy," in *The Cambridge Companion to Merleau-Ponty,* ed. Taylor Carman and Mark B. N. Hansen (New York: Cambridge University Press, 2005), 170.

22. Ibid., 169.

23. Annette Michelson, "Bodies in Space: Film as Carnal Knowledge," in *Artforum,* reprinted in *The Making of 2001: A Space Odyssey,* ed. Stephanie Schwam (New York: Modern Library, 2000), 198.

24. Ibid., 200.

25. Ibid., 205–6.

26. Such a method is fundamental to many philosophies and practices that, unlike the dominant Christian-Platonic view described earlier, refuse to leave the body behind when seeking enlightenment. A short list of these would include disciplines such as yoga and tai chi, as well as Greek and Roman Stoicism and Epicureanism, most strains of Renaissance humanism, Continental *lebensphilosophies,* the transcendentalism of Ralph Waldo Emerson and Henry David Thoreau, much of pragmatism, and the Alexander technique developed around the turn of the twentieth century by F. Matthias Alexander.

27. Shusterman, "Silent, Limping Body," 169.

28. Shusterman, "Somatic Experience," 166.

29. Ibid.

30. Sullivan, *Living across and through Skins,* 64.

31. Ibid., 70.

32. Ibid., 8.

33. See, for example, Michel Foucault, *Madness and Civilization: A History of Insanity in the Age of Reason,* trans. Richard Howard (New York: Vintage Books, 1973). Foucault analyzes how the establishment of "normality" in the medical and psychological sciences allows individuals to be classified as "pathological" and then changed at fundamental levels through institutionalization and treatment. What is key to Foucault's view, however, is that "normality" is defined by practices of "discipline and control" external to the body and do not mirror something essential about it that needs to be recaptured or regained.

34. Sullivan, *Living across and through Skins,* 74.

THE LOGIC OF *LOLITA*

Kubrick, Nabokov, and Poe

Jerold J. Abrams

Lolita, light of my life, fire of my loins. My sin, my soul. Lo-lee-ta: the tip of the tongue taking a trip of three steps down the palate to tap, at three, on the teeth. Lo. Lee. Ta.

   She was Lo, plain Lo, in the morning, standing four feet ten in one sock. She was Lola in slacks. She was Dolly at school. She was Dolores on the dotted line. But in my arms she was always Lolita.

—Humbert Humbert in
Vladimir Nabokov's *Lolita*

Umberto Eco notes that while writing his novel *The Name of the Rose,* he "had only to choose (from among the model plots) the most metaphysical and philosophical: the detective novel."¹ The detective story is also, I think, the most philosophical dimension of Vladimir Nabokov's novel *Lolita* (1955) and Stanley Kubrick's film adaptation (1962), for which Nabokov wrote the screenplay.² *Lolita* is a masterful detective story in the same tradition of Edgar Allan Poe's tales about master sleuth C. Auguste Dupin and Sir Arthur Conan Doyle's Sherlock Holmes.³ Of course, *Lolita*'s detective plot and constant references to Poe are often noted. But the distinctive detective logic at the center of the work, as it is found in Poe and Conan Doyle and formally articulated by philosopher Charles S. Peirce (who drew on Poe as well), has yet to be filled out in its entirety. Indeed, Humbert Humbert's method is not, as he claims, a logic of deduction but a logic of abduction. And it is precisely Humbert's inability to use this logic, along with his madness and his mastery of chess, that makes him such a remarkable failure as a detective.

Synopsis of the Film

Humbert Humbert (James Mason) is a European émigré and a professor and scholar of some success. He is also erotically obsessed with very young girls, whom he calls "nymphets." On summer break, he takes up lodging in Ramsdale, New Hampshire, in the house of Charlotte Haze (Shelley Winters) and her underage daughter, Lolita (Sue Lyon). Charlotte is a lonely widow and wants Humbert desperately. Humbert has nothing but contempt for Charlotte, but he marries her anyway, just to be close to Lolita. Humbert faithfully records all of this in his diary—his hatred for Charlotte, his obsession with Lolita—until Charlotte discovers it. Devastated, she runs into traffic and is killed. Meanwhile, Lolita has been away at Camp Climax (in the novel, it is Camp Q, located near Lake Climax), so Humbert must go to collect her. But he does not mention Charlotte's death until he and Lolita have had sex for the first time—initiated, in fact, by Lolita.

Now they set off in a car across country to sightsee, have sex in motels, and keep their affair a secret. But Clare Quilty (Peter Sellers), a playwright and pornographer and Humbert's "double," spots them at a hotel and begins following them. All the while, moreover, Lolita, who has been in love with Quilty for some time, keeps Quilty informed of their every move. Eventually, Lolita and Quilty escape together and leave Humbert behind. He tries to find them, but he does not even know the identity of her captor, and it is only years later that Lolita, in need of money, reveals her whereabouts to Humbert in a letter. Immediately he goes to her. By this point, Quilty is long gone, and Lolita is pregnant and living with Dick Schiller (Gary Cockrell), a good man who loves her. Humbert begs her to run away with him, but she refuses. Now, all he has left is revenge, and he refuses to give her a cent without the name of the man who took her away from him. So Lolita, the intelligent nymph—whom Humbert has always taken for a sexy little idiot who reads only comic books and magazines—cruelly reveals how she and Quilty (as a fake policeman and a fake psychologist) played Humbert for a fool all along. Degraded and furious, Humbert leaves Lolita with more money than she needs and sets off to murder Quilty.

The Importance of Poe to *Lolita*

It is not mentioned in the film, but Humbert's first childhood love, "Annabel Leigh,"[4] is an important link to Poe, whose poem "Annabel Lee" begins its second stanza, "*I* was a child and *she* was a child."[5] Nabokov repeats this early in the novel: "When I was a child and she was a child, my little Annabel was no nymphet to me; I was her equal."[6] And just as Poe's Annabel dies young—"Chilling and killing my ANNABEL LEE"—so too must Humbert's. So when Humbert tells us that Annabel was reincarnated in Lolita ("It was the same child"[7]), he also means—and Nabokov means—that the confession that is the text of *Lolita* is equally a literary "reincarnation" of Poe's "Annabel Lee" and several other Poe works besides.[8] Kubrick probably should have left this element in the film, to claim for himself yet another reincarnation: a kind of Pythagorean nymphic transmigration of the literary soul of Annabel Lee from Poe's verse to Nabokov's novel to Kubrick's film.

Nevertheless, Kubrick does recognize the importance of Poe when Humbert asks Lolita if she would like to hear some poetry from his "favorite poet." "Who's the poet?" asks Lolita. "The divine Edgar," responds Humbert, and begins reading from Poe's poem "Ulalume." Lolita is clearly unimpressed and wants to move on to other things. But notice a line from the last stanza that Humbert does not read: "Ah, what demon has tempted me here."[9] Of course, the little temptress demon is Lolita (a point to which I return shortly). Kubrick also does well with the detective element of the story, which derives partly from Poe's "The Mystery of Marie Roget" and "The Purloined Letter" but mostly from "The Murders in the Rue Morgue"—all of which are Dupin stories (the last being the best).

Within these three stories emerges the now well-known classic detective formula, which contains the following elements, usually in this order: (1) an examination of the detective's special powers of reason, often involving a certain duality of mind, and sometimes a study of games; (2) a crime, almost always a murder; (3) an examination of the crime scene and the gathering of clues by the detective; (4) interviews of suspects by the detective and his partner (if he has one); (5) a portrayal of the relations among clues, suspects, and the crime as a labyrinth; (6) a contemplative study of the case with a focus on the arrangement of clues, often through chemically induced meditation; (7) the solving of the case; and (8) the capture of the criminal, sometimes through an elaborate trap.

Nabokov's and Kubrick's "Double-Dupin"

With regard to the first element of the classic detective story—an examination of the detective's dual mind—Poe begins "The Murders in the Rue

Morgue" by dividing Dupin's character in half, twice. First, we know Dupin only through a "friend," interpretable as part of Dupin's mind. The two live alone in the narrator's mansion: "we admitted no visitors."[10] It is the same in Conan Doyle, who modeled Sherlock Holmes on Dupin: two men—Holmes, the detective, and Dr. Watson, his friend and the narrator of the stories—live together. Second, the detective's mind seems to have two selves contained within it, each with a distinctive character. As Poe writes: "His manner at these moments was frigid and abstract; his eyes were vacant in expression; while his voice, usually a rich tenor, rose into a treble which would have sounded petulant but for the deliberateness and entire distinctness of the enunciation. Observing him in these moods, I often dwelt meditatively upon the old philosophy of the Bi-Part Soul, and amused myself with the fancy of a double Dupin—the creative and the resolvent."[11] Again, we find the same division in Holmes, particularly in "The Red-headed League," where Conan Doyle essentially reproduces the passage above from Poe:

> In his singular character the dual nature alternately asserted itself, and his extreme exactness and astuteness represented, as I have often thought, the reaction against the poetic and contemplative mood which occasionally predominated in him. The swing of his nature took him from extreme languor to devouring energy; and, as I knew well, he was never so truly formidable as when, for days on end, he had been lounging in his armchair amid his improvisations and his black-letter editions. Then it was that the lust of the chase would suddenly come upon him, and that his brilliant reasoning power would rise to the level of intuition, until those who were unacquainted with his methods would look askance at him as on a man whose knowledge was not that of other mortals.[12]

So, one side of the detective's mind is dreamy and creative imagination, and the other is high energy and logic. Together, they represent two extremes and are constantly combined toward the objective of discovering whodunit. This is Poe's double-Dupin and Conan Doyle's double-Holmes—both with the bipart mind.

Clearly, Humbert is modeled on Dupin: a brilliant, European, double-man detective—even with a double name, Humbert Humbert—two men in one, living in the same house that they do not own.[13] Yet the two sides of

Humbert are not exactly like the two sides of Dupin—namely, the creative and the resolvent. Rather, the difference between Humbert 1 and Humbert 2 is that of a well-mannered intellectual-detective (like Dupin) and a criminal (unlike Dupin). Moreover, Humbert has another double whose name is just as significant: Clare Quilty, as in "clear guilty."[14] As doubles, Humbert and Quilty are very much alike: both are literary men, both have pedophilic interests, both have loved Lolita, both are detectives, and both travel to the same lodge on the same night. Yet they are also quite different when it comes to their frames of mind, which happen to correspond exactly to the two sides of the double-Dupin: the resolvent and the creative. Humbert is the resolvent, and Quilty is the creative. And here, instead of the creative and resolvent faculties working together to solve a crime, as they do in Poe and Conan Doyle, the creative detective actually shadows the resolvent—Quilty creatively tormenting every resolve of Humbert—until, suddenly, the doubles switch and the resolvent pursues the creative. So, effectively, the double-Dupin and the criminal of "The Murders in the Rue Morgue" are transposed in *Lolita*, such that the two sides of Dupin's mind become two actual persons, Humbert and Quilty, both of whom are detectives as well as criminals—and both of whom are quite mad.

Humbert's Detective Madness

Of course, madness has always been integral to the detective's genius. In "The Murders in the Rue Morgue," for example, Poe writes of Dupin's "excited" and "diseased intelligence."[15] This madness—which we find in Holmes as well—is, once again, two-sided. While hot on the trail, Dupin and Holmes appear mad with obsessive focus, but when contemplating clues in seclusion, they appear mad with hallucinatory creativity. And just as Dupin's faculties are evenly distributed between Quilty and Humbert, so too is Dupin's madness. Quilty's madness is creative: he lives his life as though he were a character in a play, except that he is always changing characters, and sometimes he is even the director. He treats Humbert and Lolita the same way—as characters to play with.

Humbert, by contrast, has none of this ability. He is always Humbert the obsessed, Humbert the resolvent, absolutely single-minded in his madness—a madness he knows well and for which he has been institutionalized more than once.[16] Humbert calls his disease "nympholepsy" and defines it as a condition arising in an older man who obsesses over the demoniacal and erotic nature of nymphets, to the point of madness and collapse. The disease appears to have two basic elements: First, the man must already have some germinal form of nymphic madness to even "see" the nymphets; they are hidden to everyone else. Second, the force of the demon within the nymphet is roughly proportional to the madness she causes within the madman. This demon force is generated in the nymphet by the tension resulting from the polarization between sweet childish innocence and erotic darkness. As Humbert says in the novel and film (narrating in voice-over): "What drives me insane is the twofold nature of this nymphet, a veteran nymphet perhaps, this mixture in my Lolita of tender, dreamy childishness and a kind of eerie vulgarity."[17] Effectively, then, it is the intensity of the duality in the nymphet that causes the intensity of the duality in the man, this latter duality being precisely the essence of his madness, with its ever-widening rift between one self and the other—ultimately rendering the other, Quilty, an autonomous person.

Also essential to this madness is a self-absorbing need to examine the intensity of the force of the nymphet on the nympholeptic's mind: "Why does the way she walks—a child, mind you, a mere child!—excite me so abominably? Analyze it. A faint suggestion of turned in toes. A kind of wiggly looseness."[18] Every physical detail is studied and cataloged; every movement she makes is recorded.[19]

Humbert's Taxonomy of Nymphic Indexes

Like cognitive duality and madness, this technique of cataloging is also universal among detectives. Holmes, for example, creates multiple databases of information about criminals and psychopaths, each with their various markings from the world. By just looking at a man, Holmes knows his profession: "By a man's finger-nails, by his coat-sleeve, by his boots, by his trouser-knees, by his callosities of his forefinger and thumb, by his shirt-cuffs—by each of these things a man's calling is plainly revealed."[20] These signs that Holmes is reading are called indexes, which Peirce defines as being physically connected to the objects that they signify; for example, a fingerprint has a physical and one-to-one connection to the object it signifies (to the detective)—namely, the finger and the person who left the print.[21]

Like Holmes and Dupin, Humbert studies indexes as well—only these are specifically nymphic indexes. By examining a little girl's various physical and social traits, Humbert can determine her status as a nymphet. And again, these nymphets are essentially hidden, like criminals; if they are to be found, they must be detected by reading their indexes. As Humbert puts it:

> A normal man given a group photograph of school girls or Girl Scouts and asked to point out the comeliest one will not necessarily choose the nymphet among them. You have to be an artist and a madman, a creature of infinite melancholy, with a bubble of hot poison in your loins and a super-voluptuous flame permanently aglow in your subtle spine (oh, how you have to cringe and hide!), in order to discern at once, by ineffable signs—the slightly feline outline of a cheekbone, the slenderness of a downy limb, and other indices which despair and shame and tears of tenderness forbid me to tabulate—the little demon among the wholesome children; *she* stands unrecognized by them and unconscious herself of her fantastic power.[22]

In the novel, Humbert returns again and again to note and catalog these nymphic indexes. And while not all of them can be listed here, among the most important are the following: (1) Nymphets live between the ages of nine and fourteen. (2) Nymphets are very thin (Humbert refers to "the slenderness of a downy limb"). (3) Nymphets have catlike features—"the slightly feline outline of a cheekbone." (4) Nymphets resemble (and really are, for Humbert) "little deadly demons." (5) Nymphets have "marvelous skin." As Humbert puts it, "Nymphets do not have acne although they gorge themselves on rich food." (6) Nymphets are not the prettiest among young girls. (7) Nymphets are very rare: "Within the same age limits [9–14] the number of true nymphets is strikingly inferior to that of provisionally plain, or just nice, or 'cute,' or even 'sweet' and 'attractive,' . . . girls." (8) Nymphets have a strange and magical or "fey grace." (9) Nymphets have a dual nature: innocence combined with "eerie vulgarity." (10) A nymphet has a "small agile rump." (11) Nymphets are "so cruel and crafty in everyday life," but have a "cheerful indifference" in formal games like tennis. (12) Nymphets are prone to dangerous heat when emotional: "Hysterical little nymphs might, I knew, run up all kinds of temperature—even exceeding a fatal count." (13) Nymphets retain some, though not all, of their nymphic traits, as they age, such as the cheekbone. Humbert can spot these postnymphs almost at a glance—for example, when he notes on the street "a delinquent nymphet shining through the matter-of-fact young whore." (14) "Nymphets do not occur in polar regions."[23]

Humbert's Detective Logic

In addition to madness and taxonomy of indexes, equally essential—perhaps most essential—is a detective's logic. In Poe and Conan Doyle, that logic is called deductive. Holmes, for example, in "A Study in Scarlet," develops a "Science of Deduction and Analysis," and then in "The Sign of the Four," he scorns guessing: "I never guess."[24] But in fact, both Dupin and Holmes are wrong. As several Peirce scholars have pointed out, their logic is "abduction." And abduction, Peirce claims, "is nothing but guessing."[25] Humbert makes the same mistake:

> But in Monique's case there could be no doubt she was, if anything, adding one or two years to her age. This I deduced from many details of her compact, neat, curiously immature body. Having shed her clothes with fascinating rapidity, she stood for a moment partly wrapped in the dingy gauze of the window curtain listening with infantile pleasure, as pat as pat could be, to an organ-grinder in the dust-brimming courtyard below. . . . Her hips were no bigger than those of a squatting lad. . . .
> . . . Dutiful little Monique (oh, she had been a nymphet, all right!). [26]

Humbert notes that he has "deduced from many details"—these are the indexes—Monique's status as a nymphet. But clearly he is not deducing anything. Nor is he using the logic of induction, that is, a generalization from a set of cases, and their corresponding results, to a universal rule about all nymphets having these various traits.[27] Rather, what Humbert is doing (abduction) looks like this:

> Premise 1: Result—The surprising fact, C [traits 1, 3, 4, 13], is observed.
> Premise 2: Rule—But if A [this girl is, or was, a nymphet] were true, C [traits 1, 3, 4, 13] would be a matter of course.
> Therefore: Case— There is reason to suspect that A is true ["oh, she had been a nymphet, all right!"].[28]

In a word, Humbert is making a guess. He is using the logic of abduction, which Peirce recognized as the fundamental logic of all detective work. It works like this: A detective begins with a startling result, a surprise, and then formulates a rule to explain the result. So, if it were the case that Monique had been a nymphet, that would explain the result. Therefore, there is reason to suspect that she was a nymphet.

Moreover, Humbert's guess takes the form of a distinct kind of abduction—one of three categorized by Eco: overcoded, undercoded, and creative abductions. All three use the same basic form but differ in how the detective arrives at the rule. In an overcoded abduction, the rule "is given automatically or semiautomatically," such as the Monique abduction. In contrast, in an undercoded abduction, the "rule is selected as the more plausible among many."[29] (For example, in "The Murders in the Rue Morgue," Dupin knows that a human killer is an option, but the clue about the rough hair is an index to the undercoded abduction of a nonhuman criminal: an ape.) In the third type, a creative abduction, the guesser invents the rule to explain the results of observation. (For example, Darwin, Freud, and Galileo create explanations rather than choosing from those already given.) Detective stories are almost always about undercoded abductions: there are several suspects, and one is selected as the killer.

I noted earlier that the Monique abduction is overcoded. Humbert is great at these—he can spot a nymph a mile away, even long past youth—but he constantly fails to make even the simplest undercoded abductions (such as, "Lolita is in league with the man following me," or "This too-well-informed man is surveilling me"). These are abductions that even Poe's inept Parisian police would make with ease.[30] But as Humbert himself points out in the film—in dialogue with Charlotte over dinner—"I am no good at guessing." Humbert is quite right.

Undercoded Abduction and Detective Play

So, why is Humbert so adept in one form of abduction and so miserable in another? The answer is simple. Undercoded abductions, unlike overcoded abductions, require a playful, experimental, and highly creative mind, which Humbert (the resolvent) clearly does not have. Dupin and Holmes both have it: after examining the clues, they enter a state of imaginative reverie, entertaining various hypotheses to explain the clues. This is the creative side of Dupin, as opposed to the resolvent; it is the poetic and contemplative side of Holmes, as opposed to the sleuth-hound. Recall Watson's remark: "he was never so formidable as when, for days on end, he had been lounging in his armchair." Peirce calls this lounging state "musement" and credits it to Poe: "those problems that at first blush appear utterly insoluble receive, in that very circumstance,—as Edgar Poe remarked in his 'The Murders in the Rue Morgue,'—their smoothly-fitting keys. This particularly adapts them to the Play of Musement."[31] In musement, the detective keeps the indexes always before his mind and then freely and artistically entertains so many possible rules to explain the result, until one presents itself as logically the best.

Of course, sometimes Humbert *appears* to muse. For example, in the film we see him lounging in a hot bath, having a stiff drink. (For Holmes, musement often involves drugs—a point Watson notes: "'Which is it to-day,' I asked, 'morphine or cocaine?'")[32] But Humbert is not really musing; rather, he is enjoying Charlotte's death and plotting how to have sex with Lolita. Similarly, in the novel Humbert actually *thinks* he has entered the musement state: "When I try to analyze my own cravings, motives, actions and so forth, I surrender to a sort of retrospective imagination which feeds the analytic faculty with boundless alternatives and which causes each visualized route to fork and re-fork without end in the maddeningly complex prospect of my past."[33] It is obvious here that Humbert is trying to sound like Dupin ("imagination feeds the analytic faculty with alternatives"), but it is also clear that Humbert has neither the analytic faculty, as Poe defines it, nor any ability to muse. Notice that he has no control of the musement state: there are too many forking routes (Nabokov's nod to Jorge Luis Borges's detective story "The Garden of Forking Paths").[34] There is simply nothing very playful or creative about Humbert.

Dupin's Analysis of Games

A clue as to why Humbert is not very playful can be found in Poe's own analysis of games and play in his various detective stories, games that include chess, checkers, cards, marbles, puzzles, and dice.[35] In "The Murders in the Rue Morgue," Dupin even says which games use which faculties—whether calculation, attention, analysis, or acumen (imaginative insight). Chess, for example, is a game of calculation and attention: "The *attention* is here called powerfully into play. If it flag for an instant, an oversight is committed, resulting in injury or defeat. The possible moves being not only manifold, but involute, the chances of such oversights are multiplied, and in nine cases out of ten, it is the more concentrative rather than the more acute player who conquers."[36]

In fact, chess—compared to cards and checkers—is a rather derivative game, at least according to Dupin: "the higher powers of the reflective intellect are more decidedly and more usefully tasked by the unostentatious game of draughts [checkers] than by all the elaborate frivolity of chess." Poe knows that most people think chess is better, but in chess, "where the pieces have different and *bizarre* motions, with various and variable values, what is only complex, is mistaken (a not unusual error) for what is profound." Chess is complex because there are so many kinds of pieces, whereas in checkers there are only a few, which allows the players to relax their attention so they can employ the faculty of acumen. To make this point, Dupin reduces a checkerboard to two kings for two equal players. The winner will be the one with the most acumen, because he "throws himself into the spirit of his opponent, identifies himself therewith, and not unfrequently sees thus, at a glance, the sole methods (sometimes indeed absurdly simple ones) by which he may deduce into error or hurry into miscalculation."[37]

It is the same with the winning detective, who must imagine himself the criminal and all the moves he would make if he were to plot a murder. This, according to Dupin, is acumen. And when it is coupled with analysis, we get Poe's ideal detective. Analysis is the ability to read subtle telltale signs and make corresponding inferences (again, Poe thinks that these are deductions). To explain this faculty, Dupin moves to cards:

Our player confines himself not at all; nor, because the game is the object, does he reject deductions from things external to the game. . . . He notes every variation of face as the play progresses, gathering a fund of thought from the differences in the expression of certainty, of surprise, of triumph, or chagrin. From the manner of gathering up a trick he judges whether the person taking it, can make another in the suit. He recognizes what is played through feint, by the manner with which it is thrown upon the table. A casual or inadvertent word; the accidental dropping or turning of a card, with the accompanying anxiety of carelessness in regard to its concealment; the counting of the tricks, with the order of their arrangement; embarrassment, hesitation, eagerness, or trepidation—all afford, to his apparently intuitive perception, indications of the true state of affairs. The first two or three rounds having been played, he is in full possession of the contents of each hand, and thenceforward puts down his cards with as absolute a precision of purpose as if the rest of the party had turned outward the faces of their own.[38]

So, it is ultimately the cardplayer who, among all game players, is closest to the detective in terms of method and ability. He has all the acumen of the checkers master and all the analytic ability to read hard "tells." The chess player, however—should he attempt the art of detective analysis—is always doomed from the start.

Games in *Lolita*

Of course, we know that Humbert loves to play chess (as did Nabokov and Kubrick), and he even seems to see his Lolita game as a chess game.[39] For example, while teaching Charlotte to play, Humbert says, rather pleased with himself, "Yes, that can leap over the other pieces"—just as he, Humbert, can simply "leap over" Charlotte to get to Lolita. And poor Charlotte thinks that they are only talking chess: "You're going to take my queen?"—as in, take Lolita. We also know that Humbert has little more than disdain for playing cards, and his early memories associate bridge with "the enemy," who will later become the bridge-playing Charlotte.[40]

Humbert's being a chess player, disdaining cards, and being a natural descendant of Dupin means that we know all this must go very badly for him. If his game were poker or even checkers, he might have had a chance.[41] As it is, however, he simply lacks that special combination of acumen and analysis (in Poe's sense) that would allow him to engage in the play of musement (in Peirce's sense) and make the appropriate undercoded abductions (in Eco's sense). And that, essentially, is the fundamental reason that Humbert must always fail as a detective. He is all calculation and drive. And in truth, his calculations are good when he is on. For example, his chess moves toward the queen of Camp Climax are very well thought out. What he cannot do is anticipate another player's moves with any real analytic imagination, which is why Lolita has to spell it all out for him at the end. Notice here that Humbert, the genius-detective who can spot a nymphet in a moving crowd, misses the clues right under his nose:

> HUMBERT: I didn't come here to play guessing games. Tell me who it was.
>
> LOLITA: Well, give me a chance to explain. . . . Do you remember

that car that used to follow us around? . . . Do you remember mother's old flame at the school dance? . . . Do you remember the guy that you talked to at that hotel on the way back from camp? He pretended that he was part of that police convention that was there. . . . And do you remember that guy that called you at the motel?

HUMBERT: The night you disappeared? Yes, I remember him very well.

LOLITA: And yet you still haven't guessed.

HUMBERT: I told you that I'm not playing games with you. Tell me who it was.

LOLITA: It was *Clare Quilty.*

HUMBERT: Who was Clare Quilty?

LOLITA: All of them, of course.

HUMBERT: You mean Dr. Zempf, he was Clare Quilty?

LOLITA: Well, congratulations. . . . I'd had a crush on him ever since the times that he used to come and visit mother. He wasn't like you and me. He wasn't a normal person. He was a genius. . . . You know that hotel that we stopped at on the way back from camp. Well, it was just by accident that he was staying there. But it didn't take him long to figure out what was going on between us. And from that moment on, he was up to every brilliant trick he could think of.

HUMBERT: And he did all these brilliant tricks for the sheer fun of tormenting me?

Of course, the audience already knows what Humbert is just finding out, because the identity of Clare Quilty was revealed at the beginning of the film (and the novel). But we still are not sure about Quilty, and that is the mystery: we do not know whether Humbert is Quilty and whether Quilty is really guilty. Nor are these answers ever definitively given. And once we have reached this point of interpretation, it is all too apparent that the game is becoming ever more complex—moving from inside the story of *Lolita,* as a game between Quilty and Humbert, to outside the story, as a game between writer and viewer (or reader).

Nabokov once said, "Satire is a lesson, parody is a game."[42] A parody is a playful imitation of a story or genre for humorous effect. So, for example, we know the answers in Poe's detective story—the ape did it. But *Lolita,* as a parody, plays with the standard character assignments: detectives and criminals combine and change places, and we are never clear on who is guilty; we never really know who the ape is. Humbert the detective certainly refers to himself as an ape—"my aging ape eyes" and "my ape ear."[43] Appel makes this point as well: "In traditional *Doppelgänger* fiction the Double representing the reprehensible self is often described as an ape. In Dostoevsky's *The Possessed* (1871), Stavrogin tells Verkhovensky, 'you're my ape'; in Stevenson's *Dr. Jekyll and Mr. Hyde* (1886), Hyde plays 'ape like tricks', attacks and kills with 'apelike fury' and 'apelike spite'; and in Poe's 'The Murders in the Rue Morgue' (1845), the criminal self is literally an ape. But 'good' Humbert undermines the doubling by often calling himself an ape, rather than Quilty, and when the two face one another, Quilty also calls Humbert an ape."[44] But Quilty is also a kind of ape, being so much like Humbert in so many ways. So just as Quilty calls Humbert an ape, Humbert also calls Quilty "subhuman."[45] And even Lolita is described as a monkey: "the monkeyish nimbleness that was typical of that American nymphet."[46] In this way, Nabokov and Kubrick take the detective story as a logical game to be played and then proceed to play a game with the very logic of the detective story. Yet, in doing so, they also establish the reader and viewer as a detective who must unravel the mysterious and playful relations between *Lolita* and "The Murders in the Rue Morgue."

The Detective Labyrinth of *Lolita*

To understand this relation, we must now delve deeper into the history of the detective story, going well beyond Poe and all the way back to the classical myth of the maze, for just as *Lolita* parodies "The Murders in the Rue Morgue," it also parodies its own mythical beginnings. In this myth, Ariadne gives her lover, Theseus, the "clue" of thread to navigate a labyrinth and kill the Minotaur inside. In *Lolita*, Lolita is Ariadne, and Quilty and Humbert are both Minotaur and Theseus. And all three must navigate their way through at least six interlocking labyrinths: (1) Most obviously, Lolita/Ariadne gives Humbert/Theseus the clue to lead him to Quilty the Minotaur at the center of his labyrinth mansion. (2) Less obvious, Humbert navigates the labyrinth of his own mind, with all its forking paths, and is always lost: "I walk in a maze."[47] (3) In the novel more than the film, the Haze house is a labyrinthine spider web, with Humbert the spider/Minotaur at its center, tapping on the silk strands to see whether Lolita is ensnared yet.[48] The silk strands, like

Ariadne's string, run from Lolita to the Minotaur. (4) Humbert and Lolita's road trip follows a zigzagging, labyrinthine path all over the United States, through mountains, hidden valleys, forests, and shrouded getaways, each road forking here and there but never really going anywhere. (5) *Lolita,* as a work, is certainly a labyrinthine experience. As Appel puts it, "The reader of *Lolita* is invited to wend his way through a labyrinth of clues in order to solve the mystery of Quilty's identity, which in part makes *Lolita* a 'tale of ratiocination,' to use Poe's phrase."[49] (6) Finally, there is within the work (the novel more than the film) a kind of labyrinth of other works. We hear about Poe often, but there are also references to Shakespeare, Goethe, Christie, Freud, Borges, Proust, Hegel, Rimbaud, Baudelaire, Eliot, Sade, Conan Doyle, *Alice in Wonderland,* Greek mythology, Joyce, even comic books and magazines—the references seem to go on ad infinitum, each meticulously cataloged in Appel's annotations. This seeming labyrinthine infinity surely derives from Borges (a great influence on Nabokov), who famously conceived the library of literature as an infinite labyrinth of ideas.

Quilty as Minotaur

Among Minotaurs, Quilty is certainly one of the most interesting in the history of the detective story, for he is capable of changing his own identity as well as the paths through the labyrinth. The moment Humbert is on to him, Quilty simply changes the form of labyrinth—always hidden, always in control. How can he do this? The answer goes back to our discussion of games and the double-Dupin: Humbert has only resolve, calculation, and attention, while Quilty has creativity, acumen, and analysis. This allows Quilty to become Humbert, but not vice versa. Indeed, Quilty is the superior game player, for he can, as Poe says, "throw himself into the spirit of his opponent" and thus "deduce Humbert into error or hurry him into miscalculation"—which, of course, Quilty does at every turn in the labyrinth game, always tripping him up. For instance, he calls Humbert in the middle of the night at a country motel:

> Uh, hello. Is that Professor Humbert? . . . How are you Professor? . . . I was just wondering if you'd been enjoying your stay in our lovely little town here. . . . Oh, my name? Oh, it doesn't matter about my name. It's really an obscure, an unremarkable name, you understand, Professor. But my department, you see, is sort of concerned, sort of

concerned with the bizarre rumors that have been circulating about you and that lovely, remarkable girl you've been traveling around with. . . . Professor, uh, tell me something. I guess all this traveling around you do, uh, you don't get much time to see a psychiatrist, regularly? Is that right? . . . You're classified in our files, Professor. . . . I wonder if you'd be prepared to give our investigators a report, uh, Professor, on your, uh, current sex life, if any.

Quilty is just batting Humbert around in all his paranoia, pretending to watch his crimes as a policeman and judge his perversions as a psychiatrist.

Here there is a parallel to *Hamlet*—a natural connection, I think, with so many references to Shakespeare in *Lolita*. Hamlet is not one man but many men, consisting of many perspectives at once; indeed, he is a man who is a player by art and by early training, being virtually raised by Yorick, the court jester. Harold Bloom makes this point: "[Hamlet] is a changeling, nurtured by Yorick, yet fathered by himself, an actor-playwright from the start," though it would not be helpful to identify him with his author."[50] The character of Quilty is also a changeling, partly modeled on Hamlet. But here it *is* reasonable to identify Quilty with his author (both Nabokov and Kubrick), for two reasons. First, Quilty (unlike Hamlet) plays with the other characters solely for his own aesthetic bliss, just as Nabokov claims to do in the famous afterword to *Lolita*.[51] Second, as Appel points out, there is a regular use of involution throughout *Lolita*, whereby the artist involves himself in the work and thus plays with the boundary separating the inside and outside of the work.[52] In *Lolita*, this occurs through identification with the character of Quilty and Quilty's constant escort, Vivian Darkbloom (Marianne Stone). Notice that her name is actually an anagram for Vladimir Nabokov. And Vivian Darkbloom, Nabokov tells us in the foreword, is in fact writing a novel entitled *My Cue* (Quilty's nickname is "Cue"). So, it appears that Vivian Darkbloom is a double for Quilty and Nabokov—her gender being the difference. Yet even this is played with in a conversation between Lolita and Humbert, who are (almost?) talking about the writer who created them: "'Sometimes,' said Lo, 'you are quite revoltingly dumb. First, Vivian is the male author, the gal author is Clare.'"[53] Humbert thinks she is lying; but is she? After all, Nabokov (Vivian) really *is* "the male author" of the story in which Humbert and Lolita exist. But does Lolita know this?

Clearly, Kubrick was attracted to this technique and, in high Nabokovian style, performs his own involutions within the film. As Humbert navigates the labyrinthine mansion, he imagines the Minotaur, Quilty, hidden "in some secret lair."[54] Kubrick, in complete control of the labyrinth-detective theme, correctly hides Quilty under sheets—so that Humbert walks right by him, with no idea how close he is. But calling out to him, Quilty quickly appears. Humbert asks, "Are you Quilty?" Quilty says, "No, I'm Spartacus. Have you come to free the slaves or somethin'?" Of course, *Spartacus* (1960) was Kubrick's previous film project. So here, Kubrick is playing with Nabokov's involution by having Quilty, who is a writer like Nabokov, but also a film director like Kubrick, refer to Kubrick's own filmography. Indeed, both Nabokov and Kubrick identify with the Hamlet-changeling director character of Quilty, the smartest man in the play who is always controlling the action, always the Minotaur, hidden behind the scenes. They are directing the game, just as Quilty is directing the game of "Roman Ping-Pong" at the beginning of the film and every subsequent game that Humbert loses. And when they recede back behind the scenes, after momentary involutions, we know that they are only temporarily masked behind Quilty, whose mask is always changing—sometimes a policeman, sometimes Kubrick himself.

In particular, we see this Hamlet-changeling nature just before Quilty's murder. Refusing to play Quilty's game of Ping-Pong, Humbert pulls a gun on him. But Quilty, with striking indifference, says, "Hey, you're a sort of bad loser, Captain. I never found a guy who pulled a gun on me when he lost a game." Quilty then calls their problem a clash of cultures: "You are either Australian or a German refugee. This is a gentile's house. You'd better run along." Humbert becomes angrier. But Quilty does not care, and in fact, he really cannot stop playing. As a changeling (like Hamlet), he simply morphs from self to self: "Gee, that's a derling lil gun ya got there," says Quilty. "That's a derling little thing." Apparently, he is now an old Texas cowboy, which infuriates Humbert all the more—so Humbert hands him a letter. "What's this," asks Quilty (using the same cowboy persona), "the deeds to the ranch?" Humbert answers, "It's your death sentence. Read it." Quilty makes fun of Humbert's fancy "book learnin.'" And then, after reading a few sentences aloud, Quilty looks up and mocks Humbert's bad writing, using the same accent: "It's getting a bit repetitious, isn't it?" So Humbert takes it away: "That's enough!"

Suddenly, Quilty becomes someone else, almost like a tough old cop: "Listen Mac, you're drunk"—when in fact, we know that Quilty is drunk. He then proceeds to put on two enormous boxing gloves and changes yet again: "I want to die like a champion," he says. So Humbert shoots him through the glove. Instantly, Quilty morphs again—this time into a musician, playing piano and singing for Humbert, his soon-to-be murderer. Crazed at being the fool, Humbert starts shooting wildly at Quilty and finally hits him. Now badly wounded, Quilty drags himself upstairs toward his best and final mask: he crawls behind a life-sized painting of Lolita herself, which Humbert drills with bullets, killing Quilty behind it. We do not see Quilty die—which is a brilliant move on Kubrick's part. As a man without a unified self, there is simply nothing left beyond the final mask.[55]

Notes

I am grateful to Elizabeth F. Cooke and Chris Pliatska for our many discussions of *Lolita*, both film and novel. I am also grateful to Elizabeth Cooke for reading and commenting on an earlier draft of this essay. Of course, any mistakes that remain are my own.

1. Umberto Eco, postscript to *The Name of the Rose*, trans. William Weaver (New York: Harcourt Brace, 1984), 524.

2. There are certainly other philosophical dimensions. See, for example, Richard Rorty, "The Barber of Kasbeam: Nabokov on Cruelty," in *Contingency, Irony, and Solidarity* (Cambridge: Cambridge University Press, 1989). In the afterword, "On a Book Entitled *Lolita*," Nabokov says, "*Lolita* has no moral in tow" (*The Annotated* Lolita, ed. Alfred Appel Jr. [New York: Vintage, 1991], 314). But Rorty disagrees: "*Lolita* does have a moral in tow" (163–64). He says, "These books [Nabokov's *Lolita* and *Pale Fire*] are reflections on the possibility that there can be sensitive killers, cruel aesthetes, pitiless poets—masters of imagery who are content to turn the lives of other human beings into images on a screen, while simply not noticing that these other people are suffering" (157).

3. Voltaire created an early template for the detective story with *Zadig*, in *The Portable Voltaire*, ed. Ben Ray Redman (New York: Penguin Books, 1977). Eco notes this point in his "Horns, Hooves, Insteps: Some Hypotheses on Three Types of Abduction," in *The Sign of Three: Dupin, Holmes, Peirce*, ed. Umberto Eco and Thomas Sebeok (Bloomington: Indiana University Press, 1983).

4. Nabokov, *The Annotated* Lolita, 11–12.

5. Edgar Allan Poe, "Annabel Lee," in *The Complete Tales and Poems of Edgar Allan Poe* (New York: Vintage Books, 1975), 957 (hereafter, *Complete Poe*). Note that Poe's "Annabel Lee" is reproduced in Appel's annotations in *The Annotated* Lolita, 329.

6. Nabokov, *The Annotated* Lolita, 17.

7. Ibid., 39.

8. The beautiful maiden dying is a constant theme in Poe. For example, in "Morella," a man's lovely, genius wife gives birth while dying. The baby, born with mental capacities

that are too great, dies herself and is buried in a tomb mysteriously empty of the first Morella: "and I laughed with a long and bitter laugh as I found no traces of the first, in the charnel where I laid the second, Morella" (*Complete Poe*, 671). In Nabokov's novel, the reincarnated Lolita also dies in childbirth, although the child is stillborn.

9. Poe, "Ulalume," in *Complete Poe*, 954.

10. Poe, "The Murders in the Rue Morgue," in *Complete Poe*, 144.

11. Ibid.

12. Arthur Conan Doyle, "The Red-headed League," in *The Complete Sherlock Holmes* (New York: Barnes and Noble, 1992), 185.

13. There are also nods to Sherlock Holmes in the novel, such as the name of the camp headmistress, Shirley Holmes (Nabokov, *The Annotated* Lolita, 100).

14. Page Stegner makes this point in *Escape into Aesthetics: The Art of Vladimir Nabokov* (New York: Dial Press, 1966), 104.

15. Poe, "The Murders in the Rue Morgue," 144.

16. As Humbert puts it, "A dreadful breakdown sent me to a sanatorium for more than a year; I went back to my work—only to be hospitalized again" (Nabokov, *The Annotated* Lolita, 32–33).

17. Humbert also tells us that one must be a "madman, a creature of infinite melancholy" to see nymphets, to understand them (Nabokov, *The Annotated* Lolita, 17).

18. Ibid., 41.

19. Yet, in another sense, Humbert studies very little of Lolita: her comic books and magazines, her school play, her dreams and fears, all mean nothing to him. Rorty makes this point rather nicely when he writes: "This particular sort of genius-monster—the monster of incuriosity—is Nabokov's contribution to our knowledge of human possibilities" (Rorty, *Contingency, Irony, and Solidarity*, 161). Humbert is simply "uncurious" about Lolita as a person, as someone who could suffer deeply in the gentle clutches of a pedophile, even while he is monstrously curious about his own mind.

20. Conan Doyle, "A Study in Scarlet," in *Complete Holmes*, 23.

21. According to Eco, semiotic indexes include imprints, symptoms, and clues. Imprints have a one-to-one physical correspondence, such as a criminal leaving a fingerprint. Symptoms are signs resulting from, but not resembling, their objects, such as bleeding from a wound. Clues are objects deposited at a scene by an agent, such as a bullet shell casing.

22. Nabokov, *The Annotated* Lolita, 17.

23. Ibid., 16, 17, 41, 17, 44, 21, 232, 240, 23, 33.

24. Conan Doyle, "A Study in Scarlet" and "The Sign of the Four," in *Complete Holmes*, 23, 93. With regard to Dupin, there are just a few places where his method is unclear. In "The Mystery of Marie Roget," the narrator tells us about "those inductions by which he had disentangled the mystery" (*Complete Poe*, 170). And in "The Purloined Letter," he discusses guessing (ibid., 215). But overall, Dupin's method is deduction: "I do not hesitate to say that legitimate deductions even from this portion of the testimony—the

portion respecting the gruff and shrill voices—are in themselves sufficient to engender suspicion which should give direction to all farther progress in the investigation" (ibid., 156). This, of course, is not a deduction but a guess.

25. Charles S. Peirce, *The Essential Peirce*, vol. 2, ed. Peirce Edition Project (Bloomington: Indiana University Press, 1998), 107.

26. Nabokov, *The Annotated* Lolita, 22.

27. David Hume first pointed out the now famous "problem of induction": the conclusion requires the presupposition of a suppressed premise about future continuity in nature, but which is also the very thing we're concluding—so induction begs the question.

28. Peirce, *The Essential Peirce*, 2:231; see also *The Essential Peirce*, vol. 1, ed. Nathan Houser and Christian Kloesel (Bloomington: Indiana University Press, 1992), 188. Here, I am fusing Peirce's two forms of abduction. Note that versions of the abductive syllogism affirm the consequent (If *P* then *Q*; *Q*; ∴ *P*), rendering it, like induction, invalid but still very useful.

29. Eco, "Horns, Hooves, Insteps," 206.

30. Poe, "The Murders in the Rue Morgue," 152: "The Parisian police, so much extolled for *acumen*, are cunning, but no more."

31. Peirce, *The Essential Peirce*, 2:439, 436.

32. Conan Doyle, "The Sign of the Four," in *Complete Holmes*, 89.

33. Nabokov, *The Annotated* Lolita, 13.

34. Jorge Luis Borges, "The Garden of Forking Paths," in *Collected Fictions*, trans. Andrew Hurley (New York: Penguin, 1999), 119.

35. See, for example, Poe, "The Purloined Letter," 215, 219; "The Mystery of Marie Roget," 207.

36. Poe, "The Murders in the Rue Morgue," 141.

37. Ibid., 141, 142.

38. Ibid., 142–43.

39. Appel writes, "Crucial to an understanding of *Lolita* is some sense of the . . . metamorphoses undergone by Lolita, H. H., the book, the author, and the reader, who is manipulated by the novel's game-element and illusionistic devices to such an extent that he too can be said to become, at certain moments, another of Vladimir Nabokov's creations—an experience which is bound to change him" (*The Annotated* Lolita, 339).

40. Humbert remembers "a bridge game was keeping the enemy busy" (Nabokov, *The Annotated* Lolita, 14). Later he says that Charlotte is "one of those women whose polished words may reflect a book club or a bridge club, or any other deadly conventionality" (ibid., 37). Angry with Charlotte, he says, "When you lead me to bridge and bourbon with the charming Farlows, I meekly follow" (ibid., 91). Also, he and Lolita "played a childish game of cards" (ibid., 174).

41. Elizabeth Phillips notes: "Humbert is an excellent chess player when he has nothing better to do; Dupin was sufficiently adept in the game to analyze its principles

in relation to the mental process in which he is interested, although he belittles it in the analysis" ("The Hocus-Pocus of *Lolita*," *Literature and Psychology* 10 [Summer 1960]: 98). But she leaves it at that, when in fact, Humbert's chess is a key to his mind.

42. Nabokov quoted in Appel's annotations in *The Annotated* Lolita, 342.

43. Nabokov, *The Annotated* Lolita, 39, 48.

44. Appel, introduction to *The Annotated* Lolita, lx–lxi.

45. Nabokov, *The Annotated* Lolita, 295.

46. Ibid., 58. See also 51 and 213, where Humbert says he "bought a bunch of bananas for my monkey."

47. Ibid., 255. This is part of the second stanza of a poem by Humbert.

48. Ibid., 49. Borges also compares the spider web to the labyrinth in "Ibn-Hakam Al-Bokhari, Murdered in His Labyrinth," in *Collected Fictions,* 137.

49. Appel, *The Annotated* Lolita, 331. Appel also writes: "Nabokov often transmuted or parodied the forms, techniques, and themes of the detective story" (ibid.).

50. Harold Bloom, *Hamlet: Poem Unlimited* (New York: Riverhead Books, 2003), 9.

51. Nabokov, "On a Book Entitled *Lolita*," in *The Annotated* Lolita, 314–15: "For me a work of fiction exists only insofar as it affords me what I shall bluntly call aesthetic bliss, that is a sense of being somehow, somewhere, connected with other states of being where art (curiosity, tenderness, kindness, ecstasy) is the norm."

52. As Appel puts it, in the novel, "all the involuted effects spiral into the authorial voice," that is, the voice of Nabokov himself. See introduction to *The Annotated* Lolita, xxx.

53. Nabokov, *The Annotated* Lolita, 221.

54. Humbert says, "The house . . . had more planned privacy than have modern glamour-boxes" (ibid., 294).

55. Humbert calls this "the end of the ingenious play staged for me by Quilty" (ibid., 305).

PART THREE

THE SUBJECT AND THE MEANING OF LIFE

Rebel Without a Cause

Stanley Kubrick and the Banality of the Good

Patrick Murray and Jeanne Schuler

> There's nothing so very great about living—all your slaves and all the animals do it. . . . Think how long now you've been doing the same as them—food, sleep, sex, the never-ending cycle.
>
> —Seneca, *Letters from a Stoic*

> Human life is to be regarded . . . as a dull pastime.
>
> —David Hume, "The Sceptic"

Surfing the Zeitgeist

Stanley Kubrick entered the annals of filmmaking just as the McCarthy crackdown on communists in Hollywood ended and the movie production code lost its power over the studios. No director was quicker to seize on unshackled topics than Kubrick was. In *Fear and Desire* (1953), soldiers behind the lines ambush a general and shoot him point-blank as he cries "surrender." In the heist film *The Killing* (1956), Kubrick uses small-timers in a story reminiscent of John Huston's *Asphalt Jungle* (1950) but lacking its humanity. In *Paths of Glory* (1957), French military officers order a suicide mission, fire on their own men, and execute three scapegoats to cover up their crimes. In *Lolita* (1962), an English professor marries a woman he hates just so he can seduce her adolescent daughter. In *Dr. Strangelove* (1964), a cold war farce ends in a nuclear holocaust. Kubrick can ignore organized crime when the so-called guardians of society—family, scholars, government, the military—harbor such corruption. Kubrick also took the

133

lead with sex, nudity, and violence; there is the matchless eroticism of the toenail-polishing sequence that opens *Lolita,* and decades later it is still harrowing to watch scenes from *A Clockwork Orange* (1971). In a sea of films that shatter cultural norms, Kubrick's stand out: the graphic or outrageous is filmed exquisitely. The audience is torn between looking away and gazing with uneasy delight. This artistic freedom would have been unthinkable just a few years earlier, yet Kubrick fled to England not to escape surveillance but to cut production costs. There he exercised his freedom, but it is an ironic, nonconformist brand of freedom that his films expose.

Kubrick confessed that his most challenging goal as an artist was to represent his age on the screen. "I know I would like to make . . . a contemporary story that really gave a feeling of the times, psychologically, sexually, politically, personally . . . it would be the hardest film to make."[1] *Eyes Wide Shut* (1999), a film that Kubrick had in mind by the early 1970s and whose release coincided with his death, came closest to realizing that dream with its tale of jealousy, sexual adventurism, and revenge within marriage. But Kubrick surfs the zeitgeist throughout his films, exploring antiwar sentiments, the sexual revolution, space travel, behavior modification, artificial intelligence, cryogenics, the arms race, youth culture, homosexuality, and women's liberation before they surface as mainstream. He anticipates emerging trends, staying ahead of the beat.

The Skeptical Vision and the Banality of the Good

The deeper idea that informs Kubrick's films is skepticism: what seems new sinks back into old stalemates. Behind the countercultural image of trendy filmmaker is a sensibility closer to Beat generation existentialism and *Mad* magazine—Kubrick was in his twenties from 1948 to 1958—linking Kubrick to ancient and modern skeptics. If knowledge exceeds our reach, reason's sole task is to debunk any claim to truth. History is not moving toward perpetual peace or a rational society. Advancement or progress is exposed as illusion. With his ruse of the state of nature, Thomas Hobbes grasped the ugly lesson: this species lives on the brink of destruction—to plunder, pillage, and rape is our natural *right*—unless some external force intervenes. Humans are natural-born killers; their best behavior is a few steps away from the natural state of war. The ultimate scheme for imposing an external force on ourselves, the Soviet's Doomsday Machine in *Dr. Strangelove,* ends up destroying the world due to a combination of party pride by the Soviets and anticommunist fanaticism by General Jack D. Ripper (Sterling Hayden). In *2001: A Space Odyssey* (1968), murder marks the "dawn of man," and the murder weapon, tossed into the air, morphs memorably into a spacecraft.

Kubrick's adoption of skeptical tropes conjoins the absurdity of human existence to the brutish nastiness of human nature. The eons of time and the immense expanse of the universe, filling the screen in *2001*, reduce our lives to insignificance. Even if plans succeed—which rarely happens—with death as our destiny, what good can be achieved? At birth we are all DOA. Each creature briefly interrupts the cosmic emptiness. Seneca observes, "We, too, are lit and put out. We suffer somewhat in the intervening period, but at either end of it there is a deep tranquility."[2] Victor Ziegler (Sydney Pollack), in *Eyes Wide Shut*, consoles Bill Harford (Tom Cruise) with our shared fate: "Life goes on, it always does, until it doesn't." If an external force could keep us from destroying one another, could it also remove the looming threat of personal extinction? Even then, if what we presently do as mortals lacks significance, wouldn't doing it ad infinitum only magnify our absurdity?

For Albert Camus, the rebel defies absurdity with a spiteful "yes" echoing through an indifferent universe. With Kubrick's take on the absurd, moral heroes represent wishful thinking. Wedged between human treachery and cosmic futility, the genuinely good, when it emerges at all, is helpless, like Colonel Dax (Kirk Douglas) in *Paths of Glory*, or doomed, like Spartacus (also Kirk Douglas). The absurd takes a toll, blurring or reversing the distinction between good and bad. For example, Alex's presumably decent parents in *A Clockwork Orange* are painful caricatures, more disturbing than their unfettered son. Humbert Humbert (James Mason), the middle-aged professor who seduces Lolita (Sue Lyon), seems benign in comparison to her scheming, middlebrow mother, Charlotte Haze (Shelley Winters). While in the bathroom getting ready for a fancy Christmas party, Alice Harford (Nicole Kidman) fishes for a compliment as she pees. She gets it, but it is false. Bill eyes himself in the mirror, the back of his head to her. The good lack grace; they are banal and unbecoming. The wicked, by contrast, have sass, like Barry Lyndon (Ryan O'Neal) plotting his next con job or conquest. Yet both good and bad characters are exaggerated and cartoonish. Characters are flat because conversation or intimacy is rare; there is little "inner" to reveal or develop. Even Bill and Alice's bedroom scenes in *Eyes Wide Shut* are more monologue than dialogue.

What brightens the screen—and Kubrick's screen is brilliant—is irony: the snicker of the narrator or the dissonance of the sound track. In *Full*

Metal Jacket, Joker (Matthew Modine) sports a peace button on his lapel while "Born to Kill" is scrawled on his helmet. In *A Clockwork Orange,* Alex (Malcolm McDowell) exults to "Singing in the Rain" while he rapes a woman and bashes her husband by turn. A little dog gets loose and an airline luggage cart veers abruptly, spilling an old suitcase and sending a blizzard of racetrack loot blowing down the runway in *The Killing.* Camus' writings wrestle with the absurd: in his spite, Sisyphus triumphs; in Kubrick's films, the absurd rules uncontested. Kubrick's rebels lack passion; they just swerve, headed nowhere in particular.

Kubrick is dogmatic in his skepticism. The skepticism that recurs throughout his films and shapes his vision is potted. Its pervasiveness reveals Kubrick's art to be a reflection of a world that it does not comprehend. Skepticism belongs to what Karl Marx calls the "bourgeois horizon," the defective philosophical stance characteristic of modern times. In embracing skepticism, Kubrick unwittingly accommodates himself to his world. Although his relatively few films span many genres, skeptical distancing and irony shine throughout. Like Arthur Schopenhauer's formless will, Kubrick's skepticism shapes countless characters and presides over their disintegration. It may be wrong to say that an artist *has* a particular philosophy; nonetheless, the ideas circulating throughout Kubrick's work follow familiar philosophic patterns. Skeptical moves structure and check his options yet, as with chess, allow for countless variations without altering the rules or objectives. But deep-seated flaws are endemic to skepticism, which is one of the most persistent strains of false philosophy.[3] Kubrick might be called the great film artist of false philosophy. His themes are hallmarks of skeptical thought: our proximity to a state of nature, the corruptness of authority and human institutions, disillusionment with ideals such as progress, the banality of the good, the pull of immediate pleasures, the divergence of appearances from reality, the seepage of the nightmare world into daily existence, and the grasping for salvation from beyond the human condition through technology or alien life.

Skepticism and Capitalism

G. W. F. Hegel wrote that philosophy expresses its time in thought; the owl of Minerva takes wing at dusk—after history has achieved new form. Like philosophy, art captures its world, but it does so concretely in image, marble, sound, plot, music, and symbol. There is ambiguity in Hegel's idea, for there is a difference between a philosophy that mirrors its age and one that points beyond it by comprehending it. Karl Marx, who at age nineteen converted to Hegel's way of thinking, probed this ambiguity in Hegel's own philosophy. Marx focused on Hegel's chief contribution to social and political philosophy, *The Philosophy of Right* (1821), and reached the conclusion that Hegel's philosophy was more an expression of his times than a comprehension of civil society, that is, modern commercial society. Marx gradually realized that to grasp the modern world, we need a critical, searching concept of capital. But Hegel lacked such a concept. Without it, social reality is systematically distorted, appearances pose as fundamental reality, and hopes are mislaid. Civil society appears as a realm of wheeling and dealing, class conflict, waning customs, and fragmented community. Poverty and wealth spiral to extremes; ideals such as liberty and equality ignite a great scramble for commercial power and empire. For Hegel, this appearance is both disturbing and integral to the freedom that is achievable only in these societies. Once history reaches the stage of civil society, social unraveling is part of the social fabric to be managed somehow. Hegel's philosophy reflects the hurly-burly of modern commerce; it does not reach its source.

In judging that Hegel's philosophy reflects modern commercial society without adequately comprehending it, Marx further concluded that Hegel's philosophy represents an unwarranted accommodation to it. As Hegel's student, Marx undertook to disclose the source of that accommodation and get past it: "if a philosopher has actually accommodated himself, his students have to clarify this out of his inner, essential consciousness."[4] In relating the films of Stanley Kubrick to skepticism and like moves made by existentialists, we try to reveal the essential form of consciousness that makes Kubrick a rebel without a cause.

In his dissertation, Marx explores how philosophy accommodates capitalism. Although he investigates the difference between the natural philosophies of Democritus and Epicurus, Marx regards this study as a point of entry for understanding the whole cycle of ancient Greek philosophy. Marx calls the Hellenistic cycle of Epicurean, Stoic, and Skeptical philosophy "the key to the true history of Greek philosophy."[5] It appears that Marx adopted Hegel's view that the world of classical Greek philosophy, culminating in Plato and Aristotle, could not cope with the demand of the human spirit for individual liberty. "Antiquity was rooted in nature, in the substantial. Nature's degradation, its profaning, marks basically the rupture of the substantial, honorable life; the modern world is rooted in spirit, and spirit can be free, other, nature set free of itself."[6] The Hellenistic philosophies, and the Epicurean in particular, expressed that demand and thereby exposed the limits of classical Greek philosophy, but they did so in an abstract, inadequate way. The creative kernel of Marx's dissertation was to see in Epicurus's doctrine of the declination or swerving of the atom the template for his entire philosophy.[7] Those swerving atoms are the original nonconformists: they assert their liberty—the prototype of bourgeois liberty's "freedom from"—by veering away from the norm, but their freedom achieves no content beyond this gesture. What Marx goes on to say about Epicurus applies to Kubrick: "The radical subjectivism of Epicurus is double-edged. Like Prometheus, Epicurus cuts down from their heaven all gods elevated over and against human consciousness, but with the same stroke he enthrones a dangerously abstract form of self-consciousness as the new idol."[8]

The skeptic's only certainties are the stream of present sensations that Sextus Empiricus calls "appearances." These sensations are given; everything subsequent arises from our efforts to name, order, analyze, and respond to appearances. This split between what is given—appearances—and what we construct anchors skepticism in futility. Reality splinters between the formless and the formed; as soon as appearances are spoken, they relocate to the other side of the divide—no longer given but subjective, fashioned by us. Language descends on the flood of experience in an impossible mission to say what it is. Just as quickly as we say what is true, good, or beautiful, the skeptic dismisses the claim as a subjective construction. Hence doubt is more defensible than any claim. The skeptic is hard-pressed to acknowledge better knowledge or higher morality, since distinctions lose all force when leveled to equally subjective posits. Every distinction is necessarily external to formless reality, a precarious imposition on the flood. Goodness sinks into banality, while evil, closer to the maelstrom, seems authentic and real.

Capitalism encourages the skeptical mind-set: ordinary reality is often *not* what it seems to be. Behind the ordinary lurks the compulsion for money to continually expand. What is good leads a double life: home is an asset, education is an investment, children are both deductions and expenses. The liberty of the market is narrowly self-centered. The indifference of money bleeds into ordinary concerns, sapping informed moral sensibilities. Irony results from the double character of capitalism: we have to pretend that our specific labors and products matter when we know that making money is all that is important. Irony thrives in capitalist culture as we rehearse convictions passed down to us, lest they slip away. What the skeptic posits as a timeless truth actually exists as a historical reality—ours is an ironic age. Alice

Harford reluctantly rebuffs a masher at the party with a coy, "I'm *married,*" as they both realize how little weight her wedding ring carries.

The Skeptical Tropes of Stanley Kubrick

In a revealing 1968 interview with Eric Nordern for *Playboy,* we find Kubrick invoking several modes of argument commonly employed by Hellenistic philosophers. Tropes involving either size or distance, or ones involving duration and death, figure prominently in his thinking: "If man merely sat back and thought about his impending termination, and his terrifying insignificance and aloneness in the cosmos, he would surely go mad, or succumb to a numbing sense of futility. Why, he might ask himself, should he bother to write a great symphony, or strive to make a living, or even to love another, when he is no more than a momentary microbe on a dust mote whirling through the unimaginable immensity of space?"[9] Compare Kubrick's observations on the futility of human existence with what David Hume wrote in the voice of an ancient Skeptic: "It is certain, were a superior being thrust into a human body, that the whole of life would to him appear so mean, contemptible, and puerile, that he never could be induced to take part in any thing, and would scarcely give attention to what passes around him."[10]

These weighty remarks should not stun us with their wisdom. If worth is measured by size and duration, then dwarfs and toddlers beware. What matters is not quantity but the form of existence: the important difference between people and microbes is not one of size. Besides, why doesn't our being alone in the cosmos—assuming that we are—make us *more* significant? It is not only life's brevity that supposedly makes it insignificant; death—whenever it comes—cancels all hope for meaning. For Kubrick, our unique capacity to project into the future is our undoing: "Man is the only creature aware of his own mortality and is at the same time generally incapable of coming to grips with this awareness and all its implications. . . . In each man's chest a tiny ferret of fear at this ultimate knowledge gnaws away at his ego and his sense of purpose."[11] Here Kubrick finds a source of the banality—or worse—of human life. That life matters is an appearance that the skeptic sees through. Hume reminds us that "death, though *perhaps* they receive him differently, yet treats alike the fool and the philosopher."[12] Seneca writes, "In the ashes all men are leveled. We're born unequal, we die equal."[13] *Barry Lyndon*'s epilogue, looking back in time, ends with a similar

sentiment about the main characters of the story: "They are all equal now."
Skeptics use such tropes to convince us that our judgments of value are
wholly subjective, while Stoics use them to convince us of the triviality of
our temporal concerns.

Skeptical "Solutions"

The skeptic cannot get past Descartes' doubt: how do we know that all we
hold certain is not a dream? Reason's demand for truth tumbles into the
nightmare. Value is purely subjective; the world and everything in it are
utterly indifferent. In the face of such paralyzing realizations, certain skeptical options remain. These skeptical moves surface throughout Kubrick's
films. The classic skeptical solution to the nightmare of reason can be found
in Hume's essay "The Sceptic." He follows up the passage cited above, in
which he claims that a superior creature forced into a human body would
find the whole business insufferably "mean, contemptible, and puerile," by
pointing out that the philosopher arrives at the same result: "Now all the
same topics of disdain towards human affairs, which could operate on this
supposed being, occur also to a philosopher. . . . While others play, he wonders at their keenness and ardour; but he no sooner puts in his own stake,
than he is commonly transported with the same passions, that he had so
much condemned, while he remained a simple spectator."[14] Hume's advice
to Descartes: when you fall into a whirlpool of doubts, leave your study for
the society found at the billiard table. Nature and custom rescue us from
reason's incapacitating insight; we soon find ourselves caring about this or
that, and so we carry on.

The foremost solution to skeptical reason, then, lies with our natural
instincts and sentiments. Parental love displays nature's power to rescue our
species from the abyss of indifference. Even a rake such as Barry Lyndon
comes under its spell. Hume observes: "Nature has given all animals a like
prejudice in favour of their offspring. As soon as the helpless infant sees
the light, though in every other eye it appears a despicable and a miserable
creature, it is regarded by its fond parent with the utmost affection, and is
preferred to every other object, however perfect and accomplished. The
passion alone, arising from the original structure and formation of human
nature, bestows a value on the most insignificant object."[15]

In his 1968 *Playboy* interview, Kubrick echoes Hume, adding a dash of
genetics: "You may stand outside your wife's hospital room during child-

birth muttering, 'My God, what a responsibility! Is it right to take on this terrible obligation: What am I really doing here?'; and then you go in and look down at the face of your child and—zap!—that ancient programming takes over and your response is one of wonder and joy and pride. It's a classic case of genetically imprinted social patterns."[16] For the skeptic, nature, with its biochemical zaps, keeps the species going, while reason, fixed on its nightmare vision, generally lacks a commensurate power.

In going along with nature's urgings, however, we fool ourselves in order to make life endurable. As Lieutenant Corby (Kenneth Harp) says to end *Fear and Desire,* "It's all a trick we perform, because we'd rather not die immediately." Hume likens the trick to playing a game; we follow rules in pursuit of goals—say, checkmating an opponent—that are all of our own artifice. He writes: "Human life . . . is to be regarded more as a dull pastime than as a serious occupation; and is more influenced by particular humour, than by general principles. Shall we engage ourselves in it with passion and anxiety? It is not worthy of so much concern. Shall we be indifferent about what happens? We lose all the pleasure of the game by our phlegm and carelessness."[17]

With this solution, we who reflect on our situation live a lie: in order to live at all, we act as though what we care about matters, when the truth is, it does not. The rituals of ordinary life cannot mask the futility; the nightmare licking beneath the ordinary is felt. In *Eyes Wide Shut,* Bill cannot be sure what happens to his friend who is whisked from the hotel. Did the woman save his life? Was she murdered? Who is following him? At the end of *The Killing,* after the loot blows away and the police close in, Johnny Clay refuses to run, muttering, "What's the difference?" Our proximity to the uncanny explains why Kubrick turns to the surreal to portray our present feel for reality: "I have always enjoyed dealing with a slightly surrealistic situation and presenting it in a realistic manner. I've always liked fairy tales and myths . . . ghost stories. . . . I think they are somehow closer to the sense of reality one feels today."[18] Here Kubrick is at his most prescient, capturing the sense in which our lives increasingly lie outside our awareness and control.

The nightmare can arise at any time. Beneath the veneer of civilization lurks the ape. Kubrick doubts that history, for all its apparent sophistication, can leave the state of nature behind. There is fighting in the War Room, in the bedroom, at the dawn of history, and in the technologically advanced future, where astronaut Dave (Keir Dullea) finally checkmates HAL (voice by Douglas Rain) after the all-too-human computer has killed the rest of the crew. Death clings to Kubrick's vision. Any social order remains external to our unruly nature. With mutual hostility as our original state, civilization, says Sigmund Freud, "is perpetually threatened with disintegration."[19] In *Eyes Wide Shut,* Bill's lost mask gives him away to Alice. What is unsettling in Kubrick's films is that, like the ax-wielding Jack Torrance (Jack Nicholson) in *The Shining,* we are always in danger of losing the masks of our civilized selves. The civilized man who sacrifices instinctual urges for security comes off the loser. Alex in *A Clockwork Orange* appeals because of the rawness of his appetites; he devours on impulse. The aggressive instinct that opposes this program of civilization cannot be deferred for long. The civilized Alex resembles a zombie: all the juice is drained out of him. The "cured" Alex fantasizes riotous coupling beneath Victorian onlookers. Marine recruits in *Full Metal Jacket* drill to the chant, "This is my rifle; this is my gun. This is for fighting; this is for fun." The hooded patriarchs in *Eyes Wide Shut* create rituals of degradation, while the proprietor of the costume store rents out his adolescent daughter after hours. Nothing *really* changes; progress is a sham.

Encountering the nightmare may put going back to "normal" life and playing our part in the "dull pastime" beyond our reach. At the close of *Fear and Desire,* Fletcher (Stephen Coit) ponders the gulf that now separates him from his former routines: "I'm all mixed up . . . I wish I wanted what I wanted before." When, at the end of *Eyes Wide Shut,* Bill and Alice Harford resolve to return from their respective adulterous nightmares to the worn confines of their marriage, we wonder how successful they will be. What options remain if the clutch slips on the "skeptical solution" and I cannot find my way home? Mac (Frank Silvera) in *Fear and Desire* cannot bear the thought of returning to his humdrum existence. Instead, he jumps at the chance to go out with a bang by killing a general: "I'm thirty-four years old, and I've never done anything important. When this is over I'm going to fix radios and refrigerators. . . . This is something for me. They dangle a general in front of you, you know it's only for this once. . . . It's better to make your life all in one night—one night, one man, one gun!" The banality of humdrum work overlays intractable existentialist banality. Mac echoes the words of Seneca: "As it is with a play, so it is with life—what matters is not how long the acting lasts, but how good it is. It is not important at what point you stop. Stop wherever you will—only make sure that you round it off with a good ending."[20] A bold suicide puts an exclamation point on an otherwise shabby existence—and Mac's role in the assassination of the general makes it a suicide mission.

Pleasure *Über Alles*

If we are not going anywhere, the present becomes all-important. For a skeptic, what would count as a good reason to defer the pleasures of the moment? "Present pleasure is always of importance; and whatever diminishes the importance of all other objects must bestow on it an additional influence and value."[21] Does this mean that the more philosophical we become, the more prone we are to seek out dissolute pleasures? Hume worries about the lure of such reasoning. Reflection on how everything is "hurried away by time" mortifies our passions, "but does it not thereby counterwork the artifice of nature, which has happily deceived us into the opinion that human life is of some importance? And might not such a reflection be employed with success by voluptuous reasoners to lead us from the paths of action and virtue and into the flowery fields of indolence and pleasure?"[22]

The skeptical solution of sliding back into ordinary life may fail, leaving only present pleasure. The list of Kubrick characters living the "snatch and grab it" conclusion of the "voluptuous reasoners" includes Clare Quilty (Peter Sellers), Alex and his droogs, Barry Lyndon, and Victor and the other masked men at the orgy in *Eyes Wide Shut*. Marx takes the quality of the sexual bond between man and woman as the barometer of an age's progress toward or away from humanizing the species: "This direct, natural, and necessary relation of person to person is the *relation of man to woman*. . . . From this relationship one can therefore judge man's whole level of development. From the character of this relationship follows how much man as a species being, as man, has come to be himself and to comprehend himself; the relation of man to woman is the most natural relation of human being to human being. It therefore reveals the extent to which the human essence in him has become a natural essence."[23]

For Kubrick, the sexual bond uniquely exposes the human capacity for cruelty. With films such as *A Clockwork Orange* and *Eyes Wide Shut*, Kubrick heralds a deeply skeptical age in which the clutch on the skeptical solution is worn out and the day of the voluptuous reasoners is at hand. In the closing scene of *Eyes*, Alice is stumped when she tries to say why the marriage should continue; neither love nor forgiveness is within reach. Instead, it is "fuck" that opens up their future. "Fuck" is Kubrick's last word on sexual relations—even inside marriage. Present pleasure *über alles*.

The Artist's Response: Create the Meaning Missing from the World

The artist sees through the hypocrisy of ordinary life, where the indifferent is treated as significant. Nature's trick lures us along. Surrendering to this artifice of nature amounts to bad faith. The artist removes the masks for a more genuine response. Dissatisfaction with the skeptical solution may lead in a direction popularized by Jean-Paul Sartre's existentialism. In answer to the question, "If life is so purposeless, do you feel that it's worth living?" Kubrick responds:

> Yes, for those of us who manage somehow to cope with our mortality. The very meaninglessness of life forces man to create his own meaning. . . . Both because of and in spite of his awareness of the meaninglessness of life, he can forge a fresh sense of purpose and affirmation. He may not recapture the same pure sense of wonder he was born with, but he can shape something far more enduring and sustaining. The most terrifying fact about the universe is not that it is hostile but that it is indifferent; but if we can come to terms with this indifference and accept the challenges of life within the boundaries of death—however mutable man may be able to make them—our existence as a species can have genuine meaning and fulfillment. However vast the darkness, we must supply our own light.[24]

This option discloses Kubrick's self-understanding as a creative artist: what is missing from the universe is supplied by the movie projector's dancing light. Meaning arises from the value added by the imagination. Kubrick's add-your-own-value formula is familiar from Sartre: "If man, as the existentialist conceives him is indefinable, it is because at first he is nothing. Only afterward will he be something, and he himself will have made what he will be. . . . Man is nothing else but what he makes of himself. Such is the first principle of existentialism."[25] Art—including art that depicts life's absurdity—offers consolation that carries us along whenever nature's "zaps" fizzle or strike us as unseemly. Since the world in itself is vacant, we must rely on ourselves to fill it. This popular way out of the conundrums of skepticism—so important to Kubrick's self-understanding as an artist—faces an irresolvable dilemma. It turns out to be a false door.

Kubrick and like-minded existentialists exploit a fallacy in skeptical thinking about value. On the one hand, the skeptic asserts that the universe is utterly valueless or indifferent *in itself*. In truth, value is something purely subjective that we foist or project on the world. But how are we to understand this projection of values? Here is where the sophism shows up. Is the world actually being changed through this projection from utter meaninglessness into significance? Where there was darkness, does our light now shine? If so, then the world is no longer dark. What is more, my world has never been dark because humans have been lighting it for untold generations. If projection adds meaning and value to a previously indifferent world, then we actually transform it into a meaningful and valuable one. But if we can do that, surely the generations who preceded us already did so, in which case the world has long since ceased to be meaningless, if it ever was. If I once thought the world was indifferent, I was simply mistaken. No skeptical solution was called for; this option pulls the rug out from under skepticism.

But the truth about skepticism and its existential progeny lies, we believe, with the other horn of the dilemma. Skepticism is not serious about projection; that is, it does not believe that we actually make the world (or any part of it) significant. Projection leaves the universe as it was: meaningless and indifferent. So, the heady talk about our supplying "genuine" meaning, of our taking it upon ourselves to "light" the dark world, is a self-deluding fantasy. Skepticism cannot escape this dilemma: either projection actually creates meaning and value, in which case skepticism's claim that the universe is indifferent is not true, or projection does not really project anything, and the idea that we can add meaning all on our own, so to speak, turns out to be a mirage.[26]

There is an additional problem with the "make your own meaning" solution: the arbitrariness of any result. According to skeptical principles, nothing of the world provides any guidance to our meaning- and value-making ventures. "It's not from the value or worth of the object, which any person pursues, that we can determine his enjoyment."[27] The true becomes the plausible; the good becomes the preferred. Whether one prefers Beethoven, a bit of the old "in and out," bum-bashing, or a fast-forwarded three-way orgy set to the William Tell Overture is a matter of indifference. As Hume puts it, "The catching of flies, like Domitian, if it give more pleasure, is preferable to the hunting of wild beasts, like William Rufus, or conquering of kingdoms, like Alexander."[28] The meaningful falls back into "whatever gives me pleasure," the outcome it was meant to escape. This skeptical solution—creating meaning—fails.

The Consolation of False Philosophy

The existentialism born of skepticism was not the only alternative in the mid-1950s, when Kubrick's artistic vision took shape. Another approach, influenced by Martin Heidegger's *Being and Time*, emerges from the writings of Herbert Marcuse (a student of Heidegger) and Erich Fromm, where history makes a difference to the kind of beings we become.[29] Humans develop through time; their prospects are not inherently fixed.[30] Marcuse speaks of a new reality principle that transforms work into play and reconciles pleasure and freedom. Fromm observes that Freud's tragic vision arises from taking aspects of his particular social world as basic human traits: "For Freud, social life and civilization are essentially in contrast to the needs of human nature as he sees it, and man is confronted with the tragic alternative between happiness based on the unrestricted satisfaction of his instincts, and security and cultural achievements based on instinctual frustration. . . . Freud's concept of human nature as being essentially competitive (and asocial) is the same as we find it in most authors who believe that the characteristics of man in modern Capitalism are his natural characteristics."[31]

Kubrick's existentialism does not draw from this alternative. Obviously, Kubrick reflects on his world; his films take advantage of an increasingly tolerant social climate to take up the topics of the day as well as those of past and future. He keenly senses those aspects of our lives that are ripe for doubt: mutually assured destruction, bored spouses, bureaucrats, sexual obsession, youth culture. But his art does not comprehend this world. These timely topics are pretexts to rehearse what does not change.

This popularized existentialism, oddly, remains a stranger to existence. It moves from one dogmatic claim to the next without bothering to look at the human creature and consider just what kind of being it is. When we are convinced that nothing can change, there is nothing to learn. Hope must come from outside, as do the aliens who spawn a new form of life at the end of *2001*. Skeptical criteria are rigged to remain one step ahead, dancing out of reach. How do we know that these criteria indeed measure truth or goodness? That question is not asked. The skeptic defends his conclusions against the evidence that human existence can offer. Dedicated to fixed claims, this skepticism makes for a false philosophy. Under the weight of foregone conclusions, even skeptical irony goes slack. It turns banal. Kubrick leaves us with stunning pictures, a filmmaker's consolation of false philosophy.

Notes

1. Thomas Allen Nelson, *Kubrick: Inside a Film Artist's Maze* (Bloomington: Indiana University Press, 1982), 4.

2. Seneca, *Letters from a Stoic,* trans. Robin Campbell (London: Penguin Books, 1969), 104.

3. Donald Livingston addresses "the dialectic of true and false philosophy" in chapter 2 of *Philosophical Melancholy and Delirium: Hume's Pathology of Philosophy* (Chicago: University of Chicago Press, 1998).

4. As cited in Patrick Murray, *Marx's Theory of Scientific Knowledge* (Atlantic Highlands, N.J.: Humanities Press International, 1988), 20.

5. Ibid., 18.

6. Ibid., 15.

7. "The declination of the atom from the straight line is in fact not a particular determination occurring accidentally in the Epicurean physics. Rather, the law which it expresses runs through the whole Epicurean philosophy" (ibid., 14–15).

8. Ibid., 12.

9. Nelson, *Kubrick,* 17.

10. David Hume, "The Sceptic," in *David Hume: The Philosophical Works,* 4 vols., ed. Thomas Hill Green and Thomas Hodge Grose (Aalen, Germany: Scientia Verlag, 1964), 3:227.

11. Gene D. Phillips, ed., *Stanley Kubrick Interviews* (Jackson: University Press of Mississippi, 2001), 69, 72.

12. Hume, "The Sceptic," 231.

13. Seneca, *Letters from a Stoic,* 182.

14. Hume, "The Sceptic," 227–28.

15. Ibid., 216.

16. Phillips, *Stanley Kubrick Interviews,* 67.

17. Hume, "The Sceptic," 231.

18. Phillips, *Stanley Kubrick Interviews,* 114.

19. Sigmund Freud, *Civilization and Its Discontents,* trans. James Strachey (New York: W. W. Norton, 1961), 59.

20. Seneca, *Letters from a Stoic,* 130.

21. Hume, "The Sceptic," 228.

22. Ibid.

23. Karl Marx, *The Economic and Philosophic Manuscripts of 1844,* trans. Martin Milligan (New York: International Publishers, 1964), 134.

24. Phillips, *Stanley Kubrick Interviews,* 73.

25. Jean-Paul Sartre, *Existentialism and Human Emotions,* trans. Bernard Frechtman (New York: Citadel Press, 1957), 15.

26. See Barry Stroud, "'Gilding and Staining' the World with 'Sentiments' and 'Phantasms,'" *Hume Studies* 19, no. 2 (November 1993): 253–72.

27. Hume, "The Sceptic," 219.

28. Ibid., 224.

29. The mid-1950s saw the publication of *Eros and Civilization* by Herbert Marcuse (New York: Vintage Books, 1955) and *The Sane Society* by Erich Fromm (Greenwich, Conn.: Fawcett Premier Books, 1955).

30. Kubrick's existentialism is a far cry from that of Heidegger in *Being and Time*. Heidegger rejects the subjectivism of value, and he sees our being-toward-death as freeing us for greater authenticity.

31. Fromm, *The Sane Society,* 74.

THE BIG SCORE

Fate, Morality, and Meaningful Life in *The Killing*

Steven M. Sanders

Stanley Kubrick's *The Killing* is an early, comparatively short, tightly coiled film that nevertheless gives some indication of the director's later productions, with their emphasis on art direction, focal lengths, and special effects. Much of the appeal of the 1956 heist melodrama is found in its temporally fragmented style as we follow each of the participants through the events leading up to and including the day that ex-con Johnny Clay (Sterling Hayden) robs a big-city racetrack of $2 million. Their stories are implicitly connected by their participation in Johnny's plan and then become rather abruptly connected on the day of the heist. Kubrick has said that he and producer James B. Harris wanted to make the film because they were so impressed by the structuring of time in Lionel White's thriller *Clean Break,* from which the script was adapted.[1] The precision required for the plan's split-second timetable is reinforced by the formal structure of the film, which overlaps and repeats events, and by voice-over narration to establish the time of each scene. When studio executives expressed dismay over this unconventional structure, Kubrick attempted to rewrite the script in a conventional, linear form and recut the film accordingly, but he simply could not get the effect he wanted, so he restored the film, and it was released in its original, nonlinear state.[2]

The Killing is widely thought to be the breakthrough film of a nascent virtuoso, and there seems to be little doubt about the distinctive sensibility at work in it. Although the film's highly delineated style is justifiably praised by critics, its philosophical significance has been largely ignored. Indeed, Spencer Selby's *Dark City: The Film Noir* may be the only place to find an in-depth discussion of the film's philosophical themes. If, as Selby believes, *The Killing* is a rich and coherent picture, this suggests that the theme of the power of the artist to control events is essential to the style of the film. It might also explain why Kubrick operates quite visibly in the deployment of his effects rather than remaining hidden behind the scenes. Ultimately, *The Killing* is philosophically noteworthy for its use of twists of fate as a plot device and a methodology for Kubrick's commentary on fate, morality, and meaningful life. Of course, Johnny Clay's absolute confidence in his criminal enterprise is the basis of the film's double irony: Clay avoids being killed because he does not anticipate the heavy traffic that makes him late for the meeting where the money from the robbery is to be divided, *and* he is ultimately captured by the police because no matter how well he has planned, he just cannot anticipate every contingency. But before we look into these matters, I want to place the film, and especially the characterization of its protagonist, in a wider context of philosophy and popular culture.

Cult of the Cool

In a recent essay, Lee Siegel lists some qualities of *cool*, "the descriptive term for an existential condition" characterized by a certain haughtiness or insolence in the treatment of authority figures; acting contrary to expectations; solitariness and unaffectedness; speaking in a measured, unexcited style; and appearing to be unaffected by external circumstances or forces. These "rudiments of cool," Siegel writes, "come straight out of Aristotle—his definition of the 'great-souled' man—Epictetus, and Montaigne," and he identifies such "bourbon-drinking Bourbons of cool" in the American cinema as Gary Cooper's sheriff in *High Noon*, Humphrey Bogart's Philip Marlowe in *The Big Sleep*, Marlon Brando's motorcycle rebel Johnny in *The Wild One*, James Dean's Jim Stark in *Rebel without a Cause*, and Paul Newman, Jack Nicholson, Warren Beatty, Samuel L. Jackson, and Nicolas Cage.[3] Siegel's observation is helpful, even if it does not capture the important distinctions among the philosophers he mentions, and I use it as a point of departure for viewing *The Killing* through the lens of the agent-based approach to ethics found in the writings of Aristotle, the Stoics, and elsewhere.

Sterling Hayden's portrayal qualifies Johnny Clay for membership in the Stoic wing of the cult of the cool.[4] To understand why, we must briefly examine some equally interesting if less central examples of the stoical cool character in 1950s, 1960s, and 1970s cinema: Robert Mitchum's down-and-out gambler Dan Milner and ex-GI Nick Cochran in *His Kind of Woman* and *Macao*, respectively; Steve McQueen's Frank Bullitt in *Bullitt*, affluent art thief Thomas Crown in *The Thomas Crown Affair,* and ex-con bank robber Doc McCoy in *The Getaway;* Michael Caine's Harry Palmer in *The Ipcress File* (except for one awful lapse, when Palmer machine-guns an American agent covertly observing the transfer of cash for an abducted British scientist); George Segal's Quiller in *The Quiller Memorandum;* Charles Bronson's contract killer Arthur Bishop in *The Mechanic;* and Warren Beatty's investigative reporter Joe Frady in *The Parallax View.* As these examples indicate, coolness transcends genre, with the stoical cool character appearing in caper flicks, espionage films, westerns, crime melodramas, paranoid thrillers, and cross-genre films such as *The Killing* and *The Asphalt Jungle* (also starring Hayden), which combine the intricate plotline and suspense of the heist film with the sense of impending doom and character-as-destiny outlook of film noir.[5]

The qualities of character found in the cool protagonist can be traced to the Stoics, who practiced what one admirer, nineteenth-century philosopher Arthur Schopenhauer, called a "spiritual dietetics." Believing that happiness cannot be attained by changing things external to us, the Stoics advocated an attitude of acceptance of our fate. Since we cannot shape the external world to fit our desires, we must turn inward and shape our desires to conform to the way things are. "This is attained," writes Schopenhauer, "by our always keeping in mind the shortness of life, the emptiness of pleasures, the instability of happiness, and also by our having seen that the difference between happiness and unhappiness is very much smaller than our anticipation of both is wont to make us believe."[6]

It does not follow, as Schopenhauer reminds us, that we must *actually* reduce our needs to a minimum. We can continue to possess the tangible goods of life and enjoy that aspect of life, as long as we keep in mind the uncertainty and transitoriness of such goods, on the one hand, and their essential worthlessness, on the other. We must "be ready at all times to give them up" and "constantly to regard possession and enjoyment as *dispensable,* and as held in the hand of chance; for then the actual privation, should it eventually occur, would not be unexpected, nor would it be a burden."[7]

The influence of Stoic ideas is reflected in the current widespread use of the term *stoical* to express one's acceptance of misfortune without rancor or remorse and, more broadly, an outlook that brings metaphysical and ethical ideas to bear on the practice of life. The Stoics, of course, had no monopoly on practice-oriented philosophy. There were the Epicureans and the Cynics, and Plato and Aristotle before them. In our own day, action-guiding philosophies such as pragmatism, Marxism, and existentialism all have their advocates. But unlike these modern outlooks, Stoic ethics makes "living according to nature" central, and the individual's realization of what is naturally appropriate for him is the basis of his moral awareness. Since the *logos*—divine providence, nature, fate—governs everything that happens, a virtuous man who fails to do right should accept this without distress or unhappiness, for his failure must have been for the best. Indeed, since moral virtue is the only good, the (perfectly) virtuous wise man, by definition, does the best he can, so he has nothing to regret.[8]

Photo Finish on a Merry-Go-Round

To find these Stoic ideas in *The Killing*, we have to replay a few of its key scenes. The heist conveys the promise that the protagonists will "make a killing" at the track and involves the killing of a racehorse as a diversionary tactic. In addition, when one of Johnny Clay's accomplices, racetrack betting-window cashier George Peatty (portrayed with nearly pathological self-effacement by Elisha Cook Jr.), discovers that he has been two-timed by his wife, he goes on a killing spree. All this gives the film's title its ambiguous reference. By the end of the film, Clay realizes that despite his careful planning and preparation, he cannot force events to happen as he wishes. Thus, he can neither anticipate nor control the psychological power that Sherry Peatty (Marie Windsor) has over her husband, from whom she extracts information about the heist and then passes it on to her lover, Val (Vince Edwards). Val arrives at the location where the money is going to be split up, intending to rob Clay and his four accomplices. Peatty, like the others, is awaiting Clay's arrival with agitated anticipation. But when Val arrives, and Peatty realizes that he has been played for a fool by his wife, he starts blasting away, killing everyone. Although Peatty is mortally wounded in the crossfire, he manages to make it back to his apartment, where he finds Sherry packing a suitcase. His worst suspicions confirmed, he shoots his wife and then collapses. Meanwhile, Clay, who had been delayed in traffic, arrives just as Peatty emerges from the brownstone where the split was to take place. Clay proceeds according to plan and drives away. He buys a suitcase in which to carry the haul from the robbery, picks up his girlfriend, Fay (Coleen Gray), and heads for the airport.

Johnny Clay is one of those fatalistic outsiders who makes his gamble at an unlucky time and comes up empty-handed. His stoical cool lies not only in the acceptance of his fate but also in his reticence over the course of the film. He plays things close to the vest, hiring Maurice Oboukhoff (Kola Kwarian), a wrestler, and Nikki Arane (Timothy Carey), a sharpshooter, to create diversions while the robbery is in progress. But Clay refuses to let them in on the bigger picture or a share of the loot. He tells them, "You don't need to know, and you'll be paid well not to ask."

Believing that planning will ensure mastery over events that, in reality, are beyond his control, Clay is foiled by some simple twists of fate. For example, at the end of the film, the suitcase containing the money from the heist drops from the luggage trolley because the driver has to swerve to avoid hitting a poodle that has run onto the tarmac. The lid pops open before the suitcase even hits the ground, and the currency spills out, flying across the runway and into the air. Commentators have surmised that this scene is lifted from John Huston's *The Treasure of the Sierra Madre* (1947), in which the Mexican bandits unwittingly scatter the gold dust to the winds. But whether the resemblance is due to imitation, homage, or coincidence, the scene assures us that Clay's future is similarly scattered to the winds as the plainclothes detectives who have staked out the airport move in with guns drawn. Clay knows that the jig is up, and rather than flee or fight, he accepts his fate, mumbling, "What's the difference?" as he surrenders.[9] This is very much in the spirit of *apatheia,* the acceptance of one's fate, as recommended by the Stoics. Such acceptance is found in film noir as well, when the protagonist recognizes that his doom is sealed by a stroke of fate.

Fate and Morality

There is a striking parallel between Stoic philosophy's view that providence operates through a deterministic causal nexus and Kubrick's introduction of coherence and control over his film's narrative, with its fragmented temporal sequences and offscreen narration.[10] Just as the Stoics provided in their philosophical outlook for the inexplicable workings of fate, Kubrick makes fateful interventions in the film through twists that, presumably, Clay could not have anticipated. These spell his doom and make for an emotionally satisfying answer to the film's central moral question: will Johnny Clay get away with it? Still, as Selby asks, why *must* Clay fail in his quest? His answer is that "Clay must fail, not because he is breaking the law, but because his innermost motives are immoral and totally misguided." The *must* here concerns Clay's moral psychology. Given the kind of person he is, "Clay's immorality is inseparable from his quest for a god-like power," and that is why fate is against him.[11]

Selby develops this interpretation to encompass the fate of Nikki Arane as well. To obtain a parking spot in the full lot (which he needs access to so that he can shoot the lead horse, thereby creating a diversion), Nikki ingratiates himself with the black attendant by giving him a big tip and appealing to his sympathy, telling the man that he is a war veteran and a paraplegic. The obliging attendant lets Nikki enter the lot. As the race is about to begin, the attendant offers Nikki a good-luck horseshoe, but Nikki has to get rid of the man so that he can carry out the plan. He dismisses him crudely with a racial epithet, and the infuriated attendant tosses the horseshoe to the ground as he storms away. Nikki then shoots the horse and attempts to make his getaway, but as he is backing up the car, a tire blows out. He tries to jump out of the car and flee but is shot by a police officer. In a panning shot reminiscent of those used to such powerful effect in the shock endings of *The Twilight Zone,* for example, the camera reveals that the fateful horseshoe has caused the flat. In Selby's words:

> This sequence is so important because it gives us the most complete information regarding the fate which we now know is Kubrick's self-conscious and premeditated manipulation of the events depicted. The horseshoe is an overt and fairly obvious symbol of the fateful control, and it is directly linked to Nikki's relationship with the black parking attendant. The implication seems to be that if he had been nice to the attendant and accepted the horseshoe, Nikki would have escaped successfully. This was, of course, impossible because of the kind of person Nikki was. He could only be nice to the attendant when he thought he needed him. . . . Though Nikki doesn't know it, the horseshoe offer really *is* an offer of the good luck which is necessary for his survival. Revealing his true feelings toward the attendant necessarily involves refusal of the gift of luck, and that's why Nikki dies.[12]

Thus, Selby argues, "As with Nikki, the fate which dooms Clay is self-consciously based on Kubrick's negative moral judgment of the character." Clay "treats people as a means to his own selfish, greedy ends. Each person that he conspires with is absolutely necessary to the success of the plan, and that is the only reason why Clay cuts them in."[13]

Friends as Means and as Ends in Themselves

Selby offers an inventive and insightful interpretation of *The Killing* and its ethical message of the need to treat people with respect and as ends in themselves, not merely as means to one's own selfish ends. He supplements his analysis with highly apposite illustrations from this absorbing film. But he does not make a completely convincing case for his interpretation. His own question—"why must Clay fail?"—is not unanswerable (at least in Kubrick's terms), but the answer is far more complex than the one Selby gives. Rather than simply dismiss those aspects of plot and character exposition that are implausible and unconvincing, I intend to give some philosophical account of their inadequacy.

We can distinguish between the evaluation of an individual's character and motives (as in the ethics of Aristotle), on the one hand, and the evaluation of an individual's actions and their outcomes (as in the ethics of John Stuart Mill), on the other. Once we do so, Selby's adverse moral evaluation of Johnny Clay becomes problematic, since *The Killing* provides grounds for a more complex assessment of his character. Granted that each of Clay's accomplices is required to carry out the heist, what better reason could he have for cutting them in than that they are "absolutely necessary for the success of the plan"? Clay does not *need* a further reason or justification to pay them off, Selby's assumption to the contrary notwithstanding. Since Maurice's and Nikki's services are indispensable to Clay's objective, and since he offers to pay them well, it is misleading to characterize Clay's motivation as "selfish" and "greedy." Of course, Clay's behavior is both illegal and immoral, but this is a judgment about what he *does,* not a judgment about who he *is*—an important distinction, since a person of good moral character may do something wrong, and a person of questionable moral character may act in a way that is morally right.

More important, it is misleading to call Clay's character into question by implying that he treats his accomplices only "as a means to his selfish, greedy ends." On the contrary, he dismisses the romantic overtures of bookkeeper Marvin Unger (Jay C. Flippen) with sensitivity (although Unger is clearly heartbroken), and he shows Maurice and Nikki respect by paying them well and explaining that, "for certain reasons, including your own protection, I'm not going to give you the whole story." He is candid about his intent to keep things close to the vest. "Twenty-five hundred dollars is a lot of dough, Maurice," he tells the wrestler. "Part of it is for not asking questions." And when Nikki wants to know what Clay's angle is, he tells him, "What my angle is, is my business. And Nikki, five thousand bucks is a lot of dough and that's what I'm paying it for, so nobody has to know my business." This indicates that Clay regards these men as rational contractors who are free to accept his offer or to turn it down, a sign of respect.

Maybe Clay plays things a little *too* close to the vest and downplays the seriousness of the risks when he tells Nikki, "And if you do get caught, what have you done? Shot a horse out of season?" Clay is not entirely blameless in failing to spell out the wider criminal context in which Nikki's actions will be undertaken. If they are caught, Nikki will likely be charged with being an accomplice to a felony. Still, nobody forces Nikki to accept Clay's offer, and he is only too happy to earn a cool $5,000. As I indicate above, Nikki has an awful, ugly moment at a crucial point in the heist, but it is unclear whether that happens because it is part of his nature, as Selby believes, or because Kubrick is stacking the deck against Clay, which seems just as likely. It is pretty clear, however, that Selby is mistaken when he claims that the parking lot attendant's offer of the horseshoe is really an offer of good luck, which is necessary for Nikki's survival, and that Nikki dies because he refuses that gift. It is far more accurate to say that Nikki dies because he is shot, and he is shot not because he refused the gift but rather because of the attendant's intervention. Nikki is unable to make his getaway because he gets a flat tire, and he gets a flat tire because the attendant threw the horseshoe on the ground. What Nikki needed was not luck but the attendant's noninterference in the first place.

Living a Meaningful Life

Questions about the meaning and point of life are central preoccupations of Johnny Clay and his accomplices, who evidently believe that money is the solution to their problems and that criminal activity (or at least one big heist) is an efficient means of achieving a meaningful life.[14] We can see why these beliefs might serve as obstacles to, rather than vehicles for, living a meaningful life. Living a meaningful life involves distinguishing between the means for realizing some appropriate purpose in an impersonal (or at least interpersonal) way and the means for achieving a particular person's specific wishes and desires. The former invokes objective standards; the latter replaces objectivity with individual inclination and idiosyncrasy, something that both the Stoics and Aristotle were quick to repudiate.

MODELS OF A MEANINGFUL LIFE

Let us leave the particular circumstances of the protagonists in *The Killing* long enough to pursue the issue more generally. Any attempt to understand the idea of a meaningful life must address the fact that there are a number of models to which ordinary people (not just philosophers) turn when thinking about the notion: exuberance, moral perfection, nirvana, and self-fulfillment, to name just a few. Based on the first model, exuberance, a meaningful life is one filled with passion, ecstasy, risk, even suffering. Its overriding aim is emotional intensity, a life driven by the will. Based on the model of moral perfection, a meaningful life is principled, conscientious, and dutiful; it is an autonomous life guided by reason—at least in those versions of the model (such as Immanuel Kant's) that link morality with practical reason. The model of nirvana typically combines detachment from one's passions and desires with the transcendence of the self in order to merge with some larger, impersonal oneness. The model of self-fulfillment is best construed as realizing one's potential. However, self-realization, or doing what is in one's nature, does not mean that there is just *one* thing it is in one's nature to do; our natures are much too complex and various for that. Still, some ways of living are far more fulfilling to us than others. The implication is that some ways of life are more meaningful (to us) than others, and this may have less to do with the external challenges we face when attempting to live any of the alternative options than it does with fulfilling what it is in our natures to be and do.

Each of these models has its advocates, its theoretical and practical advantages, and its limitations. In the remainder of this essay, I briefly contrast one version of exuberance with one version of self-fulfillment, because these models seem to be the most applicable to questions about the meaningfulness of Johnny Clay's life, given his character and the circumstances in which he finds himself.

ROMANTICISM AND RATIONALISM

What I refer to as the exuberance model is in fact one example of a more general outlook on life that might be called romanticism. As the term is used here, romanticism refers to an approach to life according to which "the will should be the overriding element in the dominant attitudes" of meaningful lives.[15] Romanticism thus places motivational supremacy in the will as opposed to the reason, as in Plato, Aristotle, and Kant. Used in this sense,

Schopenhauer, Friedrich Nietzsche, and Jean-Paul Sartre should be classified as romantics, each of whom, not coincidentally, portrayed human relationships as filled with strife, frustration, bitterness, and disappointment. This is particularly acute in Nietzsche's numerous references to women ("Toward morning, however, Zarathustra laughed in his heart and said mockingly, 'Happiness runs after me. That is because I do not run after women. For happiness is a woman.'") and in Sartre's grim depiction of personal relations in *Being and Nothingness.*[16] According to romanticism, a meaningful life can be achieved, if at all, only through an arduous struggle toward self-transformation, and only a few exceptional individuals succeed in this struggle, for immense motivational energies are required to surmount the daunting obstacles imposed by the external world. Ultimately, "the world is chaotic, not orderly; reason is not a guide to truth but a rationalization of the will," and meaningful lives must be created by individual efforts, "not found by conforming to external requirements."[17]

In contrast to all this is a view we might call rationalism, according to which the external world is not chaotic but orderly; the best guide to discerning and understanding this world is reason, and a meaningful life depends on such discernment and understanding and living one's life accordingly. Rationalists disagree about whether this order has a divine source, whether reason is empirical or a priori, whether it is possible to attain certainty, and whether individuals can exercise sufficient control over their lives to actually make them meaningful.[18] They also differ about how to think and act in light of these epistemological and metaphysical doctrines. But at the core, there is fundamental agreement among rationalists on the role of reason in living a meaningful life.

At a superficial level, Johnny Clay's approach to life reflects both romanticism and rationalism. As a career criminal, Clay is accustomed to strife, overcoming resistance, and living the kind of edgy existence endorsed by romantics in film and literature. His meticulous planning of the heist, which is his brainchild, shows the influence of rationalism on his thought. He is rational to the extent that he believes he can succeed only if he carefully plots a course of action, and to all appearances, Clay lives a purposive, goal-driven life. However, he fails to link his short-term and long-term goals, and as a result, he fails to see the folly of his ways. The risks he is willing to take are enormous, especially in light of the comparatively conventional life that seems to be his ultimate goal. We are neither shown nor told that Clay had reached a dead end in his efforts to achieve this goal by lawful means; given his evident intelligence, it is difficult to understand why Clay could not have found legitimate employment to provide the means to a secure future. Of course, Clay wants it all at once, and there lies the appeal of the perfectly planned heist—the one big score that he believes will put him on the sure path to happiness with Fay.

Character and Necessity

According to Selby, "At any time, Kubrick could have gummed up the works with an occurrence that Clay couldn't have planned for."[19] This is true, but the twists of fate that are depicted in the film as tripping Clay up are events that he *could* and *should* have anticipated, because they are so obvious. For example, Clay is capable of meticulous attention to detail in the planning of the heist and shows a high level of competence in its execution. Yet when he needs a suitcase to carry the cash, he gets one on the cheap at a pawnshop. And he knows that the suitcase does not have a reliable locking mechanism, because he tests it later when he transfers the money into it from a duffel bag. (I will not address the plausibility of depicting someone as careful as Clay failing to check the soundness of the luggage at the point of purchase, or not taking the precaution of dividing up the $2 million into two smaller bags.) In a noir film, with its typical emphasis on realism, Clay's ineptitude in this connection simply does not ring true, and his colossal errors are compounded beyond all plausibility. Perhaps Selby is correct in saying that Clay's determinative flaw lies in his hubris, his assumption that he has god-like control over all the relevant events, such as keeping Sherry Peatty in check.[20] This interpretation might explain why Clay comes to grief, but it still does not answer Selby's own question of why he *had* to fail.

The same questions of apparent character inconsistencies are left unanswered in connection with Nikki, who initially reveals great finesse in dealing with the parking lot attendant and then suddenly becomes a dunce when he needs to get rid of the well-intentioned fellow and his horseshoe gift. Instead of telling the man, "Thanks very much, I'd like to watch the seventh race alone," he infuriates him with a racial epithet. This, of course, leads to the notorious horseshoe-throwing incident. Kubrick (and Selby) would have us believe that backing up causes the horseshoe to penetrate the tire's sidewall, causing a flat. But here and elsewhere, Kubrick leaves us wondering whether he has forsaken realism for dramatic necessity.

AN ARISTOTELIAN PRINCIPLE

Philosophically, what is striking is that Kubrick has violated an important Aristotelian principle in his depiction of Johnny Clay and Nikki. According to Aristotle, virtues are characteristics we acquire by exercising them, and if a person acts habitually in accordance with the right rule, then he will do so on all occasions. I take it that this applies to the exercise of prudence as well as any of the other virtues Aristotle discusses, such as courage and temperance. Surely, if Clay and Nikki have the virtue of prudence, it is psychologically untenable to think that they would go to pieces just when it is in their best interests to keep their wits about them.[21]

Perhaps Kubrick's artistic intentions can be vindicated by the acknowledgment that the virtues of courage, self-control, initiative, and industriousness can be exercised *exclusively* self-interestedly. They can be exercised by those whose interests conflict with the interests of others and are inimical to the general good. Seen in this light, Selby's judgment that Clay's ends are "greedy and selfish" seems correct, because he wants riches that he neither earned nor inherited, that he neither won nor deserves, and he wants them at the expense of others. The fact that he is willing to give his accomplices a fair cut and share the rest with Fay, living the good life in Boston, does not make him a paragon (or even an average specimen) of moral virtue. This fact, however, gives Kubrick's "twist of fate" interventions by which Clay is punished for his immorality an even greater deus ex machina quality than if he had simply shown the social costs of Clay's illegal and immoral behavior. There are exceptions to the rule that if one is immoral one will be punished and therefore unhappy. It is not always and necessarily the case that morality and self-interest coincide, and neither we nor Kubrick can rule out the possibility of a flourishing amoralist—one who sees clearly that his happiness does not require him to be moral. Acknowledging this unfortunate fact about the moral life is a sign of realism and competence in our moral thinking, and failure to do so in order to reach a preordained conclusion undermines the plausibility of Kubrick's narrative intent.[22]

To those who are mindful of Aristotle's approach, which connects living virtuously with happiness or flourishing, we must remember that for Aristotle, the acceptance of a certain kind of social life presupposes the norms by which to judge a person's actions. With the dissolution of that traditional social life, the connection between virtue and happiness becomes precariously contingent. In this sense, Kubrick's solution is a throwback to the kind of approach that invokes divine providence to close the gap between virtue and happiness in our world. But this maneuver did not work for the moralists and theologians who tried it in the past, and it does not work for Kubrick, who has the added burden of having to rely on a totally depersonalized fate that is difficult to distinguish from coincidence.[23]

A CONDITION OF RATIONALITY

Finally, let us note that Johnny Clay is not rational in the more exacting sense of keeping his choice of ends free, well informed, and open to criticism. We have no reason to think that Clay has an open and critical attitude toward the ends he has already chosen—to enrich himself and his accomplices and to live in decorous obscurity with his soon-to-be-wife, Fay. An individual who fails to entertain a properly self-critical attitude toward his aims and goals fails to meet an important condition of rationality and, in so doing, places his chances of living a meaningful life in jeopardy. This is a matter of controversy, of course. Romantic writers such as Leo Tolstoy and D. H. Lawrence, who celebrate faith or will at the expense of reason, would repudiate the connection I have drawn between rationality and meaningfulness. For instance, in the simple and untroubled life of the Russian peasant, Tolstoy found an exemplar of meaningfulness and thus rejected reason to embrace a life of faith. Others would deny that rational choice should be understood in terms of being free, well informed, and open to criticism.

Despite these possible objections, it seems reasonable to think that in building on our dispositions, aptitudes, capacities, and talents we simultaneously develop our own distinctive individualities and we are, in the words of William James, "confronted by the necessity of standing by one of [our] empirical selves and relinquishing the rest." Many alternatives might have been available to Johnny Clay at the outset, but he had to choose because, as James colorfully puts it, "the philosopher and the lady-killer could not well keep house in the same tenement of clay."[24] However, it would have to be the case that *no* alternative was capable of realization before Clay would be justified in concluding that his life could not be meaningful if he departed from his plan. If there is a determinative flaw in Clay's thought and action, it lies in his failure to subject the empirical self he has chosen to stand by (and the course of action he has chosen to take) to the self-scrutiny needed to determine whether, in David Hume's illuminating phrase, he can "bear his own survey."[25] This capacity for self-appraisal simply is not present in Clay's conceptual repertoire, and as a consequence, he comes to grief. Although

The Killing depicts after-the-fact explanations of human actions by tracing them back to the causes that were sufficient to produce them, we must not forget that human beings make choices, respond to incentives, and seek to satisfy preferences, and that these are especially subject to the influence of reflective awareness or self-consciousness.

I have argued that Kubrick's use of the heist is suggestive but finally insufficient as a means of conveying his ideas about fate, morality, and meaningful life. Clay's lapses in planning and Nikki's racism seem more like contrivances than matters of thematic richness. There is thus a certain understated ambiguity in Kubrick's treatment of these themes that leaves us wondering where the line is to be drawn between Clay's immorality or hubris, Nikki's heavy-handedness, and sheer caprice.

Notes

My thanks to Jerold J. Abrams and Christeen Clemens for their comments on an earlier draft of this essay, and to Paul Goulart for valuable observations on *The Killing*.

1. Kubrick interview in the *Observer* (London), December 4, 1960, as cited by Spencer Selby, *Dark City: The Film Noir* (Jefferson, N.C.: McFarland Classics, 1984), 120.

2. These details are recounted in Eddie Muller, *Dark City: The Lost World of Film Noir* (New York: St. Martin's Press, 1998), 152–54.

3. Lee Siegel, "Cool Off," *TNR Online*, May 31, 2005, http://tnr.com (accessed June 7, 2005). I am grateful to Aeon Skoble for bringing this essay to my attention. Siegel identifies actors rather than their screen roles, as I have done here, except in the case of Steve McQueen, the ostensible subject of his essay, and Warren Beatty (*The Parallax View, Shampoo*).

4. Sterling Hayden also played the psychotic General Jack D. Ripper in the brilliant Kubrick film *Dr. Strangelove* (1964).

5. I discuss this aspect of film noir in "Film Noir and the Meaning of Life," in *The Philosophy of Film Noir*, ed. Mark T. Conard (Lexington: University Press of Kentucky, 2006).

6. Arthur Schopenhauer, *The World as Will and Representation*, trans. E. F. J. Payne (New York: Dover, 1966), 2:159.

7. Ibid., 156, 155.

8. See the discussion of Stoicism by R.W. Sharples in *The Oxford Companion to Philosophy* (New York: Oxford University Press, 1995), 852–53.

9. For contrast, compare the ending of Jim McBride's 1983 remake of Jean-Luc Godard's *Breathless* (1959), in which Richard Gere, playing the Jean-Paul Belmondo role, faces imminent arrest by going out in a blaze of bullets and self-justifying glory. As I explain later, this is romanticism with a vengeance.

10. The phrase "deterministic causal nexus" appears in David N. Sedley's entry on Hellenistic philosophy in *The Cambridge Dictionary of Philosophy* (New York: Cambridge University Press, 1995), 321.

11. Selby, *Dark City*, 122.

12. Ibid., 121–22.

13. Ibid., 122.

14. In this respect, my account agrees with Selby, *Dark City*, 120.

15. The present account is indebted to John Kekes's interpretation of romanticism, *The Art of Life* (Ithaca, N.Y.: Cornell University Press, 2002), 226. Kekes refers to "lives of personal excellence," whereas I am concerned with "meaningful lives," but the difference is not important for present purposes. I apply a similar distinction between rationalist and existentialist approaches to life in "Poker and the Game of Life," in *Poker and Philosophy*, ed. Eric Bronson (Chicago: Open Court, 2006), 41–51.

16. Friedrich Nietzsche, *Thus Spoke Zarathustra*, trans. Walter Kaufmann, in *The Portable Nietzsche* (Harmondsworth, England: Penguin, 1954), 275; Jean-Paul Sartre, *Being and Nothingness*, trans. Hazel E. Barnes (New York: Washington Square Press, 1966), pt. 3.

17. Kekes, *The Art of Life*, 226–27.

18. Ibid.

19. Selby, *Dark City*, 121.

20. Ibid.

21. I raise some critical questions about this Aristotelian account of psychological dispositions in "No Safe Haven: *Casino*, Friendship, and Egoism," in *The Philosophy of Martin Scorsese*, ed. Mark T. Conard (Lexington: University Press of Kentucky, 2007).

22. I explore this issue, and come to a somewhat different conclusion, in "Why Be Moral? Amorality and Psychopathy in *Strangers on a Train*," in *Alfred Hitchcock and Philosophy*, ed. David Baggett and William Drumin (Chicago: Open Court, 2007).

23. I have adapted the excellent discussion in Alasdair MacIntyre, *A Short History of Ethics* (New York: Macmillan, 1966), ch. 12.

24. William James, *Psychology* (New York: Henry Holt, 1893), 1:309, as cited by Joel Feinberg, "Absurd Self-Fulfillment," in *Time and Cause*, ed. Peter van Inwagen (Dordrecht, Netherlands: D. Reidel, 1980), 267.

25. David Hume, *A Treatise of Human Nature*, ed. L. A. Selby-Bigge (Oxford: Clarendon Press, 1965), 620.

PART FOUR

THE SUBJECT IN HISTORY

SPARTACUS AND THE SECOND PART OF THE SOUL

Gordon Braden

Roman History at the Movies

At the end of Ridley Scott's film *Gladiator* (2000), the mortally wounded Maximus (Russell Crowe), having killed the psychopathic emperor Commodus in gladiatorial combat in the Colosseum, speaks to the suddenly silent crowd: "There was a dream that was Rome. It shall be realized. These are the wishes of Marcus Aurelius." Marcus was the previous emperor and Commodus's father; Maximus is referring to a conversation with Marcus (Richard Harris) early in the film, where in his tent on the frontier Marcus had voiced his unhappiness both with Commodus as his imperial successor and with the Roman Empire itself. Marcus then asked Maximus, his greatest general, for "one more duty" after his own death: to serve as "Protector of Rome" and effect a momentous change in the capital city. "There was once a dream that was Rome," he said, and charged Maximus to use his office "to give power back to the people of Rome and end the corruption that has crippled it." Maximus asked for no more explanation. A previous scene had floated the report that sentiment for going back to the preimperial system of the Roman Republic was afoot among the senatorial order ("Rome *was* founded as a republic," according to one senator, stirringly if inaccurately), and Marcus shortly tells Commodus, "Rome is to be a republic again." This news moves Commodus to patricide. The mood at the end of the movie strongly implies that the hero's redemptive death in the arena secures the compliance of all involved finally to bring this restoration about, as Rome—literally, if the evocative final image before the credits is supposed to be a sunrise—enters a new day in its history.[1]

A certain vagueness here has something to do with this ending's being, even by the creative standards of historical fiction, radically counterfactual. Historically, we are at the point that Edward Gibbon chose as the natural beginning for *The History of the Decline and Fall of the Roman Empire*, and Hollywood condensed his title for its previous film about the death of Marcus Aurelius, Anthony Mann's *The Fall of the Roman Empire* (1964). The Republic was not restored at the death of Commodus in AD 192, nor was any such attempt made. Within six months, two new emperors were installed and murdered; there followed the eighteen-year reign of Septimius Severus, who stayed in power by giving the Principate a military cast beyond anything it had seen before. If it is, in some historical sense, morning in ancient Rome at the end of *Gladiator*, the dream being realized has to do with Maximus's valor as "a soldier of Rome" (as he is hailed at his death), not his commitment to republican government. Some critics indeed see the film as being cryptofascist in its import.[2]

This distortion mirrors a distortion in the opposite direction in *Gladiator*'s most important cinematic predecessor, Stanley Kubrick's *Spartacus* (1960). A voice-over at the start of that movie informs us: "The age of the Dictator was at hand, waiting in the shadows for the event to bring it forth." Near the end of the film, after the defeat of the slave revolt, the victorious general Marcus Licinius Crassus (Laurence Olivier) not only orders the crucifixion of six thousand surviving rebels but, assisted by the young Julius Caesar, makes his move against Roman citizens as well. Summoned to a meeting with Crassus and Caesar in an ominously darkened senate house, the populist senator Gracchus (Charles Laughton) is informed about "the new order of affairs": "The enemies of the state are known. Arrests are in progress; the prisons begin to fill. In every city and province, lists of the disloyal have been compiled. Tomorrow they will learn the cost of their terrible folly, their treason." Gracchus is told that his own name heads the list; he returns home to prepare for suicide. When Lentulus Batiatus (Peter Ustinov) shows up there with Spartacus's wife, Varinia (Jean Simmons), dangerously spirited away from Crassus's house, he confirms, "They're arresting everyone." In the film's last scene, Batiatus and Varinia leave Rome at dawn through the Appian gate, but they have a tense moment getting through a military checkpoint. We are left with the strong impression that the Roman Republic has now come to its end, supplanted by a totalitarian regime on the twentieth-century model.[3]

Generating that impression involves significant deviation not only from the historical record but also from the 1951 novel by Howard Fast on which the film is based (and which is historically accurate within much narrower limits than the film attempts to be). The final suppression of the slave revolt in 71 BC was brutal enough as far as the slaves were concerned—the figure of six thousand is well attested—but it is not known to have been accompanied by widespread proscriptions against others. Caesar (born 100 BC), though politically active at the time, was not involved in these events (and is not a character in Fast's novel); as a character in the film, he does not make much of an impression (the casting of the bland John Gavin in the role is one of the movie's weaknesses) and seems to be there for his value as one of the few figures from Roman history with secure name recognition among the general movie audience. He directs the audience's mind forward to his own imperial career, when he ruled as Dictator for four years and set the stage for the imperial regime that his nephew Octavius consolidated in 27 BC. (It was Octavius who first established the Cohortes Urbanae, apparently what is meant by the Garrison of Rome that figures in the political maneuvering in the film.) No dictatorship came in 71 BC; in the novel, Rome returns to business as usual, if a bit angrier and meaner than before. The historical Crassus found himself not in a position of political dominance but embarrassingly outshone by Gnaeus Pompeius (known in English as Pompey, and briefly mentioned in the film), who arrived at the final battle at the last minute but managed to secure the official Triumph back at Rome (Crassus had to be content with an Ovation). Political combat within the institutions of republican government resumed. If the end of *Gladiator* is anachronistically rosy, the end of *Spartacus* is anachronistically dark.

These are nevertheless not equivalent distortions; the conclusion of *Spartacus* does not so much evade Roman history as telescope it. Rome had by 71 BC known proscriptions such as those Crassus institutes in the movie during the civil wars of Marius and Sulla, and it would know them again in the aftermath of Julius Caesar's assassination (and several times later under imperial rule). In retrospect, the establishment of the Principate followed from political dysfunctions in the Republic that were already at work at the time of the slave revolt, and the film's historical prolepsis simply accelerates what came to seem inevitable. Doing so, moreover, helps secure *Spartacus*'s place as the sword-and-sandal epic with the most interesting and provocative political story to tell. In linking the end of the Republic directly to the destruction of Spartacus's army, the film shows Crassus successfully manipulating a public emergency as a way of settling old political scores with a coup d'état tricked out as a conservative restoration of order.

The film's politics have long been a focus of attention. With a script by the blacklisted Dalton Trumbo, based on a novel by a former Communist (both Trumbo and Fast served jail time for their failure to cooperate with the House Un-American Activities Committee), the finished film was the object of an attempted boycott by the American Legion and others. The decision by Kirk Douglas, whose production company made the film, to give Trumbo screen credit (he had started work under a pseudonym), combined with the movie's success at the box office, effectively ended the Hollywood blacklist and earned those involved a small but real place in American political history. (When I went to see the rereleased film in Los Angeles three decades later, the local crowd applauded when Trumbo's name appeared in the opening credits.) But internal worries about the film's political coloration had already had their effect and, together with other troubles on the set, helped generate a famously vexed production history involving constant changes in the script (with Trumbo being only one voice among several), reshoots after the first rough cut, and at least two rounds of surgery after a preview showing. The 1991 restoration put back several minutes of excised material, but the film still shows the effects of numerous unharmonized changes of direction.

There is plenty of lore about the arguments and personality conflicts involved in the making of *Spartacus,* but the publicly available information is incomplete and sometimes contradictory; it is usually difficult to be sure who was responsible for what in the final product. The fullest document is Trumbo's written response after viewing the rough cut, where he records his disagreement with numerous things he saw. What he disliked (not all of it evident in the film as we have it) is presumably the doing of others, of whom Kubrick and Douglas would have been the main voices—although Kubrick and Douglas had their own conflicts, somewhat less reliably documented (in his memoirs, Douglas categorizes Kubrick as "a talented shit"). Kubrick, working for the only time in his career without central decision-making authority, fulfilled his contract but afterward effectively disowned the film (although he cooperated in small ways with the restoration). Politically oriented critics now tend (with varying degrees of friendliness) to see the story as that of a potentially strong Marxist agenda progressively addled by Hollywood temporizing and big-budget confusion.[4]

I argue here that—against these odds, and for all its unevenness—the film as we have it has an underappreciated coherence in its picture of Roman politics, as well as a perhaps surprisingly distinguished filiation reaching back to Plato's model of the tripartite soul.

Gladiators and the Platonic Soul

There is a scheme to the plotting of *Spartacus* that seems to have evolved in stages without being any particular person's idea, although it has the advantage of pivoting on Olivier's performance, one of the film's steadiest strengths. It is related to the defining premise of the generally downscale genre of the gladiator film. A flurry of these films were made quickly and inexpensively in Italy in the early 1960s for dubbed export; they provide a bridge of sorts between *Spartacus* and *Gladiator* by exploring plot devices by which gladiators could play a significant role in ancient history. For instance, in *Gladiators Seven* (1962; *I sette gladiatori* with an Italian sound track, *Los siete espartanos* with a Spanish one), an outlaw team of gladiators travels to Greece to help Sparta throw off Roman domination and reestablish its reputation as the preeminent site of soldierly virtue. The imaginative allure of such interventions has some tenacity; in the summer of 2005 the ABC-TV miniseries *Empire* dramatized Octavius's accession to the imperial crown through the previously unrecognized assistance of the gladiator Tyrannus, whom Julius Caesar had freed from the arena to serve as his bodyguard. *Spartacus* deals with the only such story with serious historical warrant, but it also explores another level on which the uniquely Roman sport of gladiatorial combat is related to Roman politics: they mirror each other.

Sport and politics mirror each other not just in the general sense of being combative and lethal but specifically in their organization as one-on-one contests (*paria*). The usually nonlethal athletic contests in ancient Greek society that occupied roughly the same place that gladiatorial shows did for the Romans included some paired events (such as wrestling), but most Greek sports involved the simultaneous competition of a wider field of contestants. Gladiatorial fighting, in contrast, was from its origins predominantly a business of matched pairs—two men out to kill each other. One of the historical distortions in *Gladiator* is the general impression of gladiatorial combat as a kind of team sport, a nasty version of American football; there is no proper one-on-one contest until Maximus faces off with Commodus at the end. *Spartacus,* however, keeps the focus on paired combat very sharp and dramatizes it with particular force. One of the most powerful scenes in the film—and one in which Kubrick's directorial hand seems to be at its firmest—comes at the private gladiatorial show at Batiatus's school in Capua, where the first pair goes out to fight to the death while Spartacus (Kirk Douglas) and the Nubian Draba (Woody Strode) wait for their turn. Draba had earlier refused to tell Spartacus his name, saying, "Gladiators don't make friends. If we're ever matched in the arena together, I have to kill you." As the first fight can be heard and partly seen outside, the two of them wordlessly and at length face the fact that that moment is about to come, their seemingly inescapable fate.

The man who has paid to watch one of them kill the other is involved, with more relish, in the political version of such combat. Even before Crassus appears on screen, we learn of his long-standing rivalry with Gracchus—Batiatus must quickly cover a bust of Gracchus out of fear of annoying his unexpected guest—and most of the Roman business in the movie is presented as turning on this axis. At Capua, Crassus is so absorbed in discussing political strategy with his (fictional) protégé Marcus Publius Glabrus (John Dall—another unhappy casting decision) that he pays only intermittent attention to the expensive fight he has commissioned. Later, when Glabrus is disgraced, Crassus replaces him through the political seduction of Gracchus's own student, Caesar. In the long run, the Crassus-Gracchus rivalry proves to be a fight to the death. It is also one of the movie's most overt rewritings of history; the patrician-populist opposition that it is made to embody simplifies Roman politics of the time to something that a general movie audience could take in, and Gracchus himself did not exist. He is Fast's creation: Lentelus Gracchus in the novel, but simply Gracchus in the film. The name is a vague allusion to the reformist brothers Gracchi of the previous century. (In an act of cinematic homage, the more or less good senator in *Gladiator* is also named Gracchus.)

Yet these changes, like some of the others in the film, keep their own kind of faith with the historical record—in this case, with one of the most important ancient sources for these events. We have the testimony of Plutarch, the Greek essayist and biographer of the late first and early second century AD, that, at the time of the slave rebellion, Crassus was enmeshed in a rivalry with Pompey, the man who stole his Triumph; their rivalry preceded and outlasted that particular incident and, according to Plutarch, was a defining feature of this period of Roman history. The Greek words that Plutarch uses to introduce the subject (*Crassus* 6.4) are *hamilla* (contest) and *philotimia* (love of being honored; *timê* is the sign of recognition that obsesses Achilles in the *Iliad*), and they are much in evidence in his other biographies as well; *philotimia* is an almost inseparable twin to *philoneikia* (love of combat), which is essentially interchangeable with *philonikia* (love of winning), and the three function as almost technical terms in Plutarch's acute and influential analysis of the personalities and motivations of the famous generals and politicians of Greek and Roman antiquity. Time and again a rivalrous pair of males turns out to be key to an important part of the story: Agesilaus and Lysander, Aristides and Themistocles, the elder Cato and Scipio Africanus. Theseus's sense of being in competition with Heracles is supposed to have shaped his entire adult life; at Athens, the contest between Pericles and Thucydides is said to fit a pattern like that between Gracchus and Crassus in the film: "there had been from the beginning a sort of seam hidden beneath the surface of affairs, as in a piece of iron, which faintly indicated a divergence between the popular and the aristocratic program; but the emulous ambition [*hamilla kai philotimia*] of these two men cut a deep gash in the state, and caused one section of it to be called the *People*, and the other the *Few*" (*Pericles* 11.3). Of Julius Caesar, the man who eventually succeeded in changing the rules for the gladiatorial show of classical politics, Plutarch writes that he took this competitive instinct to a new level: "Caesar's many successes . . . did not divert his natural spirit of enterprise and ambition [*philotimon*] to the enjoyment of what he had laboriously achieved, but served as fuel and incentive for future achievements, and begat in him plans for greater deeds and a passion for fresh glory, as though he had used up what he already had. What he felt was therefore nothing else than emulation of himself, as if he had been another man, and a sort of rivalry [*philoneikia*] between what he had done and what he purposed to do" (*Julius Caesar* 58.4–5). Republican political combat ultimately mutates into a *hamilla* of one.[5]

Modern historians of classical antiquity depend on Plutarch for much of their information but do not necessarily accept this kind of etiology for historical events; it is their professional instinct to look for less personalized causes. Plutarch himself, however, writes with the guidance of a famous theory that posited a rigorous equivalence between the components of the state and the components of the individual psyche; his depiction of the role of *philotimia* in classical politics presumes and occasionally alludes quite specifically to Plato's *Republic* and the tripartite model of the soul. The tripartition is perhaps the most interesting part of that theory; the division is not simply into higher (rational) and lower (sensual) functions but includes another factor that tends to resist decisive translation. In English, it is usually the "passionate" or "spirited" or simply "angry" part; in Greek, it is *to thymoeides,* the part governed by the *thymos,* a semianatomical term with Homeric resonance. Plato introduces the term in the *Republic* when Socrates comes to the combative instincts needed in those who defend the state in war (2.15/375A); as he develops his analogy between the state and the individual, *to thymoeides* becomes one part of the soul of every individual, a part that interacts with the other two parts but is not reducible to either of them.[6] Without proper conditioning, it can be unstable and hostile to reason; for a while, it is treated simply as one of the irrational appetites—like those for bodily nourishment and pleasure—that the rational first part of the soul must regulate. Eventually, though, Socrates becomes very interested in the way anger can be an ally of reason in the soul's civil strife (*en têi tês psychês stasei,* 4.15/440E); *to thymoeides* may be irrational, but its irrationality differs from other irrational impulses. Plato's conceptualization of this special form of irrationality becomes clear when he begins referring to it as *philonicon* and *philotimon.* The irrational appetite that makes possible an impressive superiority to bodily pain and deprivation is competitiveness.

Plato has little to say about the abuses of this superior species of irrationality. In the *Phaedrus* (253D), the *thymos* is the splendid white horse in the soul's harness; this disposition may stand for that of classical Greco-Roman culture generally. In particular, it may stand for a political culture whose implicit faith—given institutional form in the Roman Republic—is that the rational ends of the state are best served by a vigorous competition for precedence among its players. Yet beyond his own bright metaphor, Plato's theory is quite clear that the concerns of the soul's first and second parts are essentially different: interest in being better and interest in the good are simply not the same thing, and their coincidence is at best a factional alliance. Plutarch considers himself Plato's philosophical disciple and rehearses the theory of the tripartite soul in his *Moralia;* the *Lives* is, time and again, his picture of the soul's second part in action as one of the main engines of political history from Plato's time up to the founding of the Roman Principate. It proves, thanks, among other things, to Plutarch's narrative gift, to be an extremely influential picture; it is a major source, from Shakespeare's time to our own, of a general sense of what the alpha males of classical history were like. It also explores, more acutely than Plato himself tries to do, the potential dysfunction of *to thymoeides* in politics; repeatedly, Plutarch's point in drawing attention to its operations is to explain how things went wrong. The story of the Spartan king Agesilaus is the story of almost nothing else and occasions the observation that "ambitious natures [*philotimoi physeis*] in a commonwealth, if they do not observe due bounds, work greater harm than good" (*Agesilaus* 8.4). Plutarch blames Greece's eventual loss of political independence to Rome on "the baseness and contentiousness [*philoneikiai*]" of Greek leaders who are too addicted to gaming one another to make common cause (*Flamininus* 11.3), although Rome is scarcely immune. Coriolanus, who also attracted Shakespeare's interest, provides a starkly pathological example from the early years of the Republic: "He had indulged the passionate and contentious part of his soul [*tôi thymoeidei kai philoneikôi merei tês psychês*], with the idea that there was something great and exalted in this" (*Coriolanus* 15.3), and in the process, he destroyed himself and almost destroyed his city.

Competitiveness may well be a transcultural fact of human and even animal nature, and the tendency of males in particular to sort themselves out into combative pairs is so pervasive that it could even be biologically determined. Show business is certainly a prime seminary for such behavior. Many of the stories about the making of *Spartacus* take this form (according to Ustinov, the political combat between Crassus and Gracchus was tensely reproduced on a personal level by Olivier and Laughton), and one report attributes the very existence of the film to a *hamilla* between Douglas and Charlton Heston, who had beat Douglas out for the part of Ben-Hur. The conceptual salience of Plato's theory, abstracting *to thymoeides* into a full member of the soul's triumvirate, and Plutarch's long-term relevance to our inherited image of classical antiquity (he certainly would have been on Fast's reading list, and probably Trumbo's as well) argue against reducing the matter to a gossipy commonplace. *Spartacus,* I suggest, finds its troubled way to an impressive thesis about Roman history in the later Republic when a version of Plato's theory maps itself onto an imperial landscape significantly wider than the polis that was Plato's own frame of reference.

Spartacus and Crassus

Plutarch's Crassus is only a compromised specimen of a Roman politician, a relative latecomer to *philotimia* and, in the long run, conspicuously inept at it. His reigning passion is initially *philoploutia,* love of wealth (the Greek words draw a firm distinction between political ambition and avarice), and his ultimate fate is to die in a badly conceived and executed campaign against the Parthians. In the film, though, he is the supreme embodiment of Rome's combative ruthlessness, leading the city that had lately discovered the gladiatorial fight as its favorite sport to its accursed political destiny. This perspective sets the film slightly apart from other cinematic depictions of Rome's decadence, where opulent paganism is commonly set against ascetic Christianity, and the city's rot is dramatized in terms of its sensual self-indulgence. Even Fast's rigorously secular novel pointedly contrasts the bisexual promiscuity of the upper-class Romans with Spartacus's own chaste monogamy, which he legislates as a standard for the freed slaves under his leadership. The film, however, casts a kindly look on the appetites of the soul's third part; among its justly famous moments is the conversation (authored by Ustinov, to Trumbo's displeasure) between two conspicuously unmilitary Romans, Gracchus and Batiatus ("I'm a civilian," Batiatus says later, "I'm more of a civilian than most civilians"), on the moral advantages of being overweight: "Corpulence makes a man reasonable, pleasant, and phlegmatic. Have you noticed the nastiest of tyrants are invariably thin?" In Mervyn Le Roy's *Quo Vadis* (1951), the fact that the imperial palace has become "Nero's house of women" (Nero being played, as it happens, by Ustinov) is a key sign of decay at the top and a forecast of doom. Gracchus's house in *Spartacus* has an all-female staff, and the reason is exactly what you think, but the dramatic point is not his corruption but his appealing lack of hypocrisy: "I happen to like women. I have a promiscuous nature, and unlike these aristocrats I will not take a marriage vow which I know that my nature will prevent me from keeping." Gracchus too is doomed, but his weakness for women helps earn him a chaste and gentle kiss from Varinia; his destruction takes with it the only strain of grace evident in his social class.

Yet Crassus's *hamilla* with Gracchus, though it is the most overtly Plutarchan part of the film's plot, is not the most important one in which he is involved. The others are outside the rules and catch him off guard, and the drama of the last part of the film is the way they trouble his seemingly decisive victory. Draba's long gaze at Spartacus as they await their commissioned fight to the death is in fact leading up to a momentous decision to refuse that pairing; in the arena, the victorious Draba defies an order to kill Spartacus and instead hurls his trident against the Romans who are paying for the show. Crassus holds his ground and defends himself (with a shocking bloodiness originally cut for general release), but he is clearly unnerved (at least as Olivier plays it). Ignoring his own announced principles, Draba turns his hostility away from a fellow gladiator and against his real enemy. But the social boundary between slave and patrician—which in Draba's case is also something of special significance for America in 1960, the racial boundary between black and white—is such that Crassus does not expect the attack and just barely has time to get out of the way. His lack of attentiveness haunts him for the rest of the movie, as Draba's self-sacrifice sparks the gladiatorial revolt the next day, and Crassus finds himself locked in an even more dangerous contest with a mysterious antagonist who, by the scheme of things in which Crassus lives, should not exist.

The plotting of the skewed *hamilla* between Crassus and Spartacus developed as the story moved toward the screen. Some elements are there in Fast's novel; others were apparently added by Trumbo to constitute the main action after the final battle, and it culminates in a moment that was definitely not as Trumbo would have had it. It is skewed, among other things, by the fact that until his last encounter with Crassus before the Appian gate, the fight is not personal for Spartacus; he is fighting for his army's survival against whatever Rome sends his way. But by then, the fight has already become intricately personal for Crassus. The alarm he feels at Capua returns before the final battle, when he asks Batiatus for "what up to now I have not been able to obtain, a physical description of Spartacus." "But you saw him," says Batiatus, and Crassus is stunned. "I remember the Negro," he says, but he has no memory of the other gladiator, who is now his opposing general. The distress (evident in Olivier's performance, though not explicit in the shooting script) presumably has to do with both the uncanniness of their previous shared history and the anger at an inattentiveness that deprives Crassus of information he now would very much want to have. His specific inattentiveness during the earlier fight comes with a larger resonance: a socially induced blindness that kept Crassus from thinking that there was anything in the action of slaves that might be relevant to what most concerned him. He is now in a fight to the death with an invisible man.

The *hamilla* between Crassus and Spartacus—a vertical one, as it were, across a major social divide, rather than a lateral one like most of those Plutarch writes about—takes place not only on the battlefield, where Crassus proves the master, but also in venues where Crassus finds himself defeated. It was Fast's idea to create a triangle with the two men and Varinia: Crassus finds himself obsessed first with the idea of his opponent's woman and then with her in person, and after Spartacus's death he attempts, with surprising restraint, to persuade her to love him. He fails, and Gracchus, in a last move against his longtime enemy, arranges for her abduction and release. With minor changes (such as making Batiatus the agent of her escape; the movie combines two separate characters from the book), the film keeps this plotline but adds another to make the triangle a quadrilateral and to give heightened geometrical clarity to Crassus's hopeless competition with Spartacus for the love of those near him.

The character of Antoninus is entirely new to the film and even there was something of an afterthought; according to Douglas, the character was created specifically to give Tony Curtis a part to fulfill a contractual obligation. Antoninus is introduced about an hour into the movie as a new slave in Crassus's household whom Crassus picks to be his body servant. His age is specified as twenty-six (Curtis was thirty-four), but Crassus keeps calling him "boy." In an important scene restored in 1991, Crassus makes veiled sexual overtures to Antoninus while being bathed and then, at the sight of Roman soldiers marching out of the city on the other side of the Tiber, lectures him on the masochistic erotics of Roman patriotism: "There is only one way to deal with Rome, Antoninus. You must serve her, you must abase yourself before her, you must grovel at her feet, you *must* . . . love her. Isn't that so Antoninus?" His face fills the screen as he says this; then he turns around to discover that Antoninus has disappeared. We learn before too long that Antoninus has joined the slave uprising (giving the mostly rural phenomenon at least a token urban component). Spartacus takes a particular interest in him, and the two find themselves together as prisoners after the defeat of the slave army. Historically, it appears that Spartacus did not survive the battle, although his body was never found; it is that way in the novel as well. In the film, Crassus is eager to identify Spartacus alive or dead, and that is why knowing what he looks like is critical. There are political considerations—it needs to be publicized that, one way or another, the legendary leader has been disposed of—although a more personal strain runs through Crassus's urgency. The prisoners collectively refuse to identify their general by all claiming to be him (Antoninus leading the way), but Crassus is able to answer his own question when he recognizes Antoninus as the young man he had wanted to seduce. In a flash, Crassus's jealousy tells him, accurately, that the prisoner marching next to Antoninus must be Spartacus, the man who stole his boy.

Crassus's bisexuality is overt in the novel. It clearly required some work to get it into the movie, and the initial motivation for taking the trouble was probably to make a statement about Crassus's politics; the scripting of his attempted seduction of Antoninus echoes rumors about the supposedly homoerotic roots of twentieth-century fascism. The discussion of Gracchus's sexual predilections follows immediately in the next scene; a clear contrast is intended with his genially heterosexual promiscuity. Yet as the narrative unfolds in the last part of the film, the operative contrast between Crassus and Spartacus is not really one of perverse and normal objects of love. Crassus's attraction to Varinia is mirrored in the erotic overtones of the bond between Spartacus and Antoninus. The final paired combat in the film is between them (replaying, with a different outcome, the climactic sword fight between Douglas and Curtis in Richard Fleischer's *The Vikings* two years earlier). It is a combat of love in which each is striving to spare the other the crucifixion awaiting the survivor. Antoninus receives the death blow in Spartacus's embrace, and he dies, saying, "I love you, Spartacus, as I love my own father." Spartacus replies, "I love you like my son that I'll never see." The sound of this was not Trumbo's idea, and he registered his dislike for it. Yet it seems appropriate enough within the extremity of the moment, and almost a logical consequence of the introduction of Antoninus as a character, a firming up of the fourth line of the quadrilateral.

What is systematically at work is not Crassus's homoeroticism but his competitiveness. He begins the scene coming face-to-face with Spartacus and demanding confirmation of his identity. To his silence, Crassus says, "You must answer when I speak to you." At his continued silence, Crassus unexpectedly yells and hits him in the face; Spartacus then spits in his. Even Crassus's crushing military and political victory has not settled the *hamilla*, which has now come down to the core situation of two men, one on one. After forcing Spartacus to kill Antoninus, Crassus says to Caesar within Spartacus's hearing, "I wonder what Spartacus would say if he knew that the woman Varinia and her child are slaves in my household?" He steals my boy, I steal his girl. The news has the intended effect on Spartacus (and finally gives Crassus decisive confirmation of the prisoner's identity), but in fact, as this scene unfolds, Varinia is being spirited out of Crassus's house by Gracchus's connivance. The film will end with Spartacus, crucified but still alive, learning that Varinia and their son have escaped. We are not shown Crassus's reaction to Varinia's disappearance. Gracchus anticipates it by committing suicide; Crassus unwittingly anticipates it when Caesar asks, concerning Spartacus, "Did you fear him?" and Crassus answers, "Not when I fought him. I knew he could be beaten. But now I fear him." Crassus speaks here with the audible voice of Fast's Marxism; the immediate reference is surely to Spartacus's prophecy over the body of Antoninus: "He'll come back, and he'll be millions." But Crassus's words are also nested in circumstance that makes the fear more inward and immediate than that. The second part of his soul, which rules him as he now rules Rome, is not going to rest.

Notes

1. For *Gladiator,* I used the DreamWorks DVD (2000). In his commentary, Scott actually speaks of Marcus Aurelius's plans in slightly different terms: Maximus is to be "a temporary prince-consort . . . until the Senate get everything into line and decide on . . . a successor." DreamWorks has issued an extended edition of the film on DVD (2005), but nothing in it changes or clarifies things here.

2. See, for instance, Arthur J. Pomeroy, "The Vision of a Fascist Rome in *Gladiator,*" in *Gladiator: Film and History,* ed. Martin M. Winkler (Oxford: Blackwell, 2004), 111–23. Pomeroy concludes that "we are probably justified to regard *Gladiator* as commending not an outright Fascist ideology, but a neo-conservative rural utopianism" (121).

3. For *Spartacus,* I cite the version on the Criterion Collection DVD (2001), which is that of Robert Harris's 1991 restoration; at 196 minutes, it is a partial re-creation of the 202-minute version of the film's first public showing. I also had at hand a videotape (timed at 185 minutes) of the general release version from the 1960s, and one stage of the much-revised shooting script (dated January 16, 1959, but incorporating changes dated as late as July 27).

4. The fullest published account of the film's production history is Duncan Cooper, "Who Killed Spartacus?" *Cineaste* 18, no. 3 (1991): 18–27, drawing on a fair amount of unpublished documentation. Kirk Douglas tells his version of the story in his autobiography, *The Ragman's Son* (New York: Simon and Schuster, 1988), 303–34 (the remark about Kubrick is on p. 333). Part of Trumbo's memo (reportedly eighty pages long) is reprinted as "Report on Spartacus," *Cineaste* 18, no. 3 (1991): 30–33; selections from it are also read by Matthew McConaughey as the second commentary track on the Criterion DVD. The first commentary track includes observations and reminiscences by Douglas, Ustinov, and Fast, among others; a separate interview with Ustinov (from 1992) has some excellent if not necessarily reliable storytelling from the set. In general, Trumbo wanted an idealistic, heroic, and articulate Spartacus, whereas Kubrick wanted something more brutal and grim, with less talk; Douglas appears to have gone back and forth. Cooper calls the result "a political film with scarcely any politics in it" (23) and a "shabby compromise with history" (27). For somewhat less dismissive analyses of the film's conflicted agenda (and long views on the depiction of Spartacus in literature and film), see Maria Wyke, *Projecting the Past: Ancient Rome, Cinema, and History* (New York: Routledge, 1997), 34–72, and Alison Futrell, "Seeing Red: Spartacus as Domestic Economist," in *Imperial Projections: Ancient Rome in Modern Popular Culture,* ed. Sandra R. Joshel, Margaret Malamud, and Donald T. McGuire Jr. (Baltimore: Johns Hopkins University Press, 2001), 77–118.

5. For Plutarch's *Lives*, I use the eleven-volume Loeb Library edition of Bernadotte Perrin (Cambridge, Mass.: Harvard University Press, 1914–1926). References are to chapter and subsection of the Greek text; the English translations quoted are Perrin's, with small adjustments. For more details on the reading of Plutarch offered here, see my "Plutarch, Shakespeare, and the Alpha Males," in *Shakespeare and the Classics*, ed. Charles Martindale and A. B. Taylor (Cambridge: Cambridge University Press, 2004), 188–205.

6. References to the texts of Plato are to the traditional Stephanus page numbers, although for the *Republic*, I add book and section numbers.

THE SHAPE OF MAN

The Absurd and *Barry Lyndon*

Chris P. Pliatska

> Absurdity is one of the most human things about us: a manifestation of
> our most advanced and interesting characteristics.
>
> —Thomas Nagel, "The Absurd"

The Shape of a Film

Covering several decades of the eighteenth century, *Barry Lyndon* (1975) tells
a deceptively simple and even conventional story that follows the rise and fall
of its title character, played by Ryan O'Neal. In part one of the film—which
charts the rise of our hero—a young Redmond Barry falls in love with his
cousin Nora Brady (Gay Hamilton) and enters into a duel with the rival for
her affections, Captain John Quin (the superb Leonard Rossiter). Tricked
into thinking that he has killed the cowardly Quin, Barry flees and joins the
British army, which he soon deserts. He is then conscripted into the Prussian army, and his superiors eventually engage him to spy on a suspicious
character by the name of the Chevalier de Balibari (Patrick Magee). For
reasons of his own, Barry confesses at once to the chevalier, and they soon
become partners in the professional gambling trade, divesting the aristocracy
of their money in fashionable courts all over Europe. In part two—which
follows his precipitous demise—Barry marries the beautiful Lady Lyndon
(Marisa Berenson), gaining a substantial fortune and the title Barry Lyndon in the process. Unfortunately, he quickly squanders much of his wife's
money in a vain attempt to gain peerage, and his beloved young son dies in
a tragic accident. Eventually, Barry enters into a duel with the jealous Lord

Bullington (Leon Vitali), Lady Lyndon's son from her first marriage. Barry loses the duel and is forced into exile—without his wife, his title, and what remained of his fortune. He dies penniless and alone.

Although the film's plot is relatively conventional, its cinematic structure certainly is not. The film is marked by a steadfast refusal to employ standard cinematic narrative conventions. As Robert Kolker rightly observes, *Barry Lyndon* "does not meet demands for action, clear motivation of characters, straightforward development of story in simple, dramatic terms and with a functional, unobtrusive style." In its failure to meet these demands, he concludes, the film "sets itself at odds with the traditions of American commercial filmmaking."[1] Instead of relying on the standard narrative conventions that film audiences have come to expect, Kubrick tells the story of Barry Lyndon first and foremost by employing overtly *visual* strategies. As Mario Falsetto remarks, viewers "come to know Barry through strategies of *presentation* rather than more typical character-building conventions," which leads him to suggest that the "character of Barry could not possibly exist outside the world of film."[2] Of course, Kubrick's tendency to employ visual narrative strategies is by no means confined to *Barry Lyndon*; it is a hallmark of many of his films. Hans Feldmann, for one, notes that the "substance of a Kubrick movie is always delivered through the images projected on the screen; seldom, if ever, is it delivered through dialogue."[3] Making a similar point, Kolker observes that in "Kubrick's films we learn more about a character from the way the character inhabits a particular space than (with the exception of *Dr. Strangelove*) from what the character says."[4] Yet, with the exception of *2001: A Space Odyssey*, in no other film does Kubrick more radically forsake conventional narrative strategies than he does in *Barry Lyndon*. The film thus constitutes, in the words of Kolker, "an advanced experiment in cinematic narrative structure and design."[5]

Kubrick's success—one might even say his audacity—in so radically emphasizing visual strategies while minimizing more familiar cinematic conventions presents special challenges to viewers. The use of such conventions is designed to feed into an audience's expectations, and one consequence of doing so is a tendency to induce a certain degree of unreflective passivity in the audience. We as an audience are content to follow the cinematic cues we have become so accustomed to, largely taking for granted what the film has to offer us. The more a film relies on conventional narrative strategies, the more confident we can be that the film will not place any extraordinary intellectual demands on us. By contrast, when a film bypasses conventional strategies, our expectations tend to be subverted. The subsequent unease we feel in this unfamiliar cinematic territory puts us on notice that a special effort is required to come to terms with what the film is trying to convey. Ideally, our unease should provoke a reflective engagement *with* the film instead of a relatively unthinking immersion *in* the film.[6]

Yet the special challenges of *Barry Lyndon* do not stem solely from Kubrick's heavy reliance on nonconventional cinematic strategies. Rather, they result from the goals that these strategies are partly meant to serve. In discussing the film back in 1975, Kubrick was at pains to insist that "the most important parts of the film" are "beyond the reach of reason and language."[7] The techniques that Kubrick so self-consciously and artfully employs are meant to convey to the audience a narrative that resists translation into a straightforwardly linguistic medium. As a consequence, *Barry Lyndon* is an especially challenging film just to talk (or write) about.

Still, there is much that *can* be said about the film. In particular, we can focus on the very cinematic devices that Kubrick employs and reflect on the general narrative themes that, taken together, they suggest. In what follows, I revisit three aspects of the film that have generated perhaps the most widespread critical attention: what Kolker refers to as the film's "painterly aesthetic,"[8] Kubrick's frequent use of the reverse zoom, and his use of an unidentified narrator (voiced by the late Michael Hordern). Not surprisingly, critics have interpreted these elements as representing familiar Kubrickian themes having to do with the loss of human freedom. For example, Falsetto contends that *Barry Lyndon* is "one of Kubrick's least hopeful films," expressing "his most biting critique of how social mores restrict individual freedom and are responsible for the loss of youthful energy and ideals."[9] Along similar lines, Kolker claims that "Kubrick structures a decline of vitality and loss of individual power more severe and final than in any of his other films," leaving the viewer with "an impression of permanent passivity and entrapment."[10] The picture that emerges, according to these critics, is not a pretty one. Although I do not deny the legitimacy of these interpretations, nor their philosophical significance, I focus here on another, relatively neglected theme that emerges from the cinematic composition of *Barry Lyndon*. The theme is the absurd. Specifically, I suggest that the three cinematic elements I mentioned earlier are central to generating that theme. First, however, we need to look more carefully at the idea of the absurd and distinguish between two importantly different forms it can take.

The Absurd: Conventional versus Philosophical

The natural starting point for any discussion of the absurd is Albert Camus' reflections on that idea in *The Myth of Sisyphus*. In the Greek myth, Sisyphus was eternally condemned by the gods to repeatedly push a huge boulder to the top of a mountain, only to have it roll back down again. Sisyphus thus suffered the "unspeakable penalty" of someone whose "whole being is exerted toward accomplishing nothing." And his penalty was made all the worse because he *recognized* the "whole extent of his wretched condition."[11] For Camus, Sisyphus is representative of the human condition; like him, we are condemned to a pointless existence.

As it happens, Camus' discussion contains the seeds of a distinction between two forms of absurdity—a distinction that Thomas Nagel has nicely articulated in his own ruminations on the absurd. The first is a conventional form of absurdity, and the second is a deeper, distinctly philosophical form. The former arises in ordinary life whenever there is, in Nagel's words, "a conspicuous discrepancy between pretension or aspiration and reality."[12] For example, imagine someone who commits her entire life to the pursuit of a career as a world-famous musician but who, unfortunately and unbeknownst to her, lacks any musical talent whatsoever.

Another example of conventional absurdity comes from the natural world. Consider the curious behavior of the digger wasp, or *Sphex ichneumoneus*—*Sphex* for short. The female *Sphex* digs a burrow for her eggs and buries a paralyzed insect along with them to provide food for when they hatch. Before dragging the insect into the burrow, she follows a standard routine: she first brings the insect to the burrow's opening and inspects the burrow's interior. Experiments reveal that if the insect is moved even slightly while the *Sphex* is performing her inspection, she mechanically repeats the entire routine—in one experiment, forty times.[13]

The *Sphex* highlights an important feature of conventional absurdity, one that distinguishes it from its philosophical counterpart. The *Sphex* lacks the capacity to be self-aware, and it is this lack that arguably contributes to the absurdity of her situation. If she had any self-awareness, it would surely occur to her *at some point* to pull the insect directly into the burrow—thereby escaping the absurd situation. The *Sphex* example shows that conventional absurdity does not require self-awareness.[14] Thus, although Nagel does not emphasize this point, one can be utterly unaware that one is in a conventionally absurd situation.[15]

Philosophical absurdity is another story; self-awareness is essential to it. To see why, consider that this form of absurdity arises when, in Nagel's words, "two inescapable viewpoints collide in us."[16] On the one hand, there is the viewpoint that we naturally take as participants in our lives. From this perspective, human life is permeated with meaning and value. We show intense concern about the kinds of people we are or would like to be, and we pursue myriad projects with varying degrees of interest. On the other hand, there is the viewpoint that our capacity for self-awareness makes possible. As Nagel notes, "humans have the special capacity to step back and survey themselves, and the lives to which they are committed, with the detached amazement that comes from watching an ant struggle up a heap of sand." We can adopt an external perspective on our lives and, in so doing, realize that our deepest commitments are based on "responses and habits that we never question," that "what seems to us important or serious or valuable would not seem so if we were differently constituted."[17] Thus, the lives that are ordinarily so permeated with meaning take on an arbitrary quality when viewed from the external perspective.

The philosophical form of absurdity thus consists in the tension created by these two perspectives. It consists in the fact that we can neither forsake our ordinary convictions and strivings nor cease to see them as arbitrary. We continue to adhere to commitments by which we largely define ourselves, while simultaneously acknowledging them to be groundless.[18]

Barry Lyndon

Barry Lyndon addresses both the conventional and philosophical forms of absurdity, doing so in interconnected yet subtly different ways. More specifically, numerous instances of conventional absurdity emerge during the story of Barry's rise and fall. Yet reflection on these instances encourages viewers to confront the essential role that philosophical absurdity plays in the universal human condition. In other words, reflection on the conventional absurdity *within* the film fosters a confrontation *in viewers* with the reality of philosophical absurdity. The cinematic devices that Kubrick employs and that dominate the film—the film's painterly aesthetic, the reverse zoom, and the unidentified narrator—are central to encouraging this reflection.

A PAINTERLY AESTHETIC

The choice to film a story set in the eighteenth century is not an accident, and neither is Kubrick's way of presenting the historical subject matter; both are crucial to the film's success in provoking a confrontation with the absurd. For starters, placing the story in the past automatically distances viewers from the events taking place in the film. The distance is widened by the specific choice of time period. As Feldmann notes, eighteenth-century Europe represents for Kubrick "Western civilization at its most formal stage of development. Conformity to the innumerable codes of ritualized social conduct was essential for any man wishing to establish his value as a man."[19] Although the story takes place in western Europe—a place that is both geographically and historically familiar to most viewers—the social rituals of the time are sure to appear strikingly alien to us.

Kubrick does his best to emphasize these rituals and thus alienate us from that past. He does so by (among other things) relying on what Kolker refers to as a painterly aesthetic.[20] Scenes are deliberately composed to resemble familiar paintings of the period; indeed, Ryan O'Neal reported that at one point during filming, Kubrick searched through a book of eighteenth-century art for a particular painting and then proceeded to pose O'Neal and Marisa Berenson as though they were the figures in the painting.[21] Such a self-conscious use of an eighteenth-century painterly aesthetic seeks, in the words of Alan Spiegel, "to preserve not the immediacy, but the pastness of the past, its remoteness and irretrievability."[22] Furthermore, as Kolker notes, one of the effects of relying on this aesthetic is "to recreate the forms and formalities—the rituals—of the past *as* rituals."[23] In other words, by calling attention to the rituals themselves, the aesthetic emphasizes the very *historicity* of what viewers are seeing; it thus ensures that we do not become too involved in the characters' lives and the events unfolding in the film. Keeping us at a respectful distance invites us to take a more detached perspective. We pay close attention to *how* things are said and done—to the rituals themselves—and in so doing, we become aware that the rituals give sense and meaning to *what* the characters say and do. The rituals constitute the social world the characters inhabit and within which they make sense of their lives.

How do the effects of *Barry Lyndon's* painterly aesthetic relate to the absurd? From the historically bounded perspective of the characters as they go about their day-to-day lives, the rituals they routinely follow without question are suffused with meaning. Yet, from our enforced distance, we can take an external perspective on their lives and appreciate the rituals that govern them. (Indeed, eighteenth-century Europe's obsession with formal ritual means that their lives were governed to an extreme extent.) Our external perspective thus brings a sense that there is something mechanistic about their lives, a sense that their own rituals have entrapped them. It is almost as though we are watching the *Sphex* mechanically go through the motions. As a result, we get a strong sense that their lives are absurd, at least in a conventional sense. If only they could see beyond those rituals—see beyond their historically limited perspective—they might be able to free themselves from an unthinking conformity to them and thereby escape the absurdity of their predicament.

And yet, reflecting on the quite conventional form of the characters' absurdity should yield an uneasy realization among viewers, at least if we accept the invitation the film offers us. In a sense, we are in no better a position than they are. If we think about it, we will realize that, ultimately, we do not have a sound basis for justifying the values that give sense and meaning to *our* lives. As we go about our day-to-day lives, when we are in the thick of it, we too rely on habits and responses that we never question. Our deepest values, convictions, and commitments are without any rational basis—or, at least, none that we can cite without circularity. A disheartening sense of the arbitrariness of the values by which we define ourselves begins to creep in. So if we had been born in the eighteenth century, we too would have centered our lives around those formal rituals that we now regard with detached amusement. The trouble is that our realization does not provide an avenue of escape. We can neither quell the doubts about our values nor entirely forsake them once they have been cast into doubt. So, we are forced into a confrontation with the inescapable philosophical absurdity of our own lives and into a realization that this absurdity is an essential feature of the human condition.

THE REVERSE ZOOM

Turn now to Kubrick's use of the reverse zoom. Not only is it one of *Barry Lyndon*'s most conspicuous cinematic devices, but Spiegel suggests that it is "perhaps the film's most affective visual strategy."[24] The camera begins a scene by focusing on one or more figures in close-up and then, ever so slowly, starts to pull back. The backward movement continues at a slow but deliberate pace, encompassing more and more of the scene within its frame until the figure or figures on which the camera was originally focused are framed within a larger and sometimes overwhelming visual panorama.

One way to look at Kubrick's use of the reverse zoom is as a visual metaphor for the two perspectives we can take on our lives. By starting with a close-up shot, the camera simulates the participant perspective we take when we are involved in our daily lives and in the thick of things. By ending with an extreme long shot, the camera simulates the external perspective made available by our capacity for reflexive self-awareness. Interestingly, the continuous movement of the camera suggests that these two perspectives are not radically independent of each other: *we* are the ones who can adopt *both* perspectives. The movement further reveals the inner tension created by the juxtaposition of these two perspectives. By serving as a metaphor for these two perspectives, the reverse zoom not only conveys to viewers that the characters suffer in varying degrees from a form of conventional absurdity but also invites viewers to reflect on how human beings suffer from the inescapable philosophical form of absurdity.

Let us begin by looking at how the reverse zoom suggests that Barry Lyndon himself suffers from a conventional form of absurdity. In an interview with Michael Ciment, Kubrick remarked that Barry has "an unfortunate combination of qualities which eventually lead to great misfortune and unhappiness for himself and those around him."[25] These qualities are his ambition for wealth and social position, on the one hand, and a failure to appreciate the nature of the social world he inhabits, on the other. Unfortunately for Barry, his ambitions drive him to enter into a world whose nuances he fails to comprehend. He is thus a victim of both his ambitions and the limited view he has of his situation. Of course, if he could have achieved a wider perspective, one that allowed him to understand his social world, he might not have suffered such misfortune. In other words, if only he could have taken a step back, he might have discovered a way to extricate himself from his situation. He might have realized the nature of the social forces he was up against and either found a way to navigate his world more successfully or modified his ambitions to avoid those forces altogether. Much like the hapless *Sphex,* Barry is trapped by his limited perspective and thus suffers from a conventional form of absurdity.

So, how does the reverse zoom suggest Barry's absurdity? When the camera focuses in on Barry, its proximity to him invites us to identify with his struggles and ambitions. In so doing, we are encouraged to adopt a necessarily limited participant's perspective that is akin to Barry's own.

We take Barry seriously because we share—to the extent possible—the viewpoint of a human being immersed in life. Yet, when the camera begins to pull away from him, we are distanced from his struggles and ambitions. Instead of a participant's perspective that allows us to identify with Barry, we are encouraged to adopt the stance of a detached observer. From this detached perspective, we can observe not only Barry's struggles to satisfy his ambition but also the larger world within which those struggles take place. We have access to a perspective that is unavailable to Barry and thus can comprehend the larger world of which he is mostly unaware. We are able to realize something that he cannot—namely, his own absurdity. More specifically, we can appreciate the deep tensions that exist between his ambitions and that larger world. We also recognize, however, that if Barry could appreciate what we appreciate, if he could adopt our external perspective, he would realize his own absurdity and, perhaps, be able to extricate himself from it.

A good example of this point is a brief scene that immediately follows Barry's confrontation with his stepson Lord Bullington. It is a confrontation that has been long in coming and takes place during a recital given by Lady Lyndon to a number of illustrious guests. Bullington disrupts the recital, and Barry responds by viciously beating him in front of the shocked guests. The scene that follows begins with a close-up of Barry standing outside his ornate mansion and staring off into the distance. The camera slowly pulls back until Barry's figure becomes dwarfed by the sheer size and overwhelming mass of the mansion. Having the mansion dwarf Barry's figure suggests that he is overwhelmed by the trappings of society and by social forces that he is unable to control or fully understand.

The metaphorical movement between the participant and observer perspectives helps account for the palpable sense of entrapment and melancholy that pervades the film. Our sense of Barry's entrapment is a function of our recognition that he is constrained by his inability to adopt the external perspective, a perspective that the film makes readily available to us. The sense of melancholy stems from the way the reverse zoom encourages us to adopt both the external and the participant perspectives. On the one hand, from the latter perspective, we are invited to identify with Barry's struggles; he is a human being who has ambitions and plans, as we all do. On the other hand, from the external perspective, we come to appreciate the futility of those struggles. The melancholy is a function of the tension that exists when we juxtapose those two perspectives.

Importantly, Kubrick's use of the reverse zoom does not suggest that Barry is the only character in the film that suffers from a form of absurdity. To be sure, the peculiarities of his character lead to his ultimate downfall, and his downfall is the focus of the film's story. Yet, my observations about the movement of perspectives encouraged by the reverse zoom apply to the other denizens of the film as well. The difference is that their absurdity is not a function of any personal peculiarities. Rather, we sense that their absurdity comes from the peculiarities of the historical culture within which their identities have been formed. In other words, although the intimacy of the close-up encourages us to see them from the participant perspective as fellow human beings engaged in meaningful activities and projects, the wider perspective that we naturally adopt when the camera pulls away is a historical one. In short, we are invited to see these characters through the lens of history—*sub specie historiae,* if you will. The wider perspective encourages us to view their rituals much like a historical anthropologist would. The reverse zoom thus serves much the same function as Kubrick's use of the painterly aesthetic. From our wider perspective, we recognize that the characters cannot see beyond their historically limited stance. As a result, they fail to appreciate that many of their rituals are meaningful to them *merely* (to put the point bluntly) because of their sociohistorical context. We recognize the discrepancy between the seriousness with which they engage in these rituals and the groundlessness of the rituals within the larger historical scheme of things. Our awareness of that discrepancy leads us to see them as suffering from a conventional form of absurdity.

Our recognition of the characters' conventional absurdity quickly leads to a confrontation with the inescapability of philosophical absurdity. We realize that we can take a wider perspective on our *own* lives, and from this perspective, the rituals that we consider significant will also seem trivial and arbitrary. Despite our privileged historical vantage point, we are, in an important sense, no different from the characters inhabiting the eighteenth-century world of *Barry Lyndon.* We too inhabit a certain time and place in history, and as a result, the rituals we take so seriously are partly conditioned by our sociocultural context. A creeping anxiety thus begins to sink in, prompting us to cast about for a firmer basis on which to ground those rituals. When we ultimately come up empty-handed, we recognize simultaneously our inability to justify what we take so seriously and our inability to cease taking it seriously. The unsettling tension created by this recognition constitutes our absurdity—the absurdity of the human condition.

THE NARRATOR

Kubrick's use of an unidentified narrator does several jobs in the film, and, as Sarah Kozloff notes, the commentary he provides "plays a crucial role in our experience of the film."[26] For starters, the narrator gives us information about what the characters are thinking and feeling in particular scenes. For example, after Barry's first taste of battle, during which he loses his beloved friend Captain Grogan (Godfrey Quigley), we see Barry standing alone and pensive by an outdoor fire. The narrator informs us that "Barry's thoughts turned from those of military glory to those of finding a way to escape the service, to which he was now tied for another six years." In addition to providing information about the interior lives of the characters, the narrator often anticipates events that will happen later in the film. Perhaps one of the most powerful instances occurs when we are told the fate of Barry's young son. As we watch the two playing together, the narrator informs us that Barry "loved his son with a blind partiality." He continues: "He denied him nothing. It's impossible to convey what high hopes he had for the boy, and how he indulged in a thousand fond anticipations as to his future success and figure in the world. But fate had determined that he should leave none of his race behind him and that he should finish his life poor, lonely, and childless." Finally, the narrator even goes so far as to provide a wider historical or political perspective on the events in the film. Thus, we see a ship at sea presumably transporting Barry and his regiment to fight in the Seven Years' War. The narrator begins by confessing that "it would take a great philosopher and historian to explain the causes" of that war, and he ends with the rather prosaic observation that "England and Prussia were allies and at war against the French, Swedes, the Russians, and the Austrians."

One notable feature of the narrator's commentary is that it often appears to contradict the events taking place in a given scene. Perhaps the most notorious instance is when Barry departs from a woman named Lischen (Diana Körner) after having had a brief love affair with her. In itself, the scene is romantic and heartbreaking. Yet the narrator immediately undercuts its emotional content with the cynical comment that "the heart of Lischen's was like many a neighboring town and had been stormed and occupied several times before Barry came to invest it." Such disparities—between what is seen and what is told—have led several critics to question whether the audience should trust the narrator to tell the truth.[27] The question is not an unimportant one; how we answer it shapes our experience of the film and our understanding of the narrative it is telling.

Kozloff, for one, has made a persuasive case for concluding that the narrator is basically reliable. In the first place, she quite rightly observes that our inclination to find the narrator unreliable can be explained by the simple fact that we are used to trusting what we see with our eyes rather than what we are told. Thus, she contends, "we find it hard to accept the narrator's critical comments of someone who looks as pure as Lischen or as ingenuous as Barry. After all, *we are so used to believing that the camera does not lie*, we find it easier to start mistrusting the narrator." Second, and more substantively, she stresses that judgments about the narrator's trust-worthiness can be made only within the larger narrative context of the film. Specifically, she argues that "the lack of simultaneous visual corroboration of a statement cannot be entered into evidence either way"; rather, we must determine whether the nature of the narrator's commentary is "in line with the norms of the film as a whole."[28] She claims that those norms support the view that the narrator is reliable.

As I have been urging throughout this essay, the film as a whole encourages us to view its events and characters from two different perspectives. When taking the participant perspective, we tend to identify with those characters and events; when taking an external perspective, we tend to adopt a more coolly observational stance. While the images on the screen invite us in closer, toward a more participatory perspective, the narrator pushes us away, encouraging us to take a more external perspective. In the words of Kozloff, "the narrator drives a wedge between the audience and events, and, through occasional remarks directly addressed to us, invites us to observe the story from his removed vantage point."[29]

In this play of perspectives, the narrator is crucial to our experience of absurdity in the film and also our confrontation with the absurdity of the human condition. So, when we see Barry playing with his son, we can identify with him and his love for his son. When the narrator intrudes to tell us that his son will die and that Barry's life will end in misfortune, we are jolted out of the immediacy of the moment and forced to take a more external perspective. The narrator creates an undeniable tension between the perspective of those involved in a devoted, loving relationship and the perspective of those who know what will become of it. A similar tension emerges in the remarks the narrator makes over the shot of the troopship at sea. His comment that only someone with greater knowledge could explain the causes of the Seven Years' War need not be interpreted as expressing an epistemic limitation on the part of the narrator. Rather, there is a strong suggestion that the causes of war cease to matter when viewed from the external perspective afforded to us by history.[30] What matters is not *why* there was a war but *that* there was one and who the protagonists were. The *why* has ceased to matter to us, in the sense that it is not something *we* can take seriously, even though we can appreciate that the participants took it very seriously indeed. The narrator highlights a similar point in his commentary on the skirmish in which Captain Grogan loses his life. Over a shot of British soldiers advancing along a field into a line of French soldiers, the narrator remarks that the encounter "is not recorded in any history books," but that it was nevertheless "memorable enough to those who took part." The skirmish was especially memorable for Barry, as that was when his close friend was killed.[31] Indeed, one of the few times we see Barry express emotion is the scene where Captain Grogan dies; in fact, he is overwhelmed by it. (The only other times that Barry expresses such emotion are when he first meets the Chevalier de Balibari and when his son dies. Tellingly, these are instances when Barry expresses deep sorrow.) Yet again, we recognize the absurdity of the situation. With the advance of time, the struggles of these people have ceased to matter, even though they mattered once.

One especially interesting example of the narrator's crucial role in our experience of a scene is when Barry first presents himself to the Chevalier de Balibari. Barry's Prussian superiors have conscripted him to spy on the chevalier by having him pretend to be Lazlo Zilagy, a Hungarian servant in need of employment. The scene opens with the chevalier eating at a small table with his back to the viewers. We see Barry enter from a center door at the far side of the large, ornate room. Barry approaches the chevalier and presents his credentials. While the chevalier is reading them, the narrator provides the following commentary: "It was very imprudent of him, but when Barry saw the splendor of the Chevalier's appearance, the nobleness of his manner, he felt it impossible to keep disguise with him. Those who have never been out of their country know little what it is to hear a friendly voice in captivity. And as many a man will not understand the cause of the burst of feeling which was now about to take place." This commentary is interesting in several respects. First, it anticipates Barry's emotional confession that he is in fact an Irishman spying on the chevalier for the Prussians, thereby engaging the viewers' expectations. Second, the Prussians choose Barry for this assignment because they suspect that the chevalier is Irish, and the narrator speaks to Barry's feelings at having found a fellow countryman after years of exile from his native land. The need to find a "friendly voice" among strangers is something that viewers can surely appreciate, and so we readily identify with Barry's emotional reaction here. Finally, by noting how Barry is struck by the "splendor of the Chevalier's appearance" and the "nobleness of his manner," the narrator speaks to Barry's character—his tendency to be overly impressed by wealth and social position and to covet the same for himself. Yet the chevalier's appearance no doubt strikes *us* quite differently. His face is caked with white powder, and garish red blush is strewn about his cheeks. Over his right eye is a black eye patch, and placed above and below his left are two black *mouches*. Put simply, he looks ridiculous. The narrator's comments about Barry's perception of the chevalier, together with his actual appearance, conspire to add a tinge of humor and absurdity to a scene that is otherwise quite serious and emotionally compelling.

The narration thus adds a layer of complexity and depth to what would otherwise be a rather unremarkable scene. Significantly, it encourages viewers to identify with Barry's emotional state at having found a compatriot, and yet it also encourages us to view him as vaguely absurd, thus alienating us from him. As a result, there is an undeniable tension in how viewers react to the scene.

The Shape of Man

Barry Lyndon ends with the following epilogue: "It was in the reign of George III that the aforesaid personages lived and quarreled; good or bad, handsome or ugly, rich or poor, they are all equal now." There is a strong suggestion here of the futility of life—that no matter what we do, all our achievements will ultimately come to nothing. The epilogue resonates with a scene that bookends the first part of the film. Barry has just had a pointed exchange with Sir Charles Lyndon, Lady Lyndon's ailing husband. Sir Charles has become distressed by the exchange and begins wheezing terribly. He quickly reaches for his medication, which he scatters over the table at which he is sitting. As his companions try to collect his medication and calm him, we hear the narrator over Sir Charles's still-audible wheezing: "From a report in the Saint James's *Chronicle:* Died at spa in the Kingdom of Belgium, the right honourable Sir Charles Reginald Lyndon, Knight of Bath, Member of Parliament, and for many years His Majesty's Representative at various European courts. He has left behind him a name which is endeared to all his friends."

The narrator's voice quickly fades out, and the screen goes black—as if to say that all the achievements of this illustrious man have come to nothing more than a few words in an obituary that no one will remember. The picture of life's absurdity presented both here and in the epilogue is strikingly pessimistic. In contrast, Nagel approaches the absurd with comparative equanimity. For Nagel, philosophical absurdity is no mere accidental feature of human existence. There is an essential connection between our capacity for reflexive awareness and philosophical absurdity. The capacity we have for reflexive awareness includes the capacity to take an external perspective on our lives, allowing us to see ourselves without presuppositions, *sub specie aeternitatis*. And it is precisely this perspective—and its tension with the value-laden participant perspective—that generates our philosophical absurdity. Thus, insofar as the capacity for reflexive awareness is essential to our humanity—and it is—so too is our absurdity. The two are inseparable. It is partly because of this fact that Nagel concludes with the remark that serves as the epigraph for this essay: "absurdity is one of the most human things about us: a manifestation of our most advanced and interesting characteristics."[32] Thus, Nagel finds no reason to lament or try to escape our absurd existence. To do so would be tantamount to denying who we are, to wishing our own extinction. Rather, the appropriate response to the recognition of life's absurdity is irony.

Kubrick, it seems, wants to go further; he appears to lament our predicament, wishing that there were an escape. This attitude is, I think, partly due to a picture of what the external perspective reveals. One is led to lament our predicament to the extent that one thinks that the external perspective gives us insight into the true nature of the world and leads us to believe thus that the value-laden world disclosed by the participant perspective is somehow illegitimate. Yet perhaps things are not as bad as Kubrick suggests. Nagel stresses that the external perspective does not reveal an *independent reality;* rather, it is an expression of the limitations *we* face when *we* go through the motions of trying to provide a rational basis for those values to which we commit ourselves.[33] In other words, when we take the external perspective, we do not apply some standard of value only to realize that it has not been met. Rather, the external perspective allows us to reflect on the very standards themselves, to step back and observe them working in our lives. Once we do, we realize, to our dismay, that we have very little sense of how to go about justifying the values to which we are so wholeheartedly committed, either to ourselves or to others. Or, if we do have some sense of how to go about doing so, we realize that our justifications must eventually run out, and when they do, all we can ultimately point to is that *we* find it natural to live our lives a certain way, based on values with which *we* find it natural to identify. Thus, when we take that crucial step backward and view our lives from an external perspective without presuppositions, we realize that we do not adhere to the values and commitments that give sense and meaning to our lives for any good—or, for that matter, any bad—*reasons*. The reasons eventually fall away, and we are left with our natural reactions. Thus, only when we try to transcend our limitations by taking the external perspective do we run straight into them.[34] So, if Nagel is right, we need not take an overly pessimistic outlook on our absurdity. It is (merely) one of the many interesting facets of who we are.

Notes

I am grateful to Jerold J. Abrams for several suggestions that improved the final draft of this essay. Thanks also to Elizabeth F. Cooke for comments on a previous version of the final section.

1. Robert Kolker, *A Cinema of Loneliness,* 3rd ed. (Oxford: Oxford University Press, 2000), 151.

2. Mario Falsetto, *Stanley Kubrick: A Narrative and Stylistic Analysis,* 2nd ed. (Westport, Conn.: Praeger Publishers, 2001), 155, 159.

3. Hans Feldmann, "Kubrick and His Discontents," in *Perspectives on Stanley Kubrick,* ed. Mario Falsetto (New York: G. K. Hall, 1996), 193.

4. Kolker, *A Cinema of Loneliness,* 101.

5. Ibid., 99.

6. Kubrick's use of nonconventional cinematic narrative devices bears more than a passing similarity to the familiar Brechtian use of the "alienation effect" (*Verfremdungseffekt*). For an accessible discussion of the alienation effect, see Martin Esslin, *Brecht: A Choice of Evils,* 4th ed. (London: Methuen, 1984), ch. 6.

7. Quoted in Norman Kagan, *The Cinema of Stanley Kubrick* (New York: Grove Press, 1972), 145.

8. Kolker, *A Cinema of Loneliness,* 155.

9. Falsetto, *Kubrick: A Narrative and Stylistic Analysis,* 155.

10. Kolker, *A Cinema of Loneliness,* 152.

11. Albert Camus, *The Myth of Sisyphus and Other Essays,* trans. Justin O'Brien (New York: Vintage Books, 1991), 120, 121.

12. Thomas Nagel, "The Absurd," in *Mortal Questions* (Cambridge: Cambridge University Press, 1979), 13.

13. The *Sphex* is discussed in connection with the problem of free will in Daniel C. Dennett, *Elbow Room: The Varieties of Free Will Worth Wanting* (Cambridge, Mass.: MIT Press, 1990), 10–11. Although Dennett does not explicitly use the language of the absurd when discussing the *Sphex,* he is clearly invoking the concept in his characterization of her condition. Thus, he notes, "if we did not have a clear and detailed vision of where her interests lay, her performance in the strange experiment . . . would not seem so pathetic. We measure her performance against her interests and see how poorly she does" (22).

14. To be sure, reflexive awareness does not bring any guarantees; we need only look to Sisyphus to appreciate that point.

15. The point here might seem to fly in the face of what Nagel says when he asks whether the life of a mouse, for example, could be absurd. His answer is that a mouse "is not absurd, because he lacks the capacities for self-consciousness and self-transcendence that would enable him to see that he is only a mouse. If that *did* happen, his life would become absurd, since self-awareness would not make him cease to be a mouse and would not enable him to rise above his mousely strivings" (Nagel, "The Absurd," 21). Although Nagel does not make clear which form of absurdity he is considering here, the context strongly suggests that his remarks are meant to apply to the philosophical and not the conventional form of absurdity. Of course, Nagel could think that even conventional absurdity requires self-awareness. If he is suggesting that it does, then the example of the *Sphex* provides a clear and powerful counterexample to any such claim.

16. Nagel, "The Absurd," 14. Elsewhere, Nagel refers to these two viewpoints as the "subjective" and "objective" perspectives. See his "Subjective and Objective," in *Mortal Questions.* For an extended discussion of the general philosophical problem of reconciling these two viewpoints, see Nagel's *The View from Nowhere* (New York: Oxford University Press, 1986). In the present essay I chose not to use these precise terms, because they each have connotations that I would like to avoid.

17. Nagel, "The Absurd," 15, 18.

18. According to Nagel, the absurdity that arises from the tension between the participant and external perspectives gives our lives a "peculiar flavor." Having adopted the external perspective, "we return to our familiar convictions with a certain irony and resignation" (Nagel, "The Absurd," 19–20). So, irony is absurdity's most conspicuous achievement.

19. Feldmann, "Kubrick and His Discontents," 197.

20. Kolker, *A Cinema of Loneliness,* 155.

21. See James Howard, *The Stanley Kubrick Companion* (London: B. T. Batsford, 1999), 140.

22. Alan Spiegel, "Kubrick's *Barry Lyndon,*" in Falsetto, *Perspectives on Stanley Kubrick,* 206.

23. Kolker, *A Cinema of Loneliness,* 155–56.

24. Spiegel, "Kubrick's *Barry Lyndon,*" 209.

25. Quoted in Michael Ciment, *Kubrick: The Definitive Edition* (New York: Faber and Faber, 2001), 172.

26. Sarah Kozloff, *Invisible Storytellers: Voice-over Narration in American Fiction Film* (Berkeley: University of California Press, 1988), 117.

27. The most forceful proponent of the view that the narrator is unreliable is Mark Crispin Miller. See his "Kubrick's Anti-Reading of *The Luck of Barry Lyndon*," in Falsetto, *Perspectives on Stanley Kubrick,* and "*Barry Lyndon* Reconsidered," *Georgia Review* 30 (1976).

28. Kozloff, *Invisible Storytellers,* 124 (emphasis in the original), 119.

29. Ibid., 119.

30. Kozloff makes similar comments to this effect; see ibid., 123.

31. Kolker makes a similar observation; see *A Cinema of Loneliness,* 157.

32. Nagel, "The Absurd," 23.

33. Hence my reason for avoiding the terms *subjective* and *objective*. See note 16.

34. Nagel remarks that when we take the external perspective, "our limitedness joins with a capacity to transcend those limitations in thought (thus seeing them as limitations, and as inescapable)" (Nagel, "The Absurd," 18).

THE SHINING AND ANTI-NOSTALGIA

Postmodern Notions of History

R. Barton Palmer

A Postmodern Turn from Engagement?

Early in his career, Stanley Kubrick found himself drawn to projects that reflected the vaguely existential fatalism of film noir (*Fear and Desire* [1953], *Killer's Kiss* [1955], *The Killing* [1956]). Philosopher Mark Conard traces this tradition (which is relevant to an understanding of Kubrick) back to Friedrich Nietzsche's antihumanism rather than to the less antiestablishmentarian thought of either Albert Camus or Jean-Paul Sartre.[1] Perhaps responding to a change in cinematic fashion, Kubrick soon developed an interest in politically engaged projects of a generally liberal nature. *Paths of Glory* (1957), an adaptation of Humphrey Cobb's fictional treatment of a 1916 French mutiny, offers such a scathing indictment of class antagonisms and military incompetence at the highest levels that the French government banned its exhibition. The film's animus, however, also seems directed at that element of American society that C. Wright Mills terms the "power elite," igniting a considerable controversy over the place and privilege of the military establishment.[2] *Spartacus* (1960) is a sword-and-sandal epic that preserves much of novelist Howard Fast's Marxist analysis of a Roman slave revolt and his fulminations against a corrupt political and economic system. Kubrick brings to life a Roman world (at many points indirectly referencing modern American society) that ruthlessly exploits labor and destroys human freedom so that the privileged few can gain power and profit.

In the form of the blackest comedy, *Dr. Strangelove* (1964) revisits the paranoia and psychopathology of film noir. In a series of devastating anti-

Enlightenment gestures, the film portrays the mindless self-destructiveness at work in the feckless behavior of the American ruling class, civilian and military alike, which mismanages a cold war nuclear standoff into an irremediable global catastrophe. In *Dr. Strangelove*, Kubrick again takes up an issue then exercising liberal intellectuals, especially Mills, who points out the "crackpot realism" at the heart of the strategy of mutually assured destruction, a "defense theory" that Kubrick plays with sardonically.[3] With its dystopian vision of Western society, *A Clockwork Orange* (1971) continues the critique of misguided rationalism and its most devastating social instantiation: the Skinnerian reformation of sociopathy and the channeling of human freedom into a law-abiding, defenseless automatism. In a typical Kubrickian reversal, the programmed compliance with virtue of ex-rapist Alex (Malcolm McDowell) ironically arouses the ire of the liberal elite, who restore him to original sin and hence his *cupiditas* for two strangely compatible delights: Beethoven and erotic violence. The twinned problems of freedom and desire are also explored in *Lolita* (1962), where, perhaps because of censorship difficulties, they are given a more conventional, even moralizing resolution that at least partly masks the deep ironies of Vladimir Nabokov's original conception. Even so, *Lolita* remains a provocative film that calls into question cherished traditional notions of innocence and "proper" sexual behavior, anticipating the liberal critique of personal morality then taking shape in the so-called sexual revolution.

Although the director's liberalism sometimes seems overly earnest (witness the moving all-men-are-brothers conclusion he adds to *Paths of Glory*), it does not seem to have been very deeply held. It is remarkable that, since his apprenticeship in film noir, Kubrick's artistic strategy throughout the 1970s was largely to avoid representing the present directly and the political issues it raises by using the re-creative powers of the cinema to evoke alternative and at least partly disconnected diegetic worlds. *Dr. Stangelove* and *Lolita* are only partial exceptions to this trend because, as black comedy, they avoid any but the vaguest sociological analysis of contemporary culture. Kubrick's films of the late 1960s and 1970s underscore this turn from (at least conventional) engagement. Referenced indirectly as the dehumanizing source of modern social theory in *A Clockwork Orange*, modernity is most famously bypassed in the great swath of species history that takes "mankind" from his hominid origins to a future world of interplanetary space travel in *2001: A Space Odyssey* (1968). The world of the present is not even conceived as a distant point of arrival in the elaborately hermetic reconstruction of a bygone eighteenth-century Europe in *Barry Lyndon* (1975). The film's shopworn, picaresque narrative, which delivers the erstwhile hero first up the social ladder and then to a predictable fall back into well-deserved obscurity, engages thoroughly outmoded notions of "breeding will out."

In *Clockwork Orange, 2001,* and *Barry Lyndon,* Kubrick turns toward detachment, mystery, and irony: the "birth" of the Star Child at the end of *2001* that signals either an atavistic no-exit return or a new beginning for humankind; the progressive (or is it conservative?) rejection of totalitarian social engineering in *Clockwork Orange;* and the resurrection of a world of self-congratulatory order and propriety in *Barry Lyndon* that is marked most obviously by failure, miscommunication, and fecklessness.

These themes find a place in Kubrick's *The Shining* (1980), but interestingly, this film marks a return to the present—also the setting, roughly speaking, for the director's final productions: *Full Metal Jacket* (1987) and *Eyes Wide Shut* (1999). This essay explores one way to approach this return to the present: as an exploration of the most characteristic problematic of postmodernism—the aesthetic and cultural moment under whose spell Kubrick began to fall as the American art cinema moved beyond modernism.[4] In particular, I suggest that *The Shining* foregrounds an anti-nostalgia that contests the reverentially retrospective turn taken by some forms of postmodernism toward the artistic and cultural past, making Kubrick one of those contemporary artists who, to invoke Hal Foster's description, are involved with a "counter-practice" that opposes not only "the official culture of modernism" but also the "false-normativity of a reactionary postmodernism" predicated on "a return to the verities of tradition (in art, family, religion . . .)."[5]

The Postmodern Moment

According to Fredric Jameson's influential analysis of postmodernity, one aspect of the "cultural logic of late capitalism" is this era's contradictory posture toward history. He observes (and it would be difficult to contest this assessment), "Our entire contemporary social system has little by little begun to lose its capacity to retain its own past, has begun to live in a perpetual present and in a perpetual change that obliterates traditions of the kind which all earlier social formations had had in one way or another to preserve."[6]

For Jameson, the power and reach of Enlightenment thought have trapped the postindustrial world in a perpetual present through the reification of human relations and a Taylorization of productive processes of every kind: "no society has ever been so standardized as this one," and "the stream of human, society and historical temporality has never flowed quite so homogeneously." In this time of stable instability, everything "submits to the perpetual change of fashion and media image," with the result that "nothing can change any longer."[7]

And yet, according to Jameson, postmodernity looks to the past because the present lacks "both forms and content." So "energetic artists" are forced to "cannibalize the museum and wear the masks of extinct mannerisms," with the result that the "blank parody" of pastiche (art confected from the remains of previous works) is the most characteristic postmodern art form.[8] It is striking that Jameson theorizes this turn to the past as a consequence of artistic impasse; as he puts it, production is "no longer personal or stylistic in the sense of the older modernism." This leads him to understand one of the prevalent forms of pastiche, the "nostalgia film," in exclusively expressive rather than ideological terms, specifically, as a "category mistake that confuses content with form, sets down to reinvent the style, not of an art language, but of a whole period."[9] This is true enough, perhaps, but this explanation begs the questions: Why this particular category mistake? And what is its connection to the historical moment? The answers are not far to seek. Surely in postmodernity "the past" must be seen in some sense as the object of a re-creative desire that manifested enormous power in the 1970s. This was exploited first and most notably by George Lucas's *American Graffiti* (1973) and soon thereafter became a full-blown craze engaging all forms of popular (and sometimes highbrow) culture. I return later to this important moment in American cinema and the place of *The Shining* within it.

This essay contends that it might be more revealing to see the nostalgia film, like all other artistic forms, within the larger context of what Jameson (following Sigmund Freud and Norman Holland) identifies as the "wishfulfilling" function of art, which is able to gratify "intolerable, unrealizable, properly imperishable desires only to the degree to which they can be momentarily stilled."[10] Mass art accomplishes this affective feat through the institution of the "happy ending," or, in Jameson's more precise terms, "the narrative construction of imaginary resolutions and . . . the projection of an optical illusion of social harmony." Modernism, in contrast, deals with the "fundamental social anxieties and concerns" that are the ultimate raw material of all storytelling by producing, instead of optical illusions, more "realistic" conclusions that provide satisfaction through "compensatory structures of various kinds."[11] Kubrick's *The Shining*, however, suggests that one postmodern solution to the wish-fulfilling function of narrative is both the rejection, rather than the projection, of an illusory moment of wholeness and the refusal to offer compensation of any kind. *The Shining* can be read as the demonstration that the wishes of those who occupy a depthless present for a vanished time of plenitude are truly intolerable and unrealizable, not to be granted even as fantasy.[12] In short, *The Shining* underscores the dead-endedness of postmodern nostalgia. The emptiness of the present leads only to a destructive past characterized by ontological impossibility, and the protagonist occupies the no-space between the two periods in which he no longer exists—the present (in which desire has no purchase) and a bygone era (where life, improbably enough, is nothing but an endless party).

Failure and Failing in *The Shining*

Although set in contemporary America, Stephen King's novel is essentially a kind of haunted house thriller, with obvious ties to eighteenth- and nineteenth-century Gothic traditions—staple elements of classic Hollywood filmmaking. Jack Torrance (Jack Nicholson), a former schoolteacher eager to transform himself into a writer, takes a job as the winter caretaker of the Overlook Hotel, an imposing and somewhat ancient (built in the early 1900s) Colorado mountain resort. Jack's wife, Wendy (Shelley Duvall), is somewhat fearful of her husband, a recovering alcoholic, but she is eager for the change. Their young son, Danny (Danny Lloyd), was once physically abused by his father, who shows the boy little affection. Danny possesses psychic powers and has created an imaginary playmate and second self named Tony, who appears to furnish him with knowledge about the past, present, and future. Danny "shines" to a gruesome moment in the hotel's history that terrifies him: the previous caretaker, a man named Grady, murdered his wife and two daughters with an ax before shooting himself in the head. At the hotel, Danny meets briefly with the departing cook, Dick Halloran (Scatman Crothers), who shares his gift of shining and warns Danny about the presence of malevolent spirits and ghostly "traces" in the hotel.

As winter descends and snow closes the road to the nearby town, the situation of the now completely isolated Torrance family quickly deteriorates. Danny increasingly experiences visions of the murdered Grady girls, and Jack has a nightmare in which he murders his family. When Danny is found with deep bruises on his neck, Wendy accuses Jack of hurting the child. Angry and rejected, Jack makes his way to the ballroom, where a ghostly bartender named Lloyd (Joe Turkel) appears and commiserates with him about the problems men have with their wives, pouring him the first drink he has had in several months, effectively ending his pledge to quit drinking. Wendy comes in (she cannot "see" Lloyd) to tell Jack that Danny has been attacked by a woman in room 237 and frightened into near catatonia. Jack investigates and discovers a beautiful woman in the bathtub. She attempts to seduce him but is suddenly transformed into a hideous hag, and Jack retreats in revulsion from her horrific embrace. Yet he tells Wendy that he found the room empty, and she demands that they leave the hotel. Angrily pleading his responsibilities to his employers and his role as the family's sole provider, Jack insists on remaining.

Jack is beginning to sense that he has been in the hotel before. Furious and raging (his growing mental instability conveyed by self-talk and bizarre gestures), Jack returns to find the ballroom filled with celebrants in 1920s evening clothes. There he meets again with Lloyd, downs another drink, and encounters a waiter named Grady (Philip Stone). When he accuses Grady of being the caretaker who killed his family, Jack is informed that he "has always been the caretaker. I should know, because I have always been here." Meanwhile, at home in Florida, Halloran realizes that the Torrances are in trouble and, failing to make contact with them, begins the journey back to Colorado.

While searching the hotel for whoever harmed Danny, Wendy goes to Jack's desk and finds that for weeks he has been writing, over and over again on page after page, the same line of banal prose. Sensing that her husband is slipping into madness, and presented yet again with evidence of his homicidal dissatisfaction with family life, Wendy retreats in fear when Jack comes in and admits that he wants to "bash her brains in." But she is the one who, defending herself, knocks her husband unconscious with Danny's baseball bat. Jack tumbles down the stairs (injuring his leg, it is later revealed), and Wendy drags him to the pantry and locks him in. Discovering that Jack has disabled both the radio and the snowcat used for winter travel, Wendy realizes that she and Danny are prisoners in the hotel. At a loss about what to do next, she retires to the bedroom and falls asleep but is suddenly roused by Danny, who, with "Tony" speaking for him, warns hysterically of "redrum." He writes the word on the wall with red lipstick, and when Wendy sees it in the mirror, she realizes that it spells "murder."

Jack, meanwhile, has been released from the pantry by Grady and the "others," who admonish him to "correct" Wendy and the boy "in the harshest terms" and also warn him that Halloran is attempting to interfere. Jack arms himself with an ax and goes off in pursuit of his family. Wendy and Danny manage to escape from the bedroom when Jack is distracted by the arrival of Halloran on a rented snowcat. Jack ambushes Halloran in the lobby, killing him with a single stroke from the ax, and then lopes off in pursuit of Danny, who flees to the hedge maze outside the hotel. Wendy grabs a knife and begins searching the hotel for Danny. She can now hear the voices of its ghostly inhabitants and even glimpses a pair of the spirits apparently engaged in sex. Outside, Danny eludes his father by backtracking along his own footsteps and joins Wendy at Halloran's snowcat, which they use to escape down the mountain. Exhausted, Jack freezes to death in the maze. In a dramatic concluding movement (an obvious homage to the closing shot of *Citizen Kane*), the camera swoops inside to locate Jack's face in a group picture hanging on the ballroom wall dated July 4, 1921, addressing with Wellesian reticence two related questions: Jack's identity, and the source of his dissatisfaction and emotional disconnection. Confirming rather than clearing up the existential uncertainties it exposes, *The Shining* is yet another tale to which the warning "No Trespassing" might be appended.

Kubrick and the Horror Film

Although its form of monstrosity, in at least partial violation of convention, eludes explanation, *The Shining* remains true to the horror genre in some ways. There is a concluding and hair-raising pursuit in which Jack, after demonstrating his deadliness, fails to kill the "last victim," thereby satisfying the spectator's contradictory urge to witness the monster's lethality and enjoy his ultimate defeat. The bulk of the film, however, lacks such frissons and thrills. It is unsettling and eerie rather than frightening, a slow-paced character study and mood piece that is dependent not on special effects but on the artful deployment of expressionist techniques (especially set design, lighting, and mannerist acting style). Turning his source resolutely toward psychological horror, Kubrick simply eliminates the more outrageous supernatural elements of the novel (including a nest of apparently dead wasps that suddenly revive and attack Danny, a fire hose that transforms into a snake with much the same purpose, and animal-shaped topiaries that come to life to protect the entrance to the hotel).

Kubrick also seems uninterested in suspense. *The Shining* briefly engages with the genre of the fantastic, in which extraordinary events are given two possible interpretations, either psychological or supernatural. But the question of whether Jack's encounters with Lloyd, Grady, and the room full of undead revelers are to be interpreted objectively or subjectively is quite anticlimactically resolved when he is released from the pantry where Wendy locked him. And, in yet another deviation from horror conventions and King's novel, when the film begins, Jack already seems decisively disposed toward discontent, dissatisfaction, and violence. In the novel, Jack is turned toward the past, and the evil it promotes, by his reading of the hotel's scrapbook, which eventually causes him to abandon the play he is working on. The film's opening sequences strongly suggest Jack's dissatisfaction with his lot in life, especially his lack of affection for Wendy and Danny, whom he sees as impediments to his freedom and self-fulfillment. Jack's interaction with the spirit world does little more than confirm his angry resentment of his family's demands and even their presence.

This de-dramatizing lack of interest in character development (simplifying the novel's more generic interest in "possession") contrasts with Kubrick's emphasis on King's existential uncertainties, which function in the novel as thematic MacGuffins—that is, as generically conventional questions that motor the narrative but do not require answering. Unlike the film, the novel ends spectacularly: the boiler explodes, destroying the hotel's varied collection of spirits and, in a sense, obviating any further consideration of their connection to the present. But in the film, the ontological enigma of the hotel endures, and the precise terms of the ending emphasize the finally unknowable connection between the past and the present, periods that are linked disconnectedly. How could Jack always have been the caretaker if Grady had once been the caretaker? What is the connection between the Grady who blew his brains out some years ago and the Grady who, transported back to 1921, now delivers drinks to the ghostly revelers in the hotel lounge? And, most tellingly, is the Jack whose story is dramatized in the present the same Jack whose image is evoked from the distant past? All these questions are raised but never answered.

According to Noël Carroll, viewers were "confused, bored, and angered" because, of the film's two meanings, only "the esoteric one reached its target."[13] It seems that the film's producers realized this problem very quickly and ordered twenty-three minutes cut from the release print. The intended effect of this reshaping was to "streamlin[e] the film's narrative component in conventional generic terms," notes David A. Cook, but he admits that most viewers still found the story and Kubrick's message "sometimes confusing."[14] A larger and more difficult question is: what exactly *is* the film's "esoteric" meaning?

Confusion is certainly not something that the traditional Hollywood genre film ever aims for. In fact, an essential element of genre production is that conventional elements are designed to disambiguate the communication of narrative information and theme. And confusion of the kind engendered by *The Shining*'s treatment of the connection between past and present and its conception of character was uncommon in the art cinema of the period. In fact, as he does in *2001*, Kubrick makes ambiguity or, more properly, undecidability a central feature of the experience of viewing *The Shining*. As Flo Leibowitz and Lynn Jeffress recount, "the critics' complaints that the film is damaged by too many loose ends and seemingly inexplicable details and incongruities . . . are justified, as far as they go."[15] To be sure, attempts to identify the meaning of *The Shining* through traditional forms of interpretation have proved largely unsatisfactory; any reading seems condemned to either reductive specificity or meaningless generality. What is even more remarkable about the conventional critical appreciations of Kubrick's film is how little they have in common, despite a grounding in elements and ideas that are undeniably present in the text.

The Failure of Interpretation

For Cook, the film is "less about ghosts and demonic possession than it is about the murderous system of economic exploitation which has sustained this country since, like the Overlook Hotel, it was built upon an Indian burial ground."[16] Leibowitz and Jeffress, in contrast, find no political themes in *The Shining*. They propose that Kubrick had difficulty integrating three separate levels of meaning (themes related to fantasy, family, and the psychic phenomenon of shining); in particular, elements of the horror film got in the way of a carefully developed pattern of symbolism (designed to comment on dissipation and violence in American society).[17] Observing that Kubrick and writer Diane Johnson delved deeply into Freud and Bruno Bettelheim before penning the screenplay, Christopher Hoile suggests that the film explores the discontents of "man's supposed progress beyond animism."[18] Thomas Allen Nelson offers the most detailed account of *The Shining*'s narrative and the distinctive images with which it is conveyed, but even he finds it impossible to characterize its meaning beyond evoking a connection to themes and stylistic *tours* evidenced elsewhere in the director's body of work: "in the end, *The Shining* concerns old projects and unfinished journeys, secret longings and frustrated desires, movements in reverse rather than movements forward, 'interviews' with the Self's dark but hardly imaginary friends."[19]

Nelson's remarks are general enough to characterize almost any Kubrick film and, in fact, most films made by the noted directors of the early post-studio era—what Kolker, in a telling phrase, calls a "cinema of loneliness." Summarizing the thematic preoccupations of this generation of filmmakers, Kolker remarks (in terms that suit the theme and narrative of *The Shining* perfectly) that, "for all the challenge and adventure, their films speak to a continual impotence in the world, an inability to change and to create change. When they do depict action, it is invariably performed by lone heroes in an enormously destructive and antisocial manner."[20] For all its restless exploration of space, time, and the intricacies of "self," *The Shining* concludes with immobility and undecidability, with twinned but irreconcilable images of the erstwhile protagonist: the ghastly frozen visage of a monster who has failed at everything in life—most recently, in an attempt to murder his innocent family—and the smiling, self-satisfied face of the same young man, evidently unattached, for whom life seems beautiful and full of opportunities, a "self" captured and preserved in a group photograph of a formal ballroom celebration held at the beginning of the Roaring Twenties.

For many in film culture at the time, this tale of failure and existential incoherence was itself a failure. Certainly Kubrick did not manage to deliver an authentic version of the novel that would please Stephen King fans (King himself was dissatisfied by the result and later arranged for the novel to be filmed again in 1997 as a television miniseries, with his own script and directed by Mick Garris). But the problem with the film runs deeper. Kubrick delivers the happy ending required by the genre (the characters with whom we most identify elude the monster's murderous attacks, and he self-destructs), but the director fails to provide a determining knowledge of the tale he has spun. In fact, the ostentatious homage to Orson Welles that closes the film precisely reverses the function of its reflex in *Citizen Kane;* there, in a foregrounding of the epistemological forthcomingness of the classic studio film, the camera finally answers (if inadequately) the question raised by the opening sequence. Kubrick, we might say, explains nothing, compounding rather than resolving the enigma of Jack's "nature."

Even more problematic is the film's invocation but then rejection of the nostalgic impulse, as Jack conjures up the past only to be destroyed by it. Unlike Grady, at the film's end, Jack has not managed a resurrecting return to the past: the gap between the two aspects of Jack's existence is closed by the camera, which leaves us only with the image of an image of what he used to be. *The Shining* thus constitutes itself as the true other of the nostalgic Gothic tale, such as Jeannot Szwarc's *Somewhere in Time,* also released in 1980. That film traces the journey of a young American writer backward in time to meet, as a young girl, a woman he first encounters at the end of her long life. The present, which is unpromising and unsatisfying, is abandoned for a past full of romance and intrigue, as this storybook romance plays out in (what else?) a grand, turn-of-the-century hotel. Ultimately faced with the choice between living in the present and returning through death to the past, the writer chooses self-annihilation over abandoning the woman he loves. Dripping with schmaltzy romanticism, the film quickly became a cult classic, prompting the founding of a fan club that, a quarter century later, still sponsors SIT weekends at the film's Michigan resort location, where guests are invited to dress up as characters and reenact the plot. Thus the contemporary culture of nostalgia makes room for a desire to return to the representations of nostalgia, engaging profound yearnings of the second degree.

In *The Shining,* however, Kubrick's intentions seem hardly the memorialization of the past and the grand establishments where the rich and famous of bygone eras regaled themselves. The film exemplifies, as Jameson would have it, an art in crisis, speaking incoherently and not to one and all about a cultural moment characterized by an inability to change and create change, as Kolker suggests. Instead of an interpretation, then, *The Shining* seems to demand a symptomatic analysis that identifies those elements that make it part of a postmodern cinema.

A Cinema of Allusion and Nostalgia

A notable feature of early poststudio American filmmaking (the so-called Hollywood Renaissance) is the textual prevalence of allusions to film history, including, most importantly, what Carroll terms the "memorialization of past genres" and "the reworking of past genres."[21] He opines that the allusiveness of 1970s films can be explained strictly by developments within the industry, particularly the emergence of a young adult, cine-literate viewership eager for the self-congratulatory experience of discovering, identifying, and enjoying references to classic movies. This college-educated generation of film buffs was also, in Carroll's view, consumed by a profound nostalgia for what was seen as a precious "common cultural heritage." In a contradictory oedipal gesture, "the generation that came to film consciousness in the sixties" sought to establish "a new community . . . with film history supplying its legends, myths, and vocabulary."[22]

Because nostalgia is motored by twin desires (to remember the past and to make it live again in the present), such reenactment is usually marked by a strong sense of loss, as the present becomes an era evoked or represented primarily by absence. *American Graffiti* crystallized and exemplified the desire of young adults in the early 1970s for a return to the perceived cultural stability of the late 1950s, but such a desire only undermines the sense of a re-created plenitude, because "underlying conflict and danger come primarily from the audience's own knowledge of the impending destruction of this innocent world."[23] Here is a film that, as Carroll suggests, "subtly confronts a generation with its moment in history."[24] More typically, the nostalgic effect of 1970s films is aroused by the recycling of representations of a bygone era. The rejection of establishment culture, as Carroll argues, was to be accomplished by an enthusiastic embrace of the films that had entertained the American public since the 1920s (but with a special value assigned to productions of the wartime and postwar eras). The intellectual and spiritual power of classic Hollywood was emphasized, and these films, which had seemingly been trivialized or ignored by the older generation, were transformed into "an emblem of self" central to the reformative project of "the adoption of a new sensibility."[25]

For Carroll, the radical politics of the 1960s and 1970s and the film craze of that era are the most obvious symptoms of the postwar generation's search for identity. The antiestablishmentarian affirmativeness of this new sensibility would be measured by the simultaneous embrace of traditional culture (genres to be memorialized in new productions) and dismantling of the ideological claims of studio types in generic remakes of the western, the gangster movie, and the horror film. These inherited genres would be reworked to express both a different politics and the creativity of directors who imagined themselves, in the tradition of the French nouvelle vague, as exceptional individuals with a claim on unique styles and thematic obsessions.

But, as Carroll acknowledges, the college educated, those with a deep knowledge of Hollywood history, constituted only a fraction, however influential, of the era's film audience. After a period of profound uncertainty about what kinds of films might suit an audience in transition, 1970s Hollywood once again achieved financial stability through the promotion of a cinema of popular, traditional genres that continued to appeal to viewers who would not number themselves among the cognoscenti. The most successful auteurs of the period (Francis Ford Coppola, Martin Scorsese, and Kubrick chief among them) proved adept at confecting what Carroll terms "the art film in the genre film," a mixed form that "sends an action/drama/fantasy-packed message to one segment of the audience and an additional hermetic, camouflaged, and recondite one to another."[26]

These films, to put it somewhat differently, were of the present even though they referred to and evoked the past in ways that those in the know would recognize and appreciate. Despite obvious successes (most notably, Coppola's *Godfather* [1972] and *Godfather II* [1974]—nostalgia films par excellence), such genre reworkings generally proved to be artistically unstable and economically problematic. The industry had dismaying experiences with both *Apocalypse Now* (Coppola, 1979) and especially *Heaven's Gate* (Michael Cimino, 1980), productions that remade the war film and the western, respectively, in ways that most filmgoers found unsatisfying, despite some highbrow acclaim and academic interest. If Carroll's culture of allusionism is an expression of the "utopian urgency" of youth movement politics, it may be that with the "foreclosure of the politics for utopia, allusionism loses most of its glitter," and the past becomes a burden rather than a source of liberation.[27]

"Adrift in a Kind of Weightlessness"

This oppressive sense of the past, of the sheer and intolerable weight of *res gestae* and *res scriptae*, certainly finds its reflex in *The Shining*. As Jack Torrance, the aspiring writer, delves into the historical records of the Overlook Hotel, he finds no inspiration or material therein. In a startling reversal of conventional neoromantic expectations (and a significant departure from King's novel), Jack is moved, instead, to devote his energies to an endless and furious repetition of the same phrase—one that, though not his own, expresses his anger at the obligation to do something (even though he sought the creative opportunity afforded by loneliness and minimal responsibilities): "All work and no play makes Jack a dull boy."

The project of artistic creation, although it proceeds energetically and ceaselessly (Jack does not suffer from writer's block in the ordinary sense), cannot move beyond either convention (with its sole material a traditional aphorism) or the tired modernist preoccupation with the self (here, seemingly, the writer's preemptive dissatisfaction with an oeuvre hardly begun, but already seen as oppressive). Jack's failure to say anything, and his compulsion to go on "producing" nonetheless, somewhat ironically evokes the situation of both Kubrick as artist and the American cinema of the era. Can it be an accident that Kubrick here sharpens the novel's presentation of that most hackneyed of modernist clichés: the *écrivain maudit*, alcoholic, disreputable, self-centered, and cruel, but devoted to his gift? Here that outlaw character is a very un-Kerouacian figure whose writing is truly merely typing. Jack's writerly impotence mocks the neoromantic myth of the exceptional self that both demands expression and merits attention through the singular force of its individuality.

We must thus resist the temptation to conclude, with Kolker and others, that films such as *The Shining*, with their deliberate deconstruction of central elements of the time-tested Hollywood formula, can be thoroughly explained by the American cinema's belated and skewed encounter with the aesthetic of modernism, a borrowing from the French nouvelle vague for whose directors and films Kubrick and company displayed such enthusiasm and to which they paid homage. *The Shining* certainly lacks the energy and stylistic exuberance of nouvelle vague filmmaking. Typically, there is little evidence here of modernism's critical, negative attitude toward middle-class values or its psychologizing and culturalist interest in individual character. As Kolker observes of this generation of directors, "unlike their French colleagues, the films they made only rarely explored ideas or the larger cultural contexts of their existence," even though such political concerns were at the heart of the New Wave movement.[28] What had changed in the decade or so that separated filmmakers such as Jean Luc Godard and François Truffaut from their American counterparts? Surely the emptiness, disengagement, and even anomie that constitute the subject matter of these films cannot be explained simply by the different facts of American production, with its more relentlessly commercial and anticreative traditions that were still somewhat intact even after the demise of the studio system.

With *The Shining* and other films of this tradition, we are faced not with an exhilarating modernist exploration of form and previously taboo subject matter but with a kind of postmodernist art that, in Jean Baudrillard's memorable words, finds itself "adrift in a kind of weightlessness" because of the disappearance of "the horizon of a political order, a cultural order." In such an aesthetic realm, where art has "deconstructed its entire universe," the only form of production that remains is "playing with the pieces."[29] What, then, can be said with the fragments of the cultural past? Perhaps, as Jameson observes, the main subject of the postmodern American cinema is the "very triviality of life in late capitalism," a theme (if that is the proper term) embodied in the languor that characterizes the Torrances' family life and Jack's connection with his employers. For Jameson, the director's challenge is "how to project the illusion that things still happen, that events exist, that there are still stories to tell, in a situation in which the uniqueness and irrevocability of private destinies and of individuality itself seem to have evaporated."[30] To provide such deceptive energies (of movement, of the possibility of transformation on which all narrative depends), Kubrick has recourse to a traditional genre that provides all the pieces he needs to play with.

From this viewpoint, the nostalgia films of 1970s Hollywood appear to be artistic solutions to the representational problems posed by postmodernity as well as responses to the hyper-cine-literacy of the postwar youth culture. *American Graffiti,* we might say, solves the problem of projecting "the illusion that things still happen" by returning to an era of vanished plenitude, a time when things—good things—happened, or so it can be collectively imagined. Genre memorializations such as *Body Heat* (1980) disguise their retreat from the present through a careful avoidance of contemporary references, projecting a palpable sense of false consciousness that this "time" is not what it seems. *The Shining* squarely confronts the representational problem by rejecting the appeal of the nostalgic impulse, figured in the film by Jack's wish to find a moment from the past to replace the present that affords him no comfort, either personal or artistic, including the ability to represent himself and his condition.

Trapped between Times

The Shining seeks to display the deconstruction of the nostalgic impulse in the manner typical of filmmakers of that period—that is, by invoking and critiquing generic conventions. The fundamental generic fact about *The Shining* is that it is a "ghost story"—an encounter between those who are living and those who are dead but somehow continue to exist. Ghost stories treat the "impossible" presence of the past in the here and how. It is important to note that Kubrick chose to work in this form long before he seized on King's novel as a source for his screenplay.[31] At a time when the American cinema found itself ambiguously oriented toward a golden era of cherished memory, Kubrick determined to invoke a genre that is about the mutual imbrication of distinct and incompatible times.

If the ghost story (Alfred Hitchcock's *Vertigo,* Jack Clayton's *The Innocents*) usually foregrounds the destructive designs of malevolent spirits on the living, *The Shining* emphasizes the vapidity and psychological fragility of the present. Trapped by marriage and the responsibility of supporting his family, Jack Torrance retreats to a grand emptiness that he hopes will afford him the semisolitude he needs to realize his ambition of becoming a writer. But given space and time, Jack discovers only the depthlessness of his existence; even the modernist withdrawal to the inner creative self brings to the surface no message other than a juvenile resentment at being forced to make a life that must be devoted (even minimally) to getting and having. The past that Jack's anger opens up to him offers the possibility of mindless self-indulgence, but it also demands the destruction rather than the abandonment of the present, a task that Jack utterly fails at, and whose reward (deliverance back to the self and condition he has always occupied) is denied him.

Jack Torrance thus becomes the perfect image of the failing artist in postmodernity: trapped between times, unable to find within or without anything worth saying, reduced to the exercise of primitive, pointless ressentiment at the bleak prospects of the human condition. Such ressentiment characterizes much of the Kubrickian oeuvre, but it finds a perfect, epoch-revealing realization only in *The Shining.*

Notes

1. Mark T. Conard, in *Film Noir and Philosophy* (Lexington: University Press of Kentucky, 2005), observes that "what makes truth problematic, and what makes definition impossible, according to Nietzsche—the abandonment of essences, the resulting flux metaphysics, the rejection of anything permanent and unchanging in the universe, that is, the death of God—is the same thing that makes noir what it is" (20).

2. C. Wright Mills, *The Power Elite* (Oxford: Oxford University Press, 1956).

3. C. Wright Mills, *The Causes of World War Three* (London: Secker and Warburg, 1958).

4. Fredric Jameson's "Historicism in *The Shining,*" *Social Text* 4 (1981), reprinted in his *Signatures of the Visible* (New York: Routledge, 1991), 82–98, was largely ignored

by critics who take an auteurist approach to commenting on the Kubrickian oeuvre. For the movement of Hollywood Renaissance auteurs such as Kubrick, Steven Spielberg, and Francis Ford Coppola into postmodernism, see Robert Kolker, *A Cinema of Loneliness,* 3rd ed. (New York: Oxford University Press, 2000), 3–10; this account should be supplemented with Vera Dika's penetrating analysis of the issue in *Recycled Culture in Contemporary Art and Film* (Cambridge: Cambridge University Press, 2003), 1–23, 89–121.

5. Hal Foster, "Postmodernism: A Preface" in *The Anti-Aesthetic: Essays on Postmodern Culture,* ed. Hal Foster (Port Townsend, Wash.: Bay Press, 1983), xii.

6. Fredric Jameson, "Postmodernism and Consumer Society," in Foster, *The Anti-Aesthetic,* 125.

7. Fredric Jameson, "The Antinomies of Postmodernity" in *The Cultural Turn: Selected Writings on the Postmodern, 1983–1998,* ed. Fredric Jameson (London: Verso, 1998), 59.

8. Ibid., 82–83.

9. Ibid., 84.

10. Fredric Jameson, "Reification and Utopia in Mass Culture," in *Signatures of the Visible,* 25.

11. Ibid., 25–26.

12. Dika's otherwise astute analysis of "recycled culture" on the contemporary scene is weakened somewhat by her misunderstanding of the fundamental emotional complexity of nostalgia, whose affective power draws largely on disappointment and frustration. Nostalgia's keenness derives from the acknowledgment that the past cannot be restored. Hence, Dika's theorizing of *American Graffiti* locates a form of resistance in the way that film punctures the bubble of remembrance. It is true that the "poignancy of that realization [that the Vietnam War and the sexual revolution effected undesirable changes in American values] continually underscores the events of the film" (*Recycled Culture,* 92). But this is hardly a political comment on the present desolation of American life; rather, it is the conventional manner in which the bittersweet moment of nostalgic pleasure is heightened.

13. Noël Carroll, "The Future of an Allusion: Hollywood in the Seventies (and Beyond)," *October* 20 (1982): 61.

14. David A. Cook, "American Horror: *The Shining,*" *Literature/Film Quarterly* 12, no. 1 (1984): 2–4.

15. Flo Leibowitz and Lynn Jeffress, "*The Shining,*" *Film Quarterly* 34 (1981): 49.

16. Cook, "American Horror," 2.

17. Leibowitz and Jeffress, "*The Shining.*"

18. Christopher Hoile, "The Uncanny and the Fairy Tale in Kubrick's *The Shining,*" *Literature/Film Quarterly* 12, no. 1 (1984): 5–12.

19. Thomas Allen Nelson, *Kubrick: Inside a Film Artist's Maze,* 2nd ed. (Bloomington: Indiana University Press, 2000), 211.

20. Kolker, *A Cinema of Loneliness,* 10.

21. Carroll, "The Future of an Allusion," refuses to view this trend in the American commercial film industry as postmodernist because, unlike Jameson, he sees post-modernism as essentially a high cultural movement: "Hollywood allusionism involves a two-tiered system of communication whereas these postmodernists operate on a one-tiered system of recondite meanings . . . and second, Hollywood allusionism is undertaken for expressive purposes whereas postmodernism, like modernism, refers to artifacts of cultural history for reflexive purposes. . . . Hollywood allusionists are essentially respectful of their forebears whereas postmodernist architects are repudiating their predecessors" (70 n.).

22. Ibid., 79.

23. Dika, *Recycled Culture,* 92.

24. Carroll, "The Future of an Allusion," 80.

25. Ibid.

26. Ibid., 56.

27. Ibid., 79, 80.

28. Kolker, *A Cinema of Loneliness,* 9.

29. Jean Baudrillard, "Interview: Game with Vestiges," *On the Beach* 5 (1984): 19, 24.

30. Jameson, "Historicism in *The Shining,*" 87.

31. James Howard, *The Stanley Kubrick Companion* (London: Batsford, 1999), 149, reports that Kubrick "bought a wide range of novels dealing with the supernatural, which he then methodically began to read in his office." According to his secretary, Kubrick perused and discarded many of these before he decided to adapt *The Shining.*

PART FIVE

THE SUBJECT OF THE FUTURE

NIHILISM AND FREEDOM IN THE FILMS OF STANLEY KUBRICK

Daniel Shaw

Much critical ink has been spilled over the question of whether the world-view of archetypal auteur Stanley Kubrick is nihilistic, and appropriately so. To my mind, this is one of the most important questions we can ask about genuine artists and their oeuvres. If auteur criticism is to have any validity, from a philosophical perspective, it must address such issues. True cinematic geniuses (Ingmar Bergman, Michelangelo Antonioni, Lina Wertmüller, Alfred Hitchcock, and David Cronenberg, to name a few) have something to teach us about the meaning of life, and in uncommon instances, their explorations can be genuinely philosophical. This is the case in several of Kubrick's films, but especially in his treatment of Anthony Burgess's dystopic classic *A Clockwork Orange* (1971).[1]

In what follows, I examine Kubrick's films with a single question in mind: what is his position on the issue of whether we humans have free will or are causally determined to act the way we do? This is a corollary to the much larger issue of whether Kubrick's worldview is nihilistic, since existential philosophers and Christian theologians have long agreed that our life is meaningless if we cannot exercise moral choice. After a detailed analysis of *A Clockwork Orange*, this essay briefly discusses Kubrick's other major works, focusing on whether the director depicts his major characters as deer frozen in the headlights or as moral agents with real alternatives.

Charismatic Evil

Burgess declares his own intentions in a new introduction to the 1986 edition of his novel, which he titled "A Clockwork Orange Resucked." Though admitting that "I enjoyed raping and ripping by proxy," the author continues: "But the book does also have a moral lesson and it is the weary traditional one of the fundamental importance of moral choice." Indeed, Burgess proceeds to disparage his novel for its didacticism in making that point.

Kubrick created such an indelible portrait of "little Alex" (Malcolm McDowell) that the film continues to spark controversy to this day. Copycat crimes were so rife in Britain after its release that Kubrick withdrew it from U.K. markets for more than two decades. The director came in for the usual moralistic condemnations for the way the film seems to valorize Alex's rapacious taste for ultraviolence. As is often the case, the howls of execration were based on a misunderstanding of the director's intentions.

Ironically, I find *A Clockwork Orange* to be one of Kubrick's most life-affirming works, second only to *2001: A Space Odyssey* (1968), its immediate predecessor. The final scene—where a chastened prime minister has an impressive sound system wheeled into Alex's hospital room, and the chorale finale of "Ode to Joy" booms in the background while Alex fantasizes about romping with a naked young woman as a Victorian-era upper crust applauds its approval—is one of the most ambivalently exhilarating sequences in the history of cinema. Alex is granted the last word: "I was cured, all right!"

What he is cured *from* is the inhibitory effect of the Ludovico technique. His attempt to "snuff it" (commit suicide by throwing himself out a window) causes sufficient trauma to free him from this nightmarish conditioning process (as his hilarious responses to cartoon images shown to him by a female psychologist in a previous scene foreshadow). No longer nauseated at the prospect of sex or violence, Alex is free to resume his sadistic ways. In my view, Kubrick *celebrates* Alex's recovered freedom of choice here. No matter how monstrous Alex is, even more monstrous is a state apparatus that can rob the individual of his free will. Along with free will, as Christianity has preached since Paul, comes the capacity to do evil. It is the price that even God has to pay for granting humans the dignity of moral responsibility.

Little Alex: Id Monster

A pat Freudian psychoanalysis of the behavior of Alexander DeLarge is clearly suggested by the filmic text. His father is precisely the type of weak figure that would have been unable to generate castration anxiety in his son, hence failing to trigger the primary repression from which the superego is said to result, according to Sigmund Freud. Indeed, Alex is depicted as a classic sociopath, taking his greatest pleasure from the pain of others while dealing with few pangs of conscience thereafter. Compounding his psychosexual difficulties, his credulous mother is an overindulgent woman addicted to "sleepers"; she dresses in outlandish outfits and unquestioningly accepts Alex's lame explanations of what he does at night to bring in all that disposable income. Both parents would rather look the other way than have to deal with the serpent in their midst.

Given Freud's theory that art functions as a catharsis of the repressed desires of the id, a Freudian reading of *A Clockwork Orange* would obviously focus on how identifying with Alex allows us to vicariously gratify *our* repressed desires for sadistic sex and violence. The opening sequences of the film, where Alex and his droogs beat up a drunk, thrash a rival gang, and break into a writer's house, do precisely this. Burgess himself admits that "it seems priggish or pollyannaish to deny that my intention in writing the work was to titillate the nastier propensities of my readers."[2] But the proposed Freudian reading fails to account both for the moral profundity of this work and for our palpable sense that something in the nature of an authentic intellectual inquiry is going on here.

To a Freudian, Alex's actions are as causally determined in his original ultraviolent mode as they are in the relatively brief time during which the Ludovico treatment is effective. In this view, there is nothing to celebrate at the end of the film other than a sadist's ability to return to his sadistic ways. Vincent Canby made a similar mistake in his first review of the movie for the *New York Times* when he opined that "Alex the hood is as much a product of conditioning as the denatured Alex." To be essentially characterized as a causally determined mechanism with no free choice reduces human existence to a nihilistic collocation of its chemical properties. This has long been recognized by European intellectuals; Fyodor Dostoevsky in *Notes from Underground,* Friedrich Nietzsche in *Thus Spoke Zarathustra,* and Jean-Paul Sartre in *Nausea* all came to similar conclusions. One of the few things that both Christians and atheistic existentialists can agree on is that freedom is the only ground for human meaning. As Burgess puts it, "If he [Alex] can only perform good or only perform evil, then he is a clockwork orange—meaning that he has the appearance of an organism lovely with color and juice but is in fact only a clockwork toy to be wound up by God or the Devil or (since this is increasingly replacing both) the Absolute State."[3]

Free Will and Operant Conditioning

Kubrick focuses on the free-will issue in his treatment of the story, his most literal adaptation of the many original literary sources from which he drew. The resultant screenplay often transposes whole chunks of dialogue and narration from the novel. In a 1972 interview for *Sight and Sound,* Kubrick comments:

> It was absolutely necessary to give weight to Alex's brutality, otherwise I think there would be moral confusion with respect to what the government does to him. If he were a lesser villain, then one could say: "Oh, yes, of course, he should not be given this psychological conditioning; it's all too horrible and he really wasn't that bad after all." On the other hand, when you have shown him committing such atrocious acts, and you still realize the immense evil on the part of the government in turning him into something less than human in order to make him good, then I think the essential moral idea of the book is clear. It is necessary for man to have the choice to be good or evil, even if he chooses evil. To deprive him of this choice is to make him something less than human—a clockwork orange.[4]

In the same interview, Kubrick also validates the Freudian reading (first proposed to him by Aaron Stern, practicing psychiatrist and former head of the Motion Picture Association of America rating board) that sees little Alex as giving vent to our unconscious instincts, as "man in his natural state" driven by Eros and Thanatos: "I think, in addition to the personal qualities I mentioned, there is the basic psychological, unconscious identification with Alex. If you look at the story not on the social and moral level, but on the psychological dream content level, you can regard Alex as a creature of the id. He is within all of us. In most cases, this recognition seems to bring a kind of empathy from the audience."[5]

Kubrick's own view of the "natural man" is in sharp contrast to Jean-Jacques Rousseau's vision of the noble savage, which had regained a degree of popularity in the late 1960s. The controversial director also gives credence to the catharsis theory: "There may even be an argument in support of saying that any kind of violence in films, in fact, serves a useful social purpose by allowing people a means of vicariously freeing themselves from the pent up, aggressive emotions which are better expressed in dreams, or in the dreamlike state of watching a film, than in any form of reality or sublimation."[6]

But to focus exclusively on this psychological aspect of the film is to discount the significance of the social and moral implications to which Kubrick refers. Like Burgess, Kubrick has a profound appreciation of innate depravity (otherwise known as original sin), an aspect of the human psyche that has fascinated American authors since Nathaniel Hawthorne. For Hawthorne (as is clear in the short story "The Bosom Serpent"), depravity is so profound and universal an aspect of the human condition as to seem innate, and he grapples with faith in a God who would instill such depravity in his most beloved creation. The modern age has transformed the problem of innate evil into the causal explanations of genetic or environmental determinism, which rob individuals of the ultimate moral responsibility for their actions (B. F. Skinner's *Beyond Freedom and Dignity* remains the locus classicus here). Either criminals are born with genetic disorders, or they are made into criminals by flawed parents or by our racist, classist, sexist society (or both).

But to reduce Alex to a collection of drives, and to believe that his actions are as fettered *before* the Ludovico treatment as *after* it, is to miss the real point of the film, which is stated explicitly by the prison chaplain. Troubled by the Ludovico technique from the start, the chaplain's is the only dissenting voice at the demonstration of its complete effectiveness (which involves teasing Alex with a naked woman whom he cannot touch without retching, and forcing him to lick the boot of a male tormenter): "Self-interest, the fear of physical pain, is what drove him to that grotesque act of self-abasement. . . . He ceases to be a wrongdoer; he also ceases to be a creature capable of moral choice." Kubrick claims to be following Burgess in making the chaplain the voice of reason. By the end of the sequence, it is the prime minister who is being ridiculed when he responds with a pat utilitarian justification for the procedure ("The point is, it works!").

In the novel, the chaplain asks Alex (as he considers whether to submit to the conditioning process) whether it might not be better to choose evil willingly than to do good unwillingly. The answer to that question (which the uplifting ending of the film underscores) is that indeed it is better to be capable of doing evil than to do good unwillingly. As the minister points out, Alex still *wants* to engage in sex and violence, but he is compelled by aversive conditioning techniques to do otherwise.

The ending of *Clockwork Orange* is the most exuberant sequence in the film since its opening crime spree. There, we identify with little Alex not just as the embodiment of our repressed desires but also as an immensely dynamic force of life, albeit one put to evil ends. Kubrick stacks the deck early on by making Alex's victims as unsympathetic as possible; in chronological order, they include a sodden street bum, a gang about to rape someone, a rich bleeding-heart liberal and his snooty wife, Alex's own derelict droogs, and the bony old *ptitsa* with a hundred cats, so we feel little sympathy for them when they are abused (in contrast, in the novel the gang's first victim is an academic coming out of the university library with a load of books). In the end, we rejoice that Alex has recovered his will, though we expect him to return to his old, depraved ways—this time, as a protected member of the establishment.

It is comparatively easy (or at least it was in Hollywood's golden age, a much less cynical time than our own) to affirm human existence by depicting the triumph of good over evil. It is much more difficult to convincingly affirm being in the world in the face of some of its greatest challenges. Tragedy, to my mind, is the most profound theatrical genre precisely because of its ability to be life affirming despite the injustice of the fates of its protagonists. Although the tale of little Alex is not a tragedy, *A Clockwork Orange* is a similarly profound film that celebrates human freedom while highlighting some of its most distasteful consequences. It is hence a moving and passionate artistic denial of the desolate nihilism that is implicit in mechanistic determinism.

Active and Passive Nihilism

An observation made by Kevin Stoehr in the journal *Film and Philosophy* is helpful in framing my analysis of the director's intent here: "Given Kubrick's comments in rare but revealing interviews throughout his career, it would be fair to say that he dwells upon the nihilistic condition of contemporary culture in order to *point beyond* such a condition, in the spirit of Nietzsche's active nihilism. In good dialectical fashion, he highlights the negative in order to indicate our positive capacity for creative and individualistic self-creation."[7]

Nietzsche condemned passive nihilism, which accepts the meaninglessness of existence and "blinks" indifferently, and he valorized active nihilism, which declares the hollowness of all the proposed idols of the marketplace in order to herald the superman. In *A Clockwork Orange,* Kubrick confronts us with the immoral monstrosity that is little Alex, the better to affirm the inviolability of the human will. The "Ode to Joy" at the end tells us how to read the meaning of the sequence; it would be much worse for society to rob such an individual of the *capacity* to do evil than it is to be forced to continue to deal with the *consequences* of his choosing to do so.

The Kubrick Vision

Unwilling to boil his films down to univocal interpretations, Kubrick has always been wary of engaging in conceptual analyses of them. Indeed, he hated it when interviewers asked such interpretive questions, and he would, for the most part, refuse to answer them (the *Sight and Sound* interview was a notable exception). His work has been variously described as misanthropic, misogynistic, fatalistic, technophobic, and downright antisocial. But a brief survey of his most prominent films offers a mixed bag of diverse plots and characterizations.

Killer's Kiss (1955), Kubrick's second feature (his first, *Fear and Desire* [1953] has been largely unavailable due to the director's determined efforts), is a gritty and realistic study of a romantic triangle involving a boxer, a nightclub dancer, and her gangster boss. Notable for the innovative shot compositions and dynamic editing that were to become Kubrick's trademark, it also permits its loser protagonist to survive in the end, in contrast to the ill-fated protagonists that generally populate films of this genre.

The Killing (1956), in contrast, is pure film noir fatalism, with protagonist Johnny Clay (Sterling Hayden) destined to fail at the end. When his overstuffed suitcase bursts open on the tarmac and the heist money blows away, his defeat could not have been more crushing. A spellbinding racetrack caper, the film grabbed the attention of Hollywood and led to Kubrick's collaboration with Kirk Douglas on *Paths of Glory* (1957). It also initiated the director's reputation as a bleak and cynical filmmaker. I contend, however, that this reputation is undeserved.

Kubrick made no fewer than three profoundly antiwar films, and such films are pointless unless one believes that we can make some headway in resisting our warlike tendencies. Colonel Dax (Kirk Douglas) in *Paths of Glory* is a heroic and extremely sympathetic officer, fighting the lunacy of trench warfare and the sociopathy of his commanding officer. General Mireau (George Macready) orders the artillery to fire on his own men (who are pinned down inside their trenches when the attack proves to be impossible) and then court-martials and executes three of their number to cover up his treachery. Dax's principled refusal to assume Mireau's command when the truth is revealed is depicted as noble, and his return to the troops in the trenches is valorized as well. Letting his men linger in a café to listen to the famously touching song (sung in German by Kubrick's future wife) with which the film ends, Dax is depicted as an officer with a heart. A moment of humanity and fellow feeling is privileged as possible in the midst of such madness.

Kubrick took over from a faltering Anthony Mann during the shooting of 1960's *Spartacus* (called in by a desperate Kirk Douglas at the last minute), but his next personal project was *Lolita* (1962). Humbert Humbert (James Mason) is a moral monster that both novelist Vladimir Nabokov and Kubrick choose to portray sympathetically—the director's first sociopath as protagonist. Humbert's preference for young girls may have been consciously cultivated, but his obsession with thirteen-year-old Lolita (Sue Lyon) is depicted as out of his control. It is also what ultimately destroys him. My guess is that Kubrick was drawn to *Lolita* precisely because of Nabokov's sympathetic portrayal of a character who is essentially a moral monster and a pedophile. Like Nabokov, Kubrick had a taste for offbeat protagonists and a knack for making their motives believable. One feels for Humbert when Clare Quilty (Peter Sellers) snatches his little nymphet away, leaving him to have a massive heart attack in the hospital where he seeks to retrieve her.

Dr. Strangelove, or: How I Learned to Stop Worrying and Love the Bomb (1964) is Kubrick's only foray into comedy (though black comic touches abound in his later films), but that was not his original intention. The madness of mutually assured destruction was such a perfect topic for satire that he dropped plans for a literal interpretation of the novel *Red Alert* (ultimately produced as *Fail Safe* [1964]). The satirical tone of *Dr. Strangelove* redeems what is ultimately an apocalyptic vision of weapons that have outstripped their makers' ability to control them, embodied in a Doomsday Machine that the Russians cannot disarm. That device is triggered when U.S. General Jack D. Ripper (Sterling Hayden) sends his bomb wing against the Russians because he is convinced that his impotence has been caused by their fluoridation of our water.

One of the myriad reasons it is difficult to characterize Kubrick's vision is that so many of his films are intentionally ambivalent. On the one hand, *Dr. Strangelove* seems to be saying that nuclear Armageddon is inevitable.

On the other hand, it is one of the most effective antiwar films ever made. Satirizing the madness helped us step back from the brink (the nuclear option was seriously considered during the Cuban missile crisis of 1963). The film entered the national zeitgeist and made nuclear conflict less thinkable (and more obviously laughable).

The 1968 film *2001: A Space Odyssey* traces a Nietzschean arc of human evolution from ape to human to *Übermensch*, all to the accompaniment of Richard Strauss's tone poem *Thus Spake Zarathustra*. The advanced alien race that sent the original monolith to earth and buried the second monolith where only a much advanced human race could find it fulfills a benevolent and almost Godlike role. This is most clearly symbolized when the ape's contact with the monolith (like the Sistine Chapel's depiction of God touching Adam) leads to his realization that a femur bone can be used as a weapon, thus ensuring the survival of the species.

Shattering decades of science fiction cliché, Kubrick chooses to depict aliens that are far from hostile and that literally redeem the human race at two critical junctures in our history. The major antagonist here is HAL, the all-too-human computer that develops an instinct for self-preservation and has murderous designs on the crew. The machine has the equivalent of a nervous breakdown due to the stress of being the only conscious entity that (who?) appreciates the true significance of their mission. The Star Child, the reincarnation of crewman Dave Bowman (Keir Dullea) after his trip across the universe, triumphantly makes its return to earth just as (the Arthur C. Clarke novel informs us) the human race is about to destroy itself in an all-out nuclear war. Able to exert the power of mind over matter, his horizon seems limitless. The celebratory feel of the ending is much less ambivalent than that of *A Clockwork Orange*.

Kubrick next turned to nineteenth-century satirist William Makepeace Thackeray and *Barry Lyndon* (1975). Irish ne'er-do-well Redmond Barry (a perfectly cast Ryan O'Neal) always takes the back stairs to social success. Neither hero nor villain, Barry goes from being a deserter to impersonating an officer, fighting duels for a gambler, and finally marrying the widow Lyndon (and treating her like dirt) and becoming a lord. Yet he loves his son (who dies in a riding accident) and unexpectedly chooses not to shoot his stepson in a duel when he is clearly at an advantage; as a result, Barry loses his leg, his wife, and his title and slinks out of the country broken and penniless. This is a picaresque and curiously moralistic tale for Kubrick (only Humbert Humbert is punished more severely), and Barry receives his comeuppance in full by the end. Neither noble nor completely ignoble, he is somewhat unpredictable and never a mere determined mechanism.

The Shining (1980) represents Kubrick's only explicit foray into the horror genre. Jack Torrance (Jack Nicholson) is unambiguously insane and completely out of control, and as he descends into madness, he shifts from protagonist to antagonist, from tormented alcoholic to psychotic monster. His assault on wife Wendy (Shelley Duvall) and son Danny (Danny Lloyd) is compelled either by his own inner demons or by the spirits that possess the Overlook Hotel. Yet even here, in one of his bleakest tales, Kubrick depicts Wendy as a resourceful heroine who surprises us, and hotel cook Dick Halloran (Scatman Crothers) is a truly caring person who drops everything and flies from Florida to Colorado in a fruitless (and fatal) attempt to respond to Danny's psychic call for help. *The Shining* also fulfills one of our most fundamental expectations for the genre: that the monster will be killed in the end.

The third installment in Kubrick's antiwar trilogy, *Full Metal Jacket* (1987), scathingly deconstructs the John Wayne myth (one imagines it paired with *The Green Berets* [1968] on the perfect double bill). A jarring mixture of riveting battle scenes and increasingly broad satire, *Full Metal Jacket,* though not as comedic as *Dr. Strangelove,* is rife with black humor and exaggeration. Private Joker (Matthew Modine) embodies the Jungian duality of the human spirit, as represented by his wearing of both a peace sign and a "Born to Kill" slogan. His distanced and humorous take on the proceedings allows us to appreciate the peculiar forms of insanity inherent in the Vietnam conflict.

The first forty minutes of the film depict yet another conditioning process, Marine Corps boot camp, which in this case is designed to rob the men of their individuality and mold them into a fighting unit. The necessity of this type of training is explained and celebrated in such John Wayne vehicles as *Sands of Iwo Jima* (1949), but here, the production of thoughtless killing machines is condemned. Private Leonard Lawrence (Vincent D'Onofrio) is an overweight goof that Sergeant Hartman (Lee Ermey, a former drill instructor himself) decides to focus on as an example. He hazes Lawrence—whom he has nicknamed "Private Pyle" (as in "Gomer Pyle")—mercilessly, then punishes the entire platoon when the poor guy continues to screw up. Lawrence absorbs abuse from everyone (even from his only ally, Private Joker), but he gets better at soldiering the closer he gets to insanity and ends up blowing away both Sergeant Hartman and himself. Private Joker becomes a war correspondent and has to deal daily with the official double-talk and inflated enemy casualty reports that were so characteristic of the Vietnam War. Joker is the most admirable Kubrickian protagonist since Colonel Dax. He tries his best to help Lawrence be a marine and is constantly looking out for his photographer, Rafterman. He mocks the John Wayne image with hilarious impersonations but is brave in battle and ultimately administers a merciful coup de grace to the teenaged sniper who gunned down several members of his patrol and failed to kill Joker only because her gun jams.

Full Metal Jacket is more insightful than either *Apocalypse Now* (1979) or *Platoon* (1986) about what was really at stake in this war. The grunts point out that the South Vietnamese care little about democracy and make their American allies feel unwelcome. A squad leader remarks sincerely that he respects the Vietcong more than the Army of the Republic of Vietnam. A general matter-of-factly proclaims that inside every gook is an American waiting to get out, perfectly capturing the virulent synthesis of racism and ethnocentrism that motivated our involvement there. The impact of these comments is heightened by the fact that many of them are delivered in explicit interview situations in full-face close-ups, with cameras rolling in the frame.

When Joker's platoon breaks into a rousing chorus of the theme from *The Mickey Mouse Club*, on their way back from the climactic battle, Kubrick's message is clear (all too clear, according to some critics). Though I found the sequence jarring when I first saw the film, I now consider this ending to be a stroke of genius. The nascent fascism of the Disney empire blooms in the Vietnam War. The self-righteousness of our culture, which has blithely permitted us to impose our political system on so many recalcitrant nations around the world, stems from the unambiguous moral certainties of the Disney universe. Give me the Brothers Grimm any day.

Throughout it all, Joker retains his sense of humor, as does the director. This is crucial to the distinction noted earlier between active and passive nihilism. Antiwar pictures such as *Dr. Strangelove* and *Full Metal Jacket* get us to see the black humor in the situation, the better to facilitate our real-ization of the madness of war. They move us to recognize and deplore the madness, and they leave us with the feeling that a greater degree of sanity is possible because we have been alerted to these dangers.

It was predictable that Kubrick would never retire. His last film, *Eyes Wide Shut* (1999), was completed four days before his death. It is one of the most nihilistic of his works, embodying a kind of Sartrean pessimism about our inevitable dissatisfaction with romantic love. In *Being and Nothingness,* Sartre attributes this to the contradictory aims we are pursuing. On the one hand, we want our beloved to freely choose to love us, with the attendant recognition that such a radically contingent choice can be withdrawn at any moment. On the other hand, we wish to be secure in that love, so we tend to reduce our beloved to an object with essential characteristics, one of which is his or her love for us. Sex only complicates the equation, because sexual gratification is at its best when we have a diverse array of sexual partners and when the other is reduced to an object to be used for our pleasure.

Bill and Alice Harford (Tom Cruise and Nicole Kidman) are an attractive upper-class couple who clearly take each other for granted at the beginning of the film. Readying themselves for a Christmas party, Alice asks Bill how she looks, and he responds "perfect" without even bothering to glance in her direction. Part of the power of the sequence comes from the contrast between Bill, who takes Alice's beauty as a given, and the viewer, who has just been ravished by the sight of Kidman's naked torso during the opening credits. The couple's complacency is soon shattered, however. After flirting with others at the party, they conclude the night with a passionate lovemaking session. In a later scene, they share some marijuana and engage in an engrossing conversation. First, Alice grills Bill about the two models he was flirting with at the party. When he will not admit to having a jealous reaction to his wife's flirtation with an exotic European gentleman at the party ("You're my wife, and you would never do anything like that"), she relates a fantasy she once entertained of leaving Bill and running off with a handsome naval officer she saw in a restaurant. Her admission triggers a jealous rage that either sends Bill on a sexual odyssey of epic proportions or causes a nightmarish dream. Although the final line of the film (Alice says, "You know, there is something we need to do as soon as possible . . . fuck!") seems to promise a reconciliation, there is little doubt that the Harfords will never be totally secure with each other, despite Bill's protestations that he has been woken up "forever." Their "adventures" were not constructive; rather, they seem to point to the crumbling of the foundations of their marriage (Bill notes, "A dream is never just a dream"). One might hope that the totally unfulfilling nature of Bill's nightmarish odyssey (where sexual gratification is desperately sought, often promised, but never forthcoming) will deepen his appreciation of his wife as a full-blown human being and not a possession. But even near the end, he still seems obsessed by visions of her making love to the naval officer and by her dream of being gangbanged. Bill has come to the realization (in Sartrean terms) that Alice is *pour soi* and not *en soi* (that is, she exists as a being for itself, with a self-consciousness that grants her radical freedom, and not simply as a beautiful object that he owns). This remains an unsettling realization at the end of the film.

Although it is pessimistic about the prospects of romantic love, *Eyes Wide Shut* foregrounds the radical freedom of the individual to choose not to love the beloved, a theme that Sartre made much of. It is precisely because we are free that love is such a frightening prospect. We put so much of our self-esteem in the hands of the beloved that we would like to know that his or her love will last. But we can value the beloved's recognition only because it is freely (and contingently) granted.

So, to summarize this brief survey, Stanley Kubrick depicts out-of-control psychopaths from time to time, including General Ripper, Jack Torrance, and Private Pyle. But the vast majority of his protagonists, including Colonel Dax, Dave Bowman, Redmond Barry, Wendy Torrance, Private Joker, and Bill Harford, are resourceful individuals who clearly exercise choice at crucial moments in their respective films. This fact, coupled with my claim that *A Clockwork Orange* makes sense only if it is a celebration of human freedom, adds up to the conclusion that Kubrick affirms the existence of human free will. Dehumanization is a central theme in many of Kubrick's works, and in *Paths of Glory, Dr. Strangelove, A Clockwork Orange, The Shining,* and *Full Metal Jacket,* what dehumanization amounts to is the loss of control over our lives and the absence of choice between real alternatives.

One of the last projects Kubrick worked on was an adaptation of Brian Aldiss's short story "Supertoys Last All Summer Long," which he bequeathed to Steven Spielberg shortly before his death; the script became the film *A.I.: Artificial Intelligence* (2001). Although I am sure that Kubrick would not have played up the Pinocchio parallels as heavily as Spielberg did, his interest in whether machines can feel emotions, make choices, and truly approximate human existence shows that he was still obsessed with the theme of free will and determinism right up to the end of his life.

Notes

An earlier version of this paper, entitled "Kubrick Contra Nihilism: *A Clockwork Orange*," appeared in vol. 9 of *Film and Philosophy*, the 2005 Special Edition on Philosophy and Science Fiction.

1. Anthony Burgess, *A Clockwork Orange* (1963; reprint, New York: W. W. Norton, 1995).

2. Ibid., iii.

3. Ibid., ix.

4. Stanley Kubrick, interview with Philip Strick, *Sight and Sound,* April 1972, http://www.archiviokubrick.it/english/interviews/content/index.html?main=1972 moderntimes.

5. Ibid.

6. Ibid.

7. Kevin Stoehr, "Kubrick and Ricoer on Nihilistic Horror and the Symbolism of Evil," *Film and Philosophy,* special issue on horror (2001): 90.

"PLEASE MAKE ME A REAL BOY"

The Prayer of the Artificially Intelligent

Jason T. Eberl

Increasing technological sophistication, leading eventually to the prospect of artificial intelligence, has been the subject of speculation in science fiction works for decades, from literature (Isaac Asimov) to films (Ridley Scott's *Blade Runner* [1982]) and television (Data on *Star Trek: The Next Generation* [1987–1994] and the Cylons of *Battlestar Galactica* [1978–1980, 2003–present]). Stanley Kubrick first placed his filmmaking stamp on this subject with the character of HAL 9000 (voice by Douglas Rain) in *2001: A Space Odyssey* (1968). A fuller treatment, however, did not come until Steven Spielberg's *A.I.: Artificial Intelligence* (2001), a film that Kubrick conceived and developed a number of years before his death.[1] Parallel viewing of these films reveals a number of philosophical similarities between the seemingly diabolical HAL in *2001* and the much more sympathetic character of David (Haley Joel Osment) in *A.I.*, along with some important differences. The questions considered in this essay are twofold: Can an artificially created being possess the qualities that define a *person*—a being who merits a fundamental respect and bears certain inalienable rights? Given the possibility of creating such beings, what novel issues arise when either technology or the humans that fear such technology run amok?

I argue that David and HAL provide sufficient evidence that they should be considered persons, even though the jury may still be out on whether either of them—or any of us, for that matter—has a soul. However, despite the wondrous nature of such potential "creations of our genius,"[2] Kubrick's films also demonstrate two key concerns that human society must address and overcome before we can embark on such a creative endeavor. First, both we humans and our artificially intelligent constructs may fall into a competitive trap in which each seeks subjugation over the other, much like different political, ethnic, and religious groups have sought dominance over others throughout human history. Second, just as many human groups have sought "purity" by ridding their societies of different types of people over the centuries, humans may unite to "cleanse" themselves of this new and different type of nonhuman being. Although this prejudice might not matter if we are talking about mere machines (Damn all toasters!), the possibility that artificially intelligent machines could possess those qualities that define personhood would make the pursuit of "biological supremacy" a moral crime.

"X-Ray Delta One, This Is Mission Control": Transmitting Kubrick's Message

Before embarking on our philosophical journey to "Jupiter and beyond the infinite," let us set the stage. Kubrick's *2001* begins with the evolution of intelligent human beings from our most closely related evolutionary ancestors. Two features mark this transition: the ability to use a tool and, consequently, the use of that tool to kill. Kubrick and collaborator Arthur C. Clarke hypothesize that this evolutionary jump was instigated by alien forces through a mysterious black monolith. As humans progressed and developed more impressive tools—both those used to kill other humans and those that allowed space travel—another monolith was discovered on the moon. After transmitting a powerful radio signal toward Jupiter, two astronauts and three scientists are sent to that planet to discover answers to this profound mystery. The scientists are placed in hibernation for the long interplanetary voyage, while the astronauts—Dave Bowman (Keir Dullea) and Frank Poole (Gary Lockwood)—pilot and maintain their spaceship, *Discovery,* with the assistance and company of a sophisticated computer: HAL 9000.

As the voyagers approach Jupiter, HAL begins to act abnormally. He mistakenly reports that the ship's AE-35 antenna, which allows the crew to keep in contact with Earth, is malfunctioning. But Bowman and Poole cannot verify the malfunction and are alarmed by this development because (unlike our computers, which are prone to crashing) "no 9000 computer has ever made a mistake or distorted information." Upon learning of Bowman and Poole's doubts about his ability to fulfill the mission parameters, HAL seeks to defend himself from their plans to disconnect his "higher-brain functions." He kills Poole, deactivates the life-support systems of the hibernating scientists, and then attempts to leave Bowman adrift in space in a pod. Bowman eventually gets back into *Discovery,* disconnects HAL, and journeys into a transcendent realm through the gateway of another large monolith orbiting Jupiter.

A.I. presents a much different tale in which the sympathetic protagonist is not a human being terrorized by an insane computer but an artificially intelligent robotic child who is designed to perfectly mimic the human form and human behavior. The cyberneticists who construct David even program him to imprint on a particular human being so that he can "love" him or her as his parent. After being adopted by a human couple, David's life goes fairly well until his parents' own biological child recovers from a life-threatening condition that had left him comatose. The ensuing competition between David and his "brother" leads to a near catastrophe, and David is abandoned to fend for himself. His only companion is Teddy (voice by Jack Angel), an artificially intelligent but much less sophisticated stuffed bear. David soon befriends Gigolo Joe (Jude Law), another artificially intelligent "Mecha"—one designed to pleasure human women—and sets out to find the "Blue Fairy"—an explicit allusion to the tale of Pinocchio. After dodging several dangers, including the notorious "Flesh Fair" (discussed later), David, Teddy, and Joe make their way to the ancient ruins of New York City. There, David makes several discoveries: first, he is only one of several artificially constructed Mecha "boy" models, and second, his fervent desire to find the Blue Fairy makes him special (also discussed later). After being frozen for an extended period, David is found by the descendants of the original Mechas, who allow him to fulfill his one wish made to an apparition of the Blue Fairy: to spend a perfect day with his mother, Monica (Frances O'Connor). His wish granted, David lies forever content in his mother's bed.

"If You Let Me, I'll Be So *Real* for You!" Anthropomorphizing David and HAL

"But outside he just looks so real—like he is a child," says Monica when she first encounters David. She cannot believe that something that looks so much like a human being is merely a mechanical contrivance. Her early response to David is to treat him as just that: a mere object. David, following his programming to act like a child, tries to play games with Monica. When she gets annoyed with him and puts him in a closet, he thinks it is part of a game of hide-and-seek—and he humorously turns the tables on Monica when she is in an undignified position later on. One can read this interaction in a different way, though: perhaps David is seeking to *imprint* on Monica, which requires her to speak a seven-word code.

She eventually speaks the magic words to him, one of which is *Socrates,* who lived and died by the Delphic admonition to "know thyself." This is among the earliest philosophical means of distinguishing persons from objects: persons can self-reflectively know themselves, whereas objects lack such a level of conscious awareness. This difference has long been used to differentiate human from nonhuman animals; although nonhuman animals are certainly conscious, they are not necessarily *self-*conscious. Recent experiments with dolphins, chimpanzees, apes, and birds call this supposed difference into question, however. Besides the anecdotal evidence depicted in films such as *The Wild Parrots of Telegraph Hill* (Judy Irving, 2003) and *March of the Penguins* (Luc Jacquet, 2005), researchers in animal cognition have continued to limit the number of species differentiae between Us and Them. With respect to self-consciousness, researchers have observed that a raven is capable of deceiving another raven, which requires it to be able to separate its own individual mental states—perceptions, feelings, and plans—from those of the other raven.[3]

Self-consciousness, though, is not the only criterion philosophers have used to determine whether something is a person. In the Middle Ages, the dominant concept of personhood was "an individual substance of a *rational* nature."[4] Rationality is the capacity not only to calculate and solve problems but also to understand reality in an abstract, conceptual manner. For example, it requires the ability to understand the concept "humanity" or "circularity" rather than simply perceiving individual human beings or circles, and to communicate such concepts using language. More recently, personhood has also been defined with respect to engaging in meaningful social activity and acting in an autonomous, moral fashion.[5]

Although it is not evident whether David "knows himself" or possesses any of the other definitive features of personhood, he does make an earnest attempt to mimic human behavior, including eating—which has deleterious effects on David's computerized innards—and the peculiarly human activity of laughing. HAL 9000, in contrast, does not laugh and does not attempt to eat. In fact, HAL cannot eat because he does not have a mouth or any other human physical features; rather, he is represented by a red-lit lens in a rectangular box. Nevertheless, the humans on the spaceship *Discovery* interact with HAL just as they would any other human crew member, even playing chess with him and getting his aesthetic opinion on Bowman's amateur artwork. HAL thus fulfills the social dimension of personhood and is clearly rational in at least a calculative sense—perhaps even more so than his human counterparts. It is debatable whether HAL acts in an autonomous, moral way when he decides to turn against the *Discovery* crew. Philosophical determinists doubt or outright deny that even human beings act autonomously; perhaps we act out of a genetically and environmentally determined psychological program, just as HAL acts based on his programming. When it comes to self-consciousness, it is difficult to determine whether HAL meets this criterion, even though he uses self-referential language: *I, me, my*. But is it any easier for us to determine whether another human being is self-conscious?

David and HAL seem like persons not because of their humanlike appearance (especially since HAL does not look human at all) but because of their *responses*. Each behaves and speaks as if he has genuine emotions, opinions, and desires. In some instances, their programmed responses are even more significant to the humans they are interacting with than what other humans say or do. Gigolo Joe, for example, knows all the right things to say when seducing a woman who has paid for his services. He tells one of his customers, "You are a goddess, Patricia. You wind me up inside. But you deserve much better in your life. You deserve . . . me." This contrasts with the bruises— "wounds of passion," Joe calls them—that her husband or boyfriend has apparently inflicted on her. But do such responses, however sophisticated they may be, indicate self-conscious rationality to the point of asserting that David, HAL, and Joe have minds like ours and are thereby persons like us?

In 1950 Alan Turing, who served as a code breaker for British intelligence during World War II, proposed a criterion for artificial intelligence based on how well a computer could play the "imitation game." In this game, now known as the "Turing test," an interrogator questions two beings. The three cannot perceive one another and communicate via teletype. The goal is for the interrogator, who asks a series of questions and judges the responses, to determine which of the two is a human being and which is a computer. Turing's thesis is that a digital computer has the same basic components—an information storage capacity, an executive unit to carry out operations, and a control that governs the operations by means of a "table of instructions"—as a human brain. It is also possible, Turing notes, for a digital computer to have a "random element" by which it can give the appearance of autonomy. Turing thus asserts, "The reader must accept it as a fact that digital computers can be constructed, and indeed have been constructed, according to the principles we have described, and that they can in fact mimic the actions of a human computer very closely."[6]

Turing developed his thesis when digital computers were in their infancy and behaviorism was the dominant theory among psychologists and philosophers for determining the properties of the human mind. Behaviorism ignores the "black box" of internal cognitive activity and instead focuses on observable behaviors—especially linguistic behaviors—that serve as evidence of both rationality and self-consciousness. Behaviorism also accepts that the "problem of other minds"—determining whether any being other than oneself has a mind—is irresolvable except by means of observing behavior. René Descartes famously asserted that, without a doubt, *he* is a thinking thing ("I think, therefore I am"), and of course, we each share Descartes' solipsism in knowing that our own selves are thinking things. But this raises the question of how Descartes or any of us can know that any other being is a thinking thing.[7] Turing's and behaviorism's answer is that we do not know, except by making inferences from other beings' behavior. Therefore, if a computer can pass the Turing test by replicating human linguistic behavior so well that the interrogator mistakes the computer for the human being, there is no reason to doubt that such a computer has a mind—any more than we would doubt that the human being who failed the test nevertheless has a mind. The Mechas in *A.I.* certainly seem to pass the Turing test with flying colors. Professor Hobby (William Hurt), David's creator, proclaims, "The artificial being is a reality of perfect simulacrum: articulated in limb, articulate in speech, and not lacking in human response."

But even a "perfect simulacrum" of human response misses the mark when it comes to the nature of human cognition and emotion. When Professor Hobby questions a Mecha on the nature of love, she responds, "Love is first widening my eyes a little bit . . . and quickening my breathing a little . . . and warming my skin . . . and touching my—." So, it is only fitting that behaviorism has long since faded as the dominant theory in psychology and the philosophy of mind. Part of the reason for behaviorism's obsolescence is that studies in neurophysiology have advanced our understanding of the link between the black box of cognitive activity and the increasingly observable neural activity of the human brain.

Given the capacity to create machines that can pass the Turing test, the question arises whether it is metaphysically possible that such machines' computational architecture can instantiate mental states like ours. In other words, could a Mecha, or HAL, *think* in the same self-conscious manner that we do? The possibility of machines thinking like we do, and perhaps possessing other definitive qualities of personhood, raises the questions of whether we should create such machines and how we should treat them once we do. Let us explore the potential danger in creating entities that may be persons but are of such a radically different nature that we do not recognize and thereby treat them as such.

"Life Functions Terminated": Humanity's Dependence on Technology

Both *A.I.* and *2001* show us the darker side of these technologically creative pursuits. As part of his all-too-human programming, HAL is capable of being deceptive. At one point, he begins questioning Bowman about the nature of their mission to Jupiter, the mystery surrounding it, and some "doubts" he apparently has. Bowman soon realizes what is going on and notes that HAL is working up his crew psychology report. HAL has been programmed to know humans better than they may know themselves. HAL tries to play psychologist once again when he advises Bowman to "lie down" and "take a stress pill" after Poole's death.

Realizing the dangerous extent to which HAL is malfunctioning, Bowman decides that it is time to disconnect HAL's higher-brain circuitry. HAL's response at this point goes from being a smart-ass—warning Bowman that it will be difficult for him to cross the vacuum of space and reenter *Discovery* without his space helmet—to pleading for his life as he drones, "Stop, Dave." But Bowman must be careful when disconnecting HAL's consciousness, for, as he and Poole note earlier in the film, "There's not a single part of ship operations that's not under his control." HAL is described as "the brain and central nervous system" of *Discovery,* which is akin to a big, metallic organism with HAL as its controlling organ. This picture paints Bowman, Poole, and the three hibernating scientists as microorganic parasites living off of *Discovery*'s life-support system, which, of course, is controlled by HAL. And he exercises this control when he cuts off the hibernating scientists from life support. In *A.I.,* when we first see Martin (Jake Thomas), David's human brother, he too is completely dependent on life-support machinery to live: human life in the hands of technology that we use and sometimes fear.

Kubrick's films present us with the *struggle* of humanity against artificial intelligence—a struggle that humanity has brought on itself and must endure. We human beings generally assume that we are the masters of our own creations and can exert control over them. But the relationship between humanity and our artifacts is not so simple. Bowman and Poole correctly note their dependence on HAL. They cannot exercise total control over him, for he has some control over their fate. The ability to recognize their dependence on HAL, however, is coupled with an inability to recognize HAL's self-consciousness—if, in fact, he is self-conscious. It may be partly due to Bowman and Poole's failure to recognize HAL's self-consciousness that he is driven to commit his murderous deeds.

German philosopher G. W. F. Hegel contends that when two self-conscious individuals encounter each other, they each seek *recognition* from the other as a self-conscious being: "Self-consciousness exists in and for itself when, and by the fact that, it so exists for another; that is, it exists only in being acknowledged."[8] To achieve this recognition, each seeks either the subjugation or death of the other:

> Thus the relation of the two self-conscious individuals is such that they prove themselves and each other through a life-and-death struggle. They must engage in this struggle, for they must raise their certainty of being *for themselves* to truth, both in the case of the other and in their own case. . . . The individual who has not risked his life may well be recognized as a *person,* but he has not attained to the truth of this recognition as an independent self-consciousness. Similarly, just as each stakes his own life, so each must seek the other's death, for it values the other no more than itself; its essential being is present to it in the form of an "other," it is outside of itself and must rid itself of its self-externality.[9]

In Hegel's view, a person's self-consciousness is fully achieved through a two-step process. First, another self-conscious being—recognized as such—must acknowledge the person's self-conscious existence. Second, to mitigate the external nature of this acknowledgment, the person must seek the subjugation or death of the other to attain an independent and internal recognition of his own self-consciousness. This struggle is even more acute, because the other is also attempting to recognize himself in the same way and so is struggling for his own self-recognition, as well as for his life and freedom.

We witness this struggle in *2001* as Bowman and Poole attempt to assert their mastery over HAL and subdue his higher-brain functions to avoid being dominated by an apparently flawed computer. HAL, however, asserts his mastery over first Poole and then the three hibernating scientists; finally, he attempts to do so with Bowman. Bowman wins out in the end, but he also realizes that he, HAL, and everyone else are subject to an even higher intelligence.

We human beings still struggle to coexist peacefully and accept the inherent diversity among us—including differences based on national identity, ethnicity, religious affiliation, gender, sexual orientation, *Star Trek* versus *Star Wars* fan, and so on. Hence, we should be wary of creating another group of beings who may merit respect and certain fundamental rights but are sufficiently different from us to evoke fear and competition, as well as wonder. This leads to one final consideration: what do we owe to such beings if they qualify as persons despite the fact that they are *our* creations?

"Flesh Fairs": What Do We Owe to the Artificially Intelligent?

The darker side of *A.I.* involves a role reversal from *2001*, with humans destroying Mechas at a Flesh Fair billed as a "celebration of life." Here, human beings fear Mechas' dehumanizing presence. The Flesh Fair revelers seek to arrive at "a truly human future" by "demolishing artificiality." To the fair's ringleader, Lord Johnson-Johnson (Brendan Gleeson), David represents the most foul of creations—"the latest iteration in a series of insults to human dignity"—because of his extreme likeness to the human form. But the spectators turn on Lord Johnson-Johnson when David pleads for his life. It is not that the spectators sympathize with David or experience a change of heart about how Mechas should be treated; they simply doubt that David is really a Mecha and not a human boy—and God forbid they make an irreversible mistake! If it were proved that David is not at all human, would the spectators change their minds, or would they continue to recognize in David the very qualities that separate not human from nonhuman but person from nonperson?

In the opening scene of *A.I.*, an ethically astute individual asks, "If a robot could genuinely love a person, what responsibility does that person hold toward that Mecha in return?" Subtle changes in the evolution of artificially intelligent computers and robots could result in the emergence of a conscious mind for which we would be responsible and that we would have to treat accordingly.[10] It is this concern that, ironically and misguidedly, drives the Flesh Fair revelers to treat as mere objects artificially intelligent Mechas that may warrant greater respect. At the very least, we know that they are sentient—capable of feeling pleasure and pain—because one asks another to turn off his pain receivers before being sacrificed at the fair.

The moral failure on the part of the Flesh Fair revelers is not simply a violation of so-called human rights (the very term might be considered racist, or at least "biolog-ist"); it is a denial of Mechas' ability to explore and develop their own potential—to transcend the limits, if possible, imposed by their design. Aristotle famously defined *virtue* in terms of a being fulfilling its telos—its goal to exercise its proper function excellently.[11] For humans, virtue consists in the excellent use of reason, which culminates in intellectual contemplation and, as a result, happiness. Many of us (even professional philosophers), burdened by various bodily and other needs that prevent us from pursuing pure intellectual activity, find it difficult to imagine achieving happiness or virtue so defined. Our natural inclination, however, is to transcend what we perceive as our limits with respect to rational activity: we can do more than we think we can and must strive, as the army used to say, to be all that we can be. If Mechas share a similar telos, then the moral loss resulting from Flesh Fairs and other similar debasing and destructive activities is the preclusion of Mechas' ability to pursue happiness by being all that they can be.

"I *Am*, I *Was!*" Artificial Intelligence Transcends Its Limits

David is the model of what artificial intelligence can potentially become. From the get-go, he embodies human personhood better than Joe or HAL ever could. But even he must transcend his own limitations. And such limitations are not unique to David as a mechanical being, for we biological beings also have individual and collective limitations that we strive to transcend to better ourselves as persons. In addition to those aforementioned qualities that define personhood, David possesses two other characteristics that mark him as potentially a person like us: his *faith* and his assertion of his own unique *selfhood*. When Professor Hobby encounters David toward the end of David's search for the Blue Fairy, he notes how amazed he is that David has been chasing his dream: "Until you were born, robots didn't dream, robots didn't desire unless we told them what to want." Ultimately, it is David's capacity to go beyond the limits of logic, which should lead him to the conclusion that Pinocchio is merely a fairy tale and the Blue Fairy does not exist, and make a "leap of faith" that brings him to the brink of personhood, if not actually endow him with it: "Our test was a simple one. Where would your self-motivated reasoning take you? To the logical conclusion . . . that [the] Blue Fairy is part of the great human flaw to wish for things that don't exist, or to the greatest single human gift—the ability to chase down our dreams." It may seem that a flaw in logical reasoning that results in epistemic error is not the best human quality to achieve, but it is truly a distinctive characteristic of human persons, as Gigolo Joe observes: "Only Orga [humans] believe what cannot be seen or measured. It's that oddness that separates our species." David's second moment of transcendence occurs when he encounters a duplicate "David" in Professor Hobby's office. David reacts violently to this "other" (remember Hegel) and proclaims, "I'm special! I'm unique! I'm David!" David conceives of himself as, and aggressively asserts himself to be, *his own self.* This inspires Joe to reach his own Cartesian conclusion just before being captured by the police for a murder he did not commit: "I *am.* I *was!*"

Kubrick and his collaborators—Arthur C. Clarke and Steven Spielberg— have presented us with some of the most thought-provoking depictions of artificial intelligence, both its nature and its potential relationship to human beings. Of course, these depictions are still in the realm of science *fiction*, but such things have a fascinating tendency to eventually become science *fact.* So it is eminently helpful to begin thinking about the metaphysical and ethical implications of this profound endeavor to create beings in our own image. Awareness of the fact that human beings must continue to evolve and mature to improve our behavior toward one another should make us pause and reflect on the potential cost of complicating, and perhaps retarding, our struggle for personal and collective self-improvement by introducing into the mix a new type of being whose nature we will not understand at first—Is it a person or not?—and will undoubtedly fail to treat appropriately.

Notes

I wish to thank my wife, Jennifer Vines, for helpful comments and for pointing out that ravens are more than just the most famously quoted bird in melancholy poetry, and Jerold J. Abrams, for inviting me to contribute to this volume and providing helpful comments along the way.

1. Kubrick handpicked Spielberg to direct *A.I.* and had several conversations with

him before he died. Similarly, Kubrick collaborated closely with Arthur C. Clarke in writing the screenplay for *2001*.

2. Captain Picard (Patrick Stewart) uses this phrase, in the singular, to describe Data (Brent Spiner) in an episode of *Star Trek: The Next Generation* entitled "Measure of a Man."

3. See David Berreby, "Deceit of the Raven," *New York Times Magazine,* September 4, 2005, http://www.nytimes.com/2005/09/04/magazine/04IDEA.html (accessed September 5, 2005).

4. See Boethius, *Contra Eutychen et Nestorium,* in *Tractates and The Consolation of Philosophy,* trans. H. F. Stewart, E. K. Rand, and S. J. Tester (Cambridge, Mass.: Harvard University Press, 1918), III.

5. See Immanuel Kant, *Groundwork of the Metaphysics of Morals,* ed. Mary Gregor (New York: Cambridge University Press, 1997), 41–42.

6. A. M. Turing, "Computing Machinery and Intelligence," *Mind* 59 (1950): 433–60; the quotation appears in John Haugeland, ed., *Mind Design II* (Cambridge, Mass.: MIT Press, 1997), 34.

7. René Descartes, *Meditations on First Philosophy,* rev. ed., ed. John Cottingham (New York: Cambridge University Press, 1996), Second Meditation.

8. G. W. F. Hegel, *Phenomenology of Spirit,* trans. A. V. Miller (Oxford: Oxford University Press, 1997), §178.

9. Ibid., §187. It is worth noting that Hegel thought that the master-slave dialectic had been resolved by the time he was writing, once ideas of universal equality, freedom, and the like had come into play in human history. Karl Marx, in contrast, considered the dialectic to be continuing, with the bourgeoisie as the masters and the proletariat as the slaves. Regardless of whether Marx was right or wrong in his analysis, the master-slave dialectic may be reinvigorated by the advent of artificial intelligence. I am grateful to Jerold J. Abrams for raising this point.

10. For further discussion of our potential ethical obligations to artificially intelligent beings, see Robert Arp, "'If Droids Could Think . . .': Droids as Slaves and Persons," in *Star Wars and Philosophy,* ed. Kevin S. Decker and Jason T. Eberl (LaSalle, Ill.: Open Court Press, 2005), 120–31.

11. See Aristotle, *Nicomachean Ethics,* trans. Terence Irwin (Indianapolis: Hackett, 1985), Books I–II.

Nietzsche's Overman as Posthuman Star Child in *2001: A Space Odyssey*

Jerold J. Abrams

> All beings so far have created something beyond themselves; and do you want to be the ebb of this great flood and even go back to the beasts rather than overcome man? What is the ape to man? A laughingstock or a painful embarrassment. And man shall be just that for the overman: a laughingstock or a painful embarrassment.
> —Friedrich Nietzsche, *Thus Spoke Zarathustra*

A Vision of the Future

Stanley Kubrick's *2001: A Space Odyssey* (1968) is perhaps the greatest science fiction film ever made, and certainly one of the most philosophical.[1] In moving images—and almost no dialogue—Kubrick captures the entire evolutionary epic of Friedrich Nietzsche's magnum opus *Thus Spoke Zarathustra*. From worms to apes to humans, Nietzsche tracks the movement of life as the will-to-power—ultimately claiming that it is not yet finished. We have one final stage left, the overman, a being who will look upon humanity as humanity now looks upon the apes.[2] It is well known that Nietzsche tells us little about what the overman will look like, except that he or she will emerge as a new kind of "child." So, naturally, many scholars have dismissed the prediction as wild speculation. But Kubrick saw in *Zarathustra* the vision of a true prophet and looked on the future of technology as the culmination of that vision.[3] His *2001* maps the same Nietzschean pre- and posthuman stages, beginning with ape-men, proceeding through humanity, and finally culminating in a new (beyond human) form, the "Star Child," a planet-sized superintelligent fetus. Almost four decades later, this remarkable image continues to overwhelm audiences as one of the most sublime visions in all of cinema. Yet, in the *next* four decades, that vision may itself move out of the realm of science fiction and into the realm of "science fact." According to some contemporary philosophers of artificial intelligence—such as Ray Kurzweil and Hans Moravec—a vision like Kubrick's (and Nietzsche's) may soon come to pass. In fact, Kurzweil claims that around 2045 we will witness a new kind of "birth" called the "singularity," which will mark the beginning of a new race of superintelligent beings that Moravec aptly calls the "mind children." As these mind children, or star children, come into being, questions will arise about whether we are in control of them. And once they are born, is it possible, as Nietzsche seems to intimate, that all humanity will be left behind?

Synopsis of the Film

The film *2001* begins silently, on the plains four million years ago, with "The Dawn of Man." A cave is inhabited by a group of apelike creatures. One morning, they awake to find standing outside the cave a massive black monolith. The viewer knows that it has been placed there by aliens to initiate the apelike creatures' development into humans. Almost immediately, we see the effects take hold as one ape curiously plays with a skeleton, detaches a bone, and suddenly realizes that this bone can serve as a tool or a weapon, allowing him to bludgeon a rival ape to death. The implication here is that knowledge, technology, evolution, and advanced forms of violence are all intertwined. The next scene is one of the most famous in all cinematic history, and it is set to Richard Strauss's *Also Sprach Zarathustra* (1896), also written as a tribute to Nietzsche's masterwork: "I wished to convey by means of music an idea of the development of the human race from its origin, through the various phases of its development, religious and scientific, up to Nietzsche's idea of the superman. The whole symphonic poem is intended as a[n] homage to Nietzsche's genius, which found its greatest expression in his book *Thus Spake Zarathustra*."[4]

Beautifully, perfectly, Kubrick moves to slow motion, and the triumphant ape throws its bone-hammer into the sky. Then, in one montage cut, we move four million years into the future, and the white bone is transformed into a white bone-shaped ship floating through space. From prehistory to the space age, we move from the end of one stage of evolution to the end of another stage—from the last moments of the ape-humans to the last moments of humanity.

By this point, we have reached the upper limit of human consciousness, having gone as far as we can with the human brain. So we now proceed with a powerful form of artificial intelligence: the HAL 9000 (voice by Douglas Rain), which is the brain of the spaceship *Discovery* that carries the astronauts Dave Bowman (Keir Dullea) and Frank Poole (Gary Lockwood). HAL is unlike any computer to date because he is more than capable of passing the Turing test (named after Alan Turing, who developed the test to determine whether a computer is "conscious"). A version of this test is given quite explicitly in the film when a television journalist from earth interviews HAL. He asks HAL a series of questions, hoping to see him as merely a machine rather than as a person. Yet the interviewer cannot tell the difference between HAL and a brilliant human being. In fact, HAL appears cordial, relaxed, bright, warm—even proud of never having made a mistake.

For all HAL's computational brilliance and seeming humanity, he ultimately turns on the crew, killing all but Bowman. HAL believes that this action is essential to the completion of the mission (the real purpose of which neither Bowman nor Poole knows). Now, Bowman must square off with HAL in a battle of wits that Bowman wins by crawling into HAL's brain and lobotomizing him down to the level of a babbling three-year-old. With HAL's mind and will completely out of the way, Bowman can at last access the secret files about the mission, which are buried at the base of HAL's brain.

Upon learning the truth about the mission, Bowman takes control of the ship and heads straight into the monolith, passing through it like a star gate. The next series of shots takes several minutes and involves a fantastic montage of kaleidoscopic and hallucinogenic images of shifting colors and noise and a flight over land and sea. Suddenly it stops, and Bowman finds himself in an elegant hotel room, where we see him pass through several stages of aging. In the last stage of his life as a man, lying on his deathbed in the same hotel, Bowman looks up and sees at the foot of the bed a new monolith. Now Bowman (like the ape with the bone) is prepared for the final transformation. Once again, Strauss's *Zarathustra* beats in the background as a newly born superintelligent Star Child turns gently to look at us.

The Age of Nihilism

The entire process leading toward this Star Child is designed and directed by a hidden race of aliens. But we discover them (indirectly) when we discover, beneath the surface of the moon, a massive black monolith that appears to have been "deliberately buried." This human discovery is Kubrick's analogue to Nietzsche's idea of the death of God, when modern science casts all religion into doubt. Nietzsche develops this idea in *Zarathustra* and in *The Gay Science*, where a prototype Zarathustra called the "madman" says, "'Whither is God?' . . . 'I shall tell you. *We have killed him*—you and I. All of us are his murderers.'" By "you and I," Nietzsche means the modern age of the Enlightenment, secularism, and science. But the real turning point is probably Galileo: "What did we do when we unchained this earth from its sun?" continues the madman. We now stray "through an infinite nothing" (and all the coldness of space).[5]

The real problem here is that along with the old cosmology, we have also lost the religious foundation for all our values—values that, like ourselves, seem to float hopelessly in the abyss. This is the beginning of the age of nihilism, marked by three specific losses. First, we lose our normative account of the past, the view that God created us for a purpose. Instead, now everything appears contingent, evolutionary. Second, we also lose our sense of normative groundwork in the present because there is no God-given "right" or "wrong" to guide our daily decisions. Finally, we lose our teleological end. Our future can no longer be said to lie in heaven, a messiah, or resurrection.

Recognizing this threefold loss, the madman and Zarathustra diagnose our age of nihilism and then present the necessary antidote. As the madman puts it, "How shall we, the murderers of all murderers, comfort ourselves? . . . Is not the greatness of this deed too great for us? Must not we ourselves become gods simply to seem worthy of it?"[6] In other words, we must transfer all the sublime and superhuman power of the God of the next world back into *this* world, and we must *will* by ourselves the creation of an overman. But, in the process, our reach should not exceed our grasp. That is, we should not will another God. As Zarathustra puts it, "God is a conjecture; but I desire that your conjectures should not reach beyond your creative will. Could you *create* a god? Then do not speak to me of any gods. But you could well create the overman."[7] Similarly, Kubrick signals a new loss of faith in the old story and the old ideals, just as Galileo and modernity called religion into doubt. In *2001,* the discovery of the moon monolith seals the case against religion, because we now *know* that God did not create us; we know who our creators and designers really are—namely, the aliens.

Moreover, with this discovery of our true nature and our true creators comes a political cover-up, in the same way that Galileo's new science of the planets triggered a suppression of the truth. Likely, it was a combination of this Galileo affair and the cover-up at Roswell, New Mexico, in 1947—where an alien spaceship allegedly crashed—that prompted Kubrick's own version of a political cover-up of a new scientific discovery involving both planets and aliens (that is, a monolith buried on the moon).[8] Kubrick's cover-up is a "noble lie" in Plato's sense from the *Republic:* the elite intellectuals must create and maintain a religiously based creation myth to keep people secure and stable. In *2001*, this takes the form of the government keeping secret the buried monolith, which is proof positive of the existence of aliens who seeded the earth, directed our evolution, and are likely directing it still.

The Higher Men

After establishing the death of God, Kubrick appropriately moves to the next stage of evolution in *Zarathustra*—namely, the higher men, who, according to Nietzsche, accept the death of God.[9] In fact, having overcome the religious noble lie, Kubrick's higher men feel incredibly liberated and are now confident that they can create a new kind of society—one entirely without lies. This is the Enlightenment, a new project that will free the rest of humanity from the darkness of the Middle Ages. And the higher men are the modern philosophers, such as René Descartes and Immanuel Kant, who will guide the way.

In developing their new society, however, they have one rather large problem. A gaping moral void is left after the exposure of the noble lie—the same void the madman and Zarathustra diagnose as the age of nihilism. But the higher men understand what the madman and Zarathustra mean about becoming gods in order to be worthy of our deicide. And they are going to try to do just that (even though, as I point out later, they do not succeed). So, in place of God, they put the human mind and make that the new foundation of morality and culture. And in place of religion's ascent into heaven, they take all our forward-looking spirit and transfer it back to this world in the form of an enlightened, globalized, cosmopolitan, scientific, individualistic, and technological society.

Like Nietzsche, Kubrick also separates the higher men from the "herd" (the rest of the population) and, indeed, places them quite literally "higher" up in space. Kubrick's higher men are the astronauts: Dave Bowman, Frank Poole, and Dr. Heywood R. Floyd (William Sylvester). And here, Kubrick provides an interesting twist on Nietzsche's view. In Nietzsche, the higher men must leave behind the otherworldliness of God in heaven and become masters of the earth. But in Kubrick, the higher men leave behind the earth and become masters of the otherworldly heavens, essentially taking God's place among the stars. In spite of this twist, however, it is important to point out that Kubrick's higher men are still very much like Nietzsche's, insofar as they represent the Enlightenment's values and the view of humanity as a replacement for God. The astronauts are clearly committed to democracy, science, and technology. And indeed, these higher men are impressive; they are intelligent, brave, and strong—certainly the best humanity has to offer, in Kubrick's vision, just as in Nietzsche's.

The Last Man and the Tightrope Walker

Yet ultimately, the higher men are doomed in both Nietzsche and Kubrick. They are doomed to become what Nietzsche calls the "last men." As Gilles Deleuze puts it in *Pure Immanence*: "Following the higher men there arises the last man, the one who says: all is vain, better to fade away passively!"[10] In other words, the once noble and brave higher men who fought and stood for humanistic values gradually settle into their new global, democratic, popular culture and eventually get tired and lazy. This is not to say that the higher man project did not work—certainly it did for a while, and it was essential for replacing religion with reason—but in the end, the higher man project was inadequate to replace the religious teleology of otherworldly bliss, immortality, and near omniscience. Keep in mind that the ultimate goal of the higher men—really, the goal of the Enlightenment—was merely the liberation of humanity from the old noble lie and the establishment of a secular society. But this goal is second rate at best, for once it has been achieved, according to Nietzsche, there is nowhere left to go and nothing left to hope for. And after enough time passes, one ends up with the finished product: Nietzsche's "most contemptible" last man. He is a marketplace man without any higher ideal. He lives solely for his sensuous appetites, his "little pleasure for the day and [his] little pleasure for the night."[11]

Basically, this is where we are now in secular culture with democratic capitalism—and as bad as it is, it is, in fact, going to get worse. According to Nietzsche, we have one more stage of descent to go before the philosophical vision of the overman can truly take hold of our minds. As Deleuze puts it, "Beyond the last man, then, there is still *the man who wants to die.* And at this moment the completion of nihilism (midnight), everything is ready—ready for a transmutation."[12] This last stage before the overman is signaled by the character in *Zarathustra* of the tightrope walker: he performs a high-wire act for the people of the marketplace but falls to the ground. Seeing him there, Zarathustra goes to him and cares for him. The tightrope walker is ready to die; he even wants to die. But, as he tells Zarathustra, he is afraid of going to hell and meeting the devil. Zarathustra recognizes that the tightrope walker is still in the last throes of the old noble lie. Perhaps the tightrope walker no longer hopes for heaven, but there is a lingering fear of the afterlife that occurs right at the moment of death. So, Zarathustra tells him plainly, "there is no devil and no hell." Hearing this from Zarathustra, the tightrope walker is at once appeased, as though he already knew this but needed to hear it again. He says, "If you speak the truth . . . I lose nothing when I lose my life." Now, all the tightrope walker desires is death because "he loses nothing if he loses his life." He has nothing left to live for anyway.[13]

In *Zarathustra,* the rope in the tightrope sequence is a symbol of humanity. As Nietzsche puts it, "Man is a rope, tied between beast and overman—a dangerous across, a dangerous on-the-way, a dangerous looking back, a dangerous shuddering and stopping."[14] So, when the tightrope walker falls to his death and wants to die, this really means that humanity itself is descending, as a consequence of the nihilism that began with the death of God. And that descent, which proceeds through the stage of the last man, ultimately results in the same attitude of the dying tightrope walker: having nothing left to live for, we simply give up and wish for death.

The Hotel Sequence

Kubrick clearly appropriates these two Nietzschean ideas of the last man and the tightrope walker. Ultimately, Poole, too, falls to his death, because HAL disconnects the rope and thus all his life support. Moreover, in terms of Kubrick's use of Nietzsche's text, Bowman goes to the disconnected Poole in a space pod, picks him up with mechanical arms, and carries him back through space—very much like Zarathustra, who picks up the tightrope walker's dead body and carries it over his shoulder.

The point about Bowman being a neo-Zarathustra character, however, should not be taken too far. His role can be seen more explicitly as that of the higher man who descends into the stage of the last man.[15] We see this role especially after Bowman has passed through the monolith star gate and then suddenly appears in a comfortable hotel room. Like Nietzsche's last man, Bowman is no longer a higher man. His government-issued spacesuit has been transformed into an evening robe. He no longer eats the prepackaged food on the *Discovery,* intended only to keep him healthy and focused on his mission. Rather, he enjoys fine cuisine and wine. He is descending into decadence and enjoying, as the last man does, his "little pleasure for the day and [his] little pleasure for the night." He lives in isolation from the rest of humanity and is indeed quite literally the "last man" in space (the rest of the crew having been murdered by HAL).

Bowman continues this descent of the last man until, finally, he is a very old man lying on his deathbed, wanting to give in to death, just like the tightrope walker. Of course, there is a temptation not to conceive of Bowman as the tightrope walker because Poole is so clearly this character, but it is important to keep in mind that Bowman *also* performs a tightrope walk. He journeys out through space to retrieve Poole and then must make an additional and extremely treacherous spacewalk from the pod, through the bay doors, across an abyss. This is a potentially fatal maneuver because he has no life support, having been cut off from the *Discovery* by HAL. Indeed, both Poole and Bowman begin as higher men and become tightrope walkers (Poole, however, does not pass through the last man stage).[16]

Finally, in a scene taken almost directly out of Nietzsche, we see the dying Bowman look up to find the final black monolith standing over him, in exactly the same way Zarathustra emerges at the moment of the tightrope walker's death to stand over him. The monolith has come to transform Bowman into the Star Child, just as Zarathustra has come to humanity to prepare us to go forward into the next stage of the overman. In both *Zarathustra* and *2001,* it is only after humanity completes its descent into darkness that we can move onto another plane of existence. We must first see the ultimate limit of the project of the higher men before a new form of existence is possible, even if only in principle. We must watch one ideal fail completely before another can be fully grasped and achieved.

Motivation and Design

In Nietzsche, the movement beyond the last man to the overman requires a fourfold recognition: (1) we cannot stay as we are and, if left to our own devices, we will continue to decline; (2) we cannot go back to the religion of the Middle Ages, because the myth has been debunked; (3) we can only go forward; and (4) we have no ideal to guide us forward, since God is dead: "the one goal is lacking. Humanity still has no goal."[17] All other ideals of humanism (for example, socialism) are powerless to solve the last man problem. So, as Zarathustra puts it, we must create a new ideal, and this is the overman: "The time has come for man to set himself a goal. The time has come for man to plant the seed of his *highest* hope."[18]

So, effectively, the motivation toward the overman is ethical, in two senses. Negatively, we want to overcome the problem of the last man; positively, we must create an ideal worthy of our aim. And Nietzsche's overman just might give us both. We would have all the old superhumanity (of religion) and none of the otherworldly immateriality, all the futuristic perfectionism and none of the superstitious metaphysics of rebirth in another world. It is the perfect substitute for what we lost: the same sublime ecstasy of the divine, newly transferred from the "next world" to this one, in the form of a new kind of superior being who will provide us with a substitute for nihilism. Of course, as already noted, Nietzsche provides little information about what the overman will look like. But it seems clear, at the very least, that the overman will be superintelligent compared with humans, specifically with regard to rationality, creativity, and the will to power—yet with none of the guilt and resentment that characterize humanity.

Here, however, there is a strong break between Nietzsche and Kubrick on the point about moral nihilism being a motivating factor for the push toward the overman. We are *not*, in *2001,* motivated by the death of God or its consequent last man. The death of God, the last man, and the tightrope walker certainly appear in the film, and they are clearly integral to the plot. But neither nihilism nor the last man as its consequence appears to motivate the coming to be of the Star Child. In other words, Kubrick's *2001,* in contrast to Nietzsche's *Zarathustra,* is not a story about moral nihilism at all. Rather, *2001* is about metaphysics and epistemology.

Metaphysically, the aliens have constructed everything, beginning with a massive black monolith that enhances the primitive brains of the apes. However, this direct influence quickly becomes indirect. Apparently, the aliens have designed us to become intelligent through technology; consequently, we become curious about anomalies such as the monoliths and the aliens themselves. In the final movement from Bowman to Star Child, these two forms of influence—indirect and direct—coalesce. Bowman is drawn (due to an alien design) to know the mind of HAL and to know the inner workings of the monolith. And he proceeds to complete his mission alone—even after his entire crew has been murdered—without permission or direction from earth. As he does so, the aliens and the monolith act directly on Bowman's mind and transform him into the Star Child.

The Singularity and the Mind Children

Both Nietzsche and Kubrick intend their respective visions to be deeply prophetic. And here, it is reasonable to ask whether Kubrick or Nietzsche might turn out to be right. Should we expect Nietzsche's overman or Kubrick's Star Child? I think perhaps we should, but not for the reasons Nietzsche and Kubrick give—that is, not necessarily because of moral nihilism or because of aliens directing evolution.

Of course, Nietzsche is quite right in his diagnosis of the age of nihilism, and much of popular culture certainly resembles the stage of the last man. But it seems rather implausible that a new form of being will appear on the horizon—out of the blue, or even as motivated by problems of the last man—and render humanity as primitive as the apes are to us, as Nietzsche predicts. A superior and brilliant man or woman is hardly genetically out of the question—and may even be likely. But this would not count as a *new kind* of being. Moreover, although humanity may be in a last man stage, Nietzsche's view of our descent into absolute darkness may be a little overstated. It seems just as likely that we will continue to develop toward the modern (higher man) ideal of democratic cosmopolitanism, perhaps becoming increasingly stable and maybe even a little happier.

Kubrick's account of our next stage is a little far-fetched as well. Like Nietzsche's overman, it is also in the realm of logical possibility, but it does not appear to be the way things are going. We may have discovered a spaceship at Roswell, and there are certainly many UFO sightings around the world. But these facts, taken together, do not add up to the conclusion that an alien race has been guiding our entire evolutionary process from early primates toward a Star Child. That *may* be the case, but the scientific community certainly has not even hinted at this picture. So, at this point, there is little reason to accept this specific view.

Kubrick's view of artificial intelligence, however, is an entirely different story. HAL, though not an overman or a supermind, is certainly superior to humans in intelligence, at least in some ways. It is true that Bowman outwits HAL, but the idea of a HAL-type entity that is more intelligent than humans is a real possibility for our species. In our highly technological society, we have already dedicated great resources and intellectual power toward the pursuit of a mind such as HAL's. But we do not do this out of an aching nihilistic religious void, nor do we do this because aliens are guiding us. Rather, we do it because our minds are intrinsically bound up with technology. Tool use marks the ascent of consciousness from our early primate beginnings to our current state of humanity, just as Kubrick portrays it—only without the monoliths' influence.

In fact, we are not really *that* far away from HAL at the moment. No computer or artificially intelligent personality can pass the Turing test like HAL can, and surely none is as charismatic. But HAL's chess ability is already within our reach. Remember, Poole and HAL play a friendly game of chess, and HAL wins (which is a foreshadowing of HAL's murder of Poole). At the time of the film's release, such a game was mere fiction. In 1968 computers were more theory than practice, more science fiction than household reality. But of course, everything changed in 1989 when a computer named Deep Blue beat world champion Gary Kasparov in a game of chess. Everyone was shocked—everyone, that is, except for Ray Kurzweil, who had predicted precisely such an event a decade earlier (virtually to the date). Insiders had long known about Kurzweil's mysterious and uncanny powers of prediction, but this was simply off the charts. So, everyone started listening.

What Kurzweil was doing was simply extrapolating from Moore's law, which states, in general terms, that computer power doubles about every eighteen months. This law works on a nonlinear curve, sort of like a bent knee. Presently, we are just rounding the bend of the knee, but once we round that bend, Moore's law will attain a kind of "racing ahead" feel, and technology will evolve very quickly. This law governs virtually everything that occurs in computer technology today, and because computer technology governs much of the evolution of science, the scientific community also pays close attention. Indeed, the ability to know the future of the computer industry attracts many bright young minds today. But no one is better at it than Kurzweil. Virtually the entire computer community is in agreement on this.[19]

Given Kurzweil's impressive success in predicting the future, it is not surprising that the high-tech community is swarming around his most recent statement about what Moore's law will do next. In his book *The Singularity Is Near: When Humans Transcend Biology*, Kurzweil claims that we are heading for a major revolutionary advance in technology—one that begins with a massive-scale birth (on a par with *2001*'s birth) and results in an entirely new kind of child. As Kurzweil puts it, "I set the date for the Singularity—representing a profound and disruptive transformation in human capability—as 2045. The nonbiological intelligence created in that year will be *one billion* times more powerful than all human intelligence today."[20] Yes, that is correct: an intelligence one billion times the sum of all human brains today. The question quite naturally arises: could this be Kubrick's Star Child?

Some will no doubt cast this prediction aside as too outrageous or simply crazy. But similar things were said about airplanes, cloning, computers, the Internet, space travel, nanotechnology, the Hubble telescope, and robots that can run like humans and drive cars—all of which are part of our common language today. Others will insist that the possibility of artificial intelligence is no different from any previous form of technology; we have never made a machine that is truly conscious, and we probably never will, because consciousness simply is not machine based. But, as it is often countered, the onus is on the critics to establish why the presence of protein and fat (in our brains) is a necessary, and not merely sufficient, condition for consciousness.[21] And even if we do require fat and protein today (in the short run), no one really doubts that nanotechnology will eventually be used *within* human brains to enhance them well beyond their present power. This enhancement will take place primarily through what are called "assemblers": nanotechnological robots with tiny arms capable of reorganizing the positions of atoms—placing them in alternative arrangements. And because everything we see around us is built of atoms, in theory, assemblers can rearrange anything to become anything else: apples can become oranges, and perhaps our minds can be enhanced as well.

This vision of the future can be seen as quite Nietzschean, especially in the writings of Hans Moravec, who, as it turns out, was later to become a favorite author of Kubrick's. In his books *Mind Children* and *Robot: Mere Machine to Transcendent Mind*, Moravec—also relying on Moore's law—describes the emergence of a whole new kind of "child" (not unlike Kubrick's Star Child). Indeed, Moravec claims that there will be an entirely new *race* of "mind children."[22] The mind children will be "our" children in four distinct ways. First, they will be beings created by us, meaning that we will "give birth" to them in the form of the singularity.

Second, the mind children will bear many marks of their lineage. That is, for all their uniqueness, they will not be entirely alien to us. Like the Star Child, the mind children will possess cognitive powers well beyond ours, but we will also recognize ourselves in them, just as we recognize ourselves in the massive Star Child, with its human eyes and its human fetal shape. As Moravec puts it, "I consider these future machines our progeny, 'mind children' built in our image and likeness, ourselves in more potent form."[23] Here, a key difference with Kubrick's Star Child should be pointed out. The Star Child is made to look like us because the aliens direct it. So, in effect, the aliens made us first in their image and then directed us to become like them, in a greater (perhaps more approximate) image of the aliens them-selves. In contrast, Moravec's mind children are like us not because of aliens but because we will make them in our image.

Third, the mind children represent our greatest reasonable hope for a better future: "Like biological children of previous generations, they will embody humanity's best chance for a long-term future."[24] Here, Moravec means that because the mind children are not protein based, they will have significant advantages over all previous human beings; they will not be mortal, nor will they be fundamentally limited in intelligence, as we are. Indeed, they will not even be confined to earth and will likely move off the planet into space to colonize other galaxies as their intelligence grows.[25] "Unleashed from the plodding pace of biological evolution," writes Moravec, "the children of our minds will be free to grow to confront immense and fundamental challenges in the larger universe."[26]

Fourth, and connected to point three, we will also live on in the mind children. But note that this kind of "immortality" is not merely metaphori-cal, like a parent living on through his or her child or someone becoming immortal through his or her work. And it is not the kind of immortality (if we may call it that) found in Nietzsche's *Zarathustra* either: "what can be loved in man is that he is an *overture* and a *going under*."[27] In Nietzsche's view, humanity's ultimate decline is a necessary stage for a greater end, and the overman will remember us as his parents. In Moravec, by contrast, the point is literal. We are *literally* going to live on in the mind children by fusing our now-biological brains with them.[28] We will actually pass into a new and higher form, in much the same way that Bowman becomes the Star Child.

This is what is known as "posthumanity," a state in which we are no longer, strictly speaking, human: we are beyond human—immortal, superintelligent, and not confined to earth.

Perhaps, then, Kubrick's vision (and Nietzsche's) is not as far off as some may think. In fact, in light of current research into the field of artificial intelligence, Kubrick and Nietzsche might actually be as prophetic as they thought they were. An overman does appear to be on the horizon who may indeed render the history of humanity primitive and apelike. This new stage of the child, moreover, will mark the end of death and a new kind of supermind, precisely in the way that Nietzsche and Kubrick claim—though perhaps not for any of the reasons they give.

Aliens and Monoliths

A final question presents itself, considering the possibility that Kubrick's vision may come to pass. Why does Kubrick—a man acutely aware of the future of technology—use the idea of aliens as the driving force behind human evolution? Of course, some will claim that because we do not actually see the aliens in the film, and because the monoliths have a kind of dark blankness about them (that is, they are not personified), the monoliths may represent human technology itself. After all, the scene of the ape-humans making an evolutionary leap forward with the discovery of tools is not so difficult to imagine being true *without* the aliens and monoliths. But if Kubrick's monoliths (and the aliens controlling them) are merely metaphors for human technology and innovation, what about the moon monolith being *deliberately* buried? Who else would have been able to bury it in outer space but aliens? The interpretation of the monoliths as technology also raises questions about why HAL, the most advanced form of human technology to date, must ultimately be destroyed in order for humanity to develop *technologically* into the Star Child. Indeed, it seems clear that Kubrick intended for nonhuman beings to be running the show from behind the scenes. And the plot simply becomes untenable without interpreting the cause of the monoliths and our future development as alien life.

And yet it also seems likely that Kubrick was aware that alien designers would not be necessary for future advances toward an overman-like future—assuming that HAL is not the end of the line of technology in *2001* or in real life. So, there is an oddity about *2001,* interpreted in light of Nietzsche's *Zarathustra* (on which Kubrick obviously based his film). Aliens may make for a better science fiction epic, but being "replacement gods" (as we may call them), they obscure what is perhaps the most fundamental insight in *Zarathustra*. There is, of course, much in Nietzsche that can be safely reinterpreted to capture the essence of his philosophical vision in space, but perhaps the death of God is not one of them. Now, as noted earlier, Kubrick *does* use his own version of the death of God (a death also achieved through science) when the moon monolith is discovered. But in an age in which the idea of God is not so widely held—certainly compared with the Middle Ages—why does Kubrick replace the old idea of a designer with a new one? The aliens may not be omniscient and omnipotent, but Kubrick gives them many of the properties of the old worldview. They are not only designers but also creators, guiding their created designs toward a new and higher form of being; they are also, like God, quite hidden. Indeed, Kubrick presents them beautifully by *not* presenting them—by presenting only the monoliths and their effects, giving *2001* an eerie, mysterious feeling. But the introduction of a new kind of extraterrestrial god must, ultimately, render Kubrick's higher men, last man, and tightrope walker conceptually thin reflections of the Nietzschean personas on which they are so clearly based.

Notes

I am grateful to Elizabeth F. Cooke and Chris Pliatska for conversations and comments on this essay and to Elizabeth Cooke for reading and commenting on it.

1. Screenplay by Stanley Kubrick and Arthur C. Clarke. Clarke's original story was written in 1948 and titled "The Sentinel."

2. Here, I am using "apes" because that is what Nietzsche uses. Of course, biologists today inform us that the apes are our cousins rather than our great-grandparents. We did not descend from them.

3. Kubrick considered the computer "one of man's most beautiful inventions." This quotation is cited by Andrew Bailey, "A Clockwork Utopia," *Rolling Stone,* January 20, 1972, 16, and Alison Castle, "Stanley Kubrick's A.I.," in *The Stanley Kubrick Archives* (made in cooperation with Jan Harlan, Christiane Kubrick, and the Stanley Kubrick estate), ed. Alison Castle (Los Angeles: Taschen, 2005), 517. In 1971 Kubrick told Alexander Walker: "One of the fascinating questions that arises envisioning computers more intelligent than men is at what point machine intelligence deserves the same considerations as biological intelligence. . . . You could be tempted to ask yourself in what way is machine intelligence any less sacrosanct than biological intelligence, and it might be difficult to arrive at an answer flattering to biological intelligence." Alexander

Walker, *Stanley Kubrick, Director* (New York: W. W. Norton, 2000), 32; also cited in Castle, "Stanley Kubrick's A.I.," 504.

4. Richard Strauss, program for *Also Sprach Zarathustra,* Op. 30 (1896), in Bernard Jacobson's essay "Also Sprach Zarathustra" for the American Symphony Orchestra, http://www.americansymphony.org/dialogues_extensions/99_2000season/2000_03_08/strauss.cf (accessed October 30, 2005).

5. Friedrich Nietzsche, *The Gay Science,* trans. Josefine Nauckhoff, ed. Bernard Williams (Cambridge: Cambridge University Press, 2001), 119–20.

6. Ibid., 120. See also Friedrich Nietzsche, *Thus Spoke Zarathustra: A Book for None and All,* trans. Walter Kaufmann (New York: Modern Library, 1995), 13. One of the first mentions of this idea appears in Hegel's *Phenomenology,* just before the final section on Absolute Mind: here we have "the painful feeling of the Unhappy Consciousness that *God himself is dead"* (G. W. F. Hegel, *Phenomenology of Spirit,* trans. A. V. Miller [New York: Oxford University Press, 1977], 476). See also Nietzsche's *Zarathustra:* "God is dead; God died of his pity for man" (90); and "'I recognize you well,' he said in a voice of bronze; '*you are the murderer of God!* Let me go. You could not bear him who saw you—who always saw you through and through, you ugliest man! You took revenge on your witness!'" (264).

7. Nietzsche, *Zarathustra,* 84.

8. In terms of the Roswell cover-up, there are several possible explanations. For example, from a political perspective, if aliens *were* discovered, suppressing the truth might be seen as necessary for political stability and the protection of certain technological secrets—which was crucial in the post–World War II era, just as we were entering the cold war. And if aliens *were not* discovered, the rumor could serve to cover up something else that needed to be hidden. Colonel Philip J. Corso, a member of President Eisenhower's National Security Council and head of the Foreign Technology Desk at the U.S. Army's Research and Development Department, allegedly saw everything. In his *The Day after Roswell* (New York: Pocket Books, 1997), Corso relies on personal experience and materials recently declassified through the Freedom of Information Act to explain in detail how an alien spaceship *did* crash; he claims that many saw it and that there was a great deal of alien technology onboard that we continue to use.

9. Leonard Wheat also makes this point about Bowman and Poole being higher men in his book *Kubrick's 2001: A Triple Allegory* (Lanham, Md.: Scarecrow Press, 2000). Wheat's basic thesis is that there are three allegories at work in the film: (1) the allegory of Nietzsche's *Zarathustra,* (2) the allegory of Homer's *Odyssey,* and (3) the allegory of human-computer fusion as it is found in Arthur C. Clarke (who collaborated with Kubrick on the film). Wheat's analysis of the relation between *2001* and *Zarathustra* is perhaps the best in the literature.

10. Gilles Deleuze, *Pure Immanence: Essays on a Life,* trans. Anne Boyman (New York: Zone Books, 2001), 82. Deleuze also notes, "the distinction between the last man

and the man who wants to die is fundamental in Nietzsche's philosophy: in *Zarathustra*"
(ibid., 101 n. 8).

11. Nietzsche, *Zarathustra*, 17, 18.

12. Deleuze, *Pure Immanence*, 82.

13. Nietzsche, *Zarathustra*, 20.

14. Ibid., 14.

15. As noted earlier, Wheat and I agree on Bowman and Poole being the higher men,
but we part ways on the idea of the last man and his relation to the tightrope walker, a
difference that can be localized in the hotel sequence near the end of *2001*. Wheat's take
does not seem to include the last man: "The five Bowmans in the hotel room (just three
or four Bowmans in some instances) collectively symbolize (1) the aging (maturation)
and birth of the fetus, (2) cell division (first four Bowmans), (3) the five stages of evolution (worm, ape, lower man, higher man, and overman), (4) Zarathustra's parable of the
shepherd, the black serpent, and the light-surrounded being (last three Bowmans only),
and (5) Zarathustra's three metamorphoses (camel, lion, and child) metaphor (last three
Bowmans)" (Wheat, *Kubrick's* 2001, 155). There is, I admit, a remarkable collection of
symbols drawn from *Zarathustra*—with references to characters such as the shepherd,
the serpent, the lion, the camel, and many others. But I tend to see this sequence as the
descent of the higher man into the last man. The last man does not appear to play a
strong role in Wheat's analysis, even though it is one of the most important characters
in both *Zarathustra* and *2001*.

16. In making the Poole–tightrope walker connection, Wheat supports his view by
using what he calls a "90% anagram." He suggests that we can rearrange the last nine
of the ten letters of "[F]rank Poole," and get "[W]alk on rope" (Wheat, *Kubrick's* 2001,
95). By dropping the *F* and adding a *W*, we can get what we want: namely, something
Nietzsche almost says, in a literary form that does not really exist.

17. Nietzsche, *Zarathustra*, 60.

18. Ibid., 17; emphasis added.

19. Bill Gates is quoted on the dust jacket blurb for Ray Kurzweil's *The Singularity
Is Near: When Humans Transcend Biology* (New York: Viking, 2005): "Ray Kurzweil is
the best person I know at predicting the future of artificial intelligence. His intriguing
new book envisions a future in which information technologies have advanced so far
and fast that they enable humanity to transcend its biological limitations—transforming
our lives in ways we can't yet imagine."

20. Kurzweil, *The Singularity Is Near*, 136. Furthermore, even President George
W. Bush's Bioethics Commission recognizes the coming changes. See, for example,
Francis Fukuyama, *Our Posthuman Future: Consequences of the Biotechnology Revolution* (New York: Farrar, Straus and Giroux, 2002), and Leon Kass, *Life, Liberty, and
the Defense of Dignity: The Challenge for Bioethics* (San Francisco: Encounter Books,
2002). Both warn about the potential dangers of going forward into posthuman-

ity. Other groups, more sympathetic to the transition, are also busy planning for posthumanity. These include the Extropians, led by Max More and Natasha Vita More (www.extropy.org), and the World Transhumanist Association, led by Nick Bostrom out of Oxford University (www.transhumanism.org/index.php/WTA/index/). These pro-posthuman groups are, of course, quite aware of the Nietzschean philosophical roots of their ideas. Max More makes this point explicitly and claims that the basic transhumanist-posthumanist philosophy derives from Nietzsche's vision in *Thus Spoke Zarathustra*. As More puts it, "I resonate to Nietzsche's declaration that 'Man is a rope, fastened between animal and overman—a rope over an abyss. . . . What is great in man is that he is a bridge and not a goal." Further on, More continues, "*A bridge, not a goal*. That nicely summarizes a transhumanist perspective" (Max More, "Max More and Kurzweil on the Singularity," http://www.kurzweilai.net/meme/frame.html?m=1). See also Ray Kurzweil, *Are We Spiritual Machines? Ray Kurzweil vs. the Critics of Strong A.I.*, ed. Jay W. Richards (Seattle: Discovery Institute, 2002). For a critique of artificial intelligence, see Hubert Dreyfus, *What Computers* Still *Can't Do: A Critique of Artificial Reason* (Cambridge, Mass.: MIT Press, 1993).

21. As Dr. Chandra (Bob Balaban) puts it aptly in *2001*'s sequel, *2010: The Year We Make Contact* (Peter Hyams, 1984): "Whether we are based on carbon or silicon makes no fundamental difference. We should each be treated with appropriate respect."

22. Hans Moravec, *Mind Children: The Future of Robot and Human Intelligence* (Cambridge, Mass.: Harvard University Press, 1988).

23. Hans Moravec, *Robot: Mere Machine to Transcendent Mind* (New York: Oxford University Press, 1999), 13.

24. Ibid. Kubrick could not have read Moravec's *Mind Children* before he made *2001*, but it is clear that *Mind Children* was an important text for Kubrick when he was writing *A.I.: Artificial Intelligence*. For example, Kubrick highlighted this sentence in his own copy of Moravec's *Mind Children*: "Complex robots will sometimes get into trouble on their own initiative" (see Castle, "Stanley Kubrick's A.I.," 507). One can certainly see the relevance of that line to *A.I.*'s David (Haley Joel Osment) and Gigolo Joe (Jude Law), who get into quite a bit of trouble on their own initiative.

25. Moravec, *Robot*, 13–14.

26. Moravec, *Mind Children*, 1.

27. Nietzsche, *Zarathustra*, 15.

28. Kurzweil (*The Singularity Is Near*, 375) touches on this subject in the following dialogue with Bill Gates:

> RAY: Once we saturate the matter and energy in the universe with intelligence, it will "wake up," be conscious, and sublimely intelligent. That's about as close to God as I can imagine.
>
> BILL: That's going to be silicon intelligence, not biological intelligence.
>
> RAY: Well, yes, we're going to transcend biological intelligence. We'll merge

with it first, but ultimately the nonbiological portion of our intelligence will predominate. By the way, it's not likely to be silicon, but something like carbon nanotubes.

In addition, according to Kurzweil, we will need a new form of religion: "Yes, well, we need a new religion. A principal role of religion has been to rationalize death, since up until just now there was little else constructive we could do about it" (ibid., 374).

Filmography

Flying Padre (1951; nonfeature, 8½ minutes)
Day of the Fight (1951; nonfeature, 16 minutes)
The Seafarers (1953; nonfeature, 30 minutes)
Fear and Desire (1953; first feature-length film, 68 minutes)
Killer's Kiss (1955)
The Killing (1956)
Paths of Glory (1957)
Spartacus (1960)
Lolita (1962)
Dr. Strangelove, or: How I Learned to Stop Worrying and Love the Bomb (1964)
2001: A Space Odyssey (1968)
A Clockwork Orange (1971)
Barry Lyndon (1975)
The Shining (1980)
Full Metal Jacket (1987)
Eyes Wide Shut (1999)
A.I.: Artificial Intelligence (2001; completed by Steven Spielberg)

Contributors

JEROLD J. ABRAMS is assistant professor of philosophy at Creighton University in Omaha, Nebraska. His essays have appeared in the journals *Modern Schoolman, Philosophy Today, Human Studies,* and *Transactions of the Charles S. Peirce Society* and the volumes *James Bond and Philosophy* (Open Court, forthcoming), *Woody Allen and Philosophy* (Open Court, 2004), *Star Wars and Philosophy* (Open Court, 2005), and *The Philosophy of Film Noir* (University Press of Kentucky, 2005).

GORDON BRADEN is Linden Kent Memorial Professor of English at the University of Virginia. He is the author of *Sixteenth-Century Poetry: An Annotated Anthology* (Blackwell, 2004), *Petrarchan Love and the Continental Renaissance* (Yale, 1999), *The Idea of the Renaissance* (with William Kerrigan; Johns Hopkins, 1989), *Renaissance Tragedy and the Senecan Tradition: Anger's Privilege* (Yale, 1985), and *The Classics and English Renaissance Poetry: Three Case Studies* (Yale, 1978).

MARK T. CONARD is assistant professor of philosophy at Marymount Manhattan College in New York City. He is the coeditor of *The Simpsons and Philosophy* (Open Court, 2001) and *Woody Allen and Philosophy* (Open Court, 2004) and the editor of *The Philosophy of Film Noir* (University Press of Kentucky, 2005). He is the author of "*Kill Bill: Volume 1,* Violence as Therapy," "*Kill Bill: Volume 2,* Mommy Kills Daddy," and "*Pulp Fiction:* The Sign of the Empty Symbol," all published on Metaphilm.com. He is also the author of the novel *Dark as Night* (UglyTown, 2004).

ELIZABETH F. COOKE is associate professor of philosophy at Creighton University. She researches in the areas of epistemology, philosophy of science, and American pragmatism. She is the author of "Be Mindful of the *Living* Force," in *Star Wars and Philosophy* (Open Court, 2005), "Rorty on Conversation as an Achievement of Hope" (*Contemporary Pragmatism,* 2004), "Peirce, Fallibilism, and the Science of Mathematics" (*Philosophia Mathematica,* 2003), and *Peirce's Pragmatic Theory of Inquiry: Fallibilism and Indeterminacy* (Continuum Press, forthcoming).

KEVIN S. DECKER is assistant professor of philosophy at Eastern Washington University near Spokane, Washington. He is the author of a number of articles on pragmatism, Continental philosophy, and social theory and is the coeditor (with Jason Eberl) of *Star Wars and Philosophy* (Open Court, 2005).

JASON T. EBERL is assistant professor of philosophy at Indiana University–Purdue University Indianapolis. He has published essays on metaphysics, bioethics, and medieval philosophy and has contributed to *Harry Potter and Philosophy* (Open Court, 2004), *Metallica and Philosophy* (Open Court, forthcoming), and *Bioethics through Film* (Johns Hopkins University Press, forthcoming). He is coeditor (with Kevin Decker) of *Star Wars and Philosophy* (Open Court, 2005).

KAREN D. HOFFMAN is assistant professor of philosophy at Hood College in Frederick, Maryland. Specializing in ethics, she has a particular interest in the topics of forgiveness and evil, as well as in philosophy of and in film. Her recent publications include "Evil and the Despairing Individual: A Kierkegaardian Account," in *Minding Evil* (Rodopi, 2005), and *"The Last Temptation of Christ* and *Bringing out the Dead*: Scorsese's Reluctant Saviors," in *The Philosophy of Martin Scorsese* (University Press of Kentucky, forthcoming).

JASON HOLT is assistant professor of communication at Acadia University in Nova Scotia. He is the author of *Blindsight and the Nature of Consciousness* (Broadview Press), which was short-listed for the 2005 Canadian Philosophical Association Book Prize, as well as a number of scholarly articles, two novels, and four books of poetry. His work in popular culture and philosophy includes essays on *Seinfeld, The Simpsons, The Matrix,* Woody Allen, film noir, and Alfred Hitchcock.

PATRICK MURRAY is professor of philosophy at Creighton University. He is the author of *Marx's Theory of Scientific Knowledge* and editor of *Reflections on Commercial Life.* His research interests center on the relationship between capitalism and modern philosophy and include the British empiricists, Hegel, Marx, and the Frankfurt School. With Jeanne Schuler, he is working on a series of articles on the dogmas of bourgeois philosophy and on *False Moves in Philosophy,* a study of the ways dualisms between the subjective and the objective breed skepticism.

R. BARTON PALMER is Calhoun Lemon professor of literature at Clemson University, where he also directs the Film Studies program. Among his many books on film and literary topics are *Hollywood's Dark Cinema: The American Film Noir* (2nd ed., University of Illinois Press, forthcoming), *Joel and Ethan Coen* (University of Illinois Press, 2004), *David Cronenberg* (University of Illinois Press, forthcoming), *Perspectives on Film Noir* (G. K. Hall, 1996), *After Hitchcock: Imitation/Influence/ Intertextuality* (with David Boyd; University of Texas Press, 2006), *Hollywood's Tennessee: Tennessee Williams on Screen* (with Robert Bray; University of Texas Press, forthcoming), and the two volumes *Nineteenth-* and *Twentieth-Century American Fiction on Screen* (Cambridge University Press, forthcoming). Along with Linda Badley, Palmer serves as general editor of the *Traditions in World Cinema* series (Edinburgh University Press).

CHRIS P. PLIATSKA is assistant professor of philosophy at Creighton University. His main scholarly interests are the metaphysics of autonomy and responsibility and issues related to the Holocaust and the nature of evil.

STEVEN M. SANDERS is emeritus professor of philosophy at Bridgewater State College in Massachusetts. He is the author, most recently, of "Film Noir and the Meaning of Life," in *The Philosophy of Film Noir* (University Press of Kentucky, 2006), and "Sunshine Noir: Postmodernism and *Miami Vice*," in *The Philosophy of Neo-Noir* (University Press of Kentucky, 2007), as well as forthcoming essays on the films of Alfred Hitchcock and Martin Scorsese. His work in progress includes volumes on television noir and science fiction feature films.

JEANNE SCHULER is associate professor of philosophy at Creighton University. She has published articles on the history of philosophy and critical theory, including works on David Hume, Immanuel Kant, G. W. F. Hegel, Karl Marx, Hannah Arendt, Iris Murdoch, and Jürgen Habermas. With Patrick Murray, she is working on a series of articles on the dogmas of bourgeois philosophy and on *False Moves in Philosophy*, a study of the ways dualisms between the subjective and the objective breed skepticism.

DANIEL SHAW is professor of philosophy and film at Lock Haven University of Pennsylvania and managing editor of the print journal *Film and Philosophy*. He has published articles on aesthetics, Continental philosophy, and the philosophy of film in such venues as the *Journal of Aesthetics and Art Criticism, International Philosophical Quarterly, Film and History, Literature/Film Quarterly*, and the *Film-Philosophy* (U.K.) and *Senses of Cinema* (Australia) Web sites. His anthology *Dark Thoughts: Philosophic Reflections on Cinematic Horror* (coedited with Steven Schneider) was published by Scarecrow Press in 2003.

Index

abduction, 4, 109, 116, 128n. 28;
    overcoded, 117; undercoded, 117, 120;
    creative, 117
absurd, the, v, 5, 9, 10, 13–15, 19–20, 30,
    135–36, 185, 197, 199; conventional
    versus philosophical, 1, 86–87
absurdity, 2, 135; of the human condition,
    192, 194
akrasia, 53–54
Aldiss, Brian, 233
Allen, Woody, 53
American Graffiti, 204, 212, 215, 217n. 12
anger, 15, 17, 63, 91, 174, 177, 213, 216
"Annabel Lee," 110–11
anonymous bodies, 104–5
Antonioni, Michelangelo, 221
appearances, 93, 96–97, 136, 137, 138
Apocalypse Now, 213, 231
Ariadne, 122
Aristotle, 45n. 2, 54, 94, 137, 150, 155, 156,
    157, 160, 244
artificial intelligence, 6, 134, 235, 239, 242,
    244–45, 246, 248–49, 257–58, 260,
    263n. 19, 264n. 20
Asphalt Jungle, The, 133, 151
authenticity, 51–54, 56, 148; problem of, 49
autonomy, 240

bad faith, 28, 51, 52, 144
banality, 136, 138, 139, 142
Baudrillard, Jean, 218n. 29
Beat generation, 134
Beatty, Warren, 150, 162n. 3
Beethoven, Ludwig van, 101, 145, 202
behaviorism, 240
being, 3, 35, 38, 46n. 16, 94, 95, 186, 233,
    242
Bergman, Ingmar, 221
Bettelheim, Bruno, 209

Bloom, Harold, 124
Body Heat, 215
Bogart, Humphrey, 150
Borges, Jorge Luis, 123, 129n. 48
bourgeois horizon, 136
Bowman, Dave, 100, 229, 233, 236–37,
    241–43, 249, 252–54, 256–57, 259
boxing, 3, 87, 90, 92
Brando, Marlon, 150
Bronson, Charles, 151
Burgess, Anthony, 221–23, 225

Cage, Nicolas, 150
Caine, Michael, 151
Camus, Albert, 2, 9, 13–15, 18–20, 22, 25,
    28–30, 135, 136, 186, 201
Canby, Vincent, 223
capitalism, 136–38, 146, 203, 215, 253
Carroll, Noël, 208, 211–13
Ciment, Michael, 45n. 6, 82n. 14, 190
Citizen Kane, 207, 210
Clarke, Arthur C., 99, 229, 236, 245,
    262n. 9
Clayton, Jack, 216
Cobb, Humphrey, 50, 201
cognitive science, 95
cold war, 2, 22, 23, 27, 133, 202, 262n. 8
Conan Doyle, Sir Arthur, 109, 112, 113,
    116, 123; "The Purloined Letter," 111;
    "The Red-Headed League," 112; "The
    Sign of the Four," 116; "A Study in
    Scarlet," 127nn. 20, 24
Conard, Mark T., 201
contingency, 20–21, 85, 92, 99, 106
Cook, David A., 208–9
Cook, Elisha, Jr., 152
Cooper, Duncan, 180n. 4
Cooper, Gary, 150
Coppola, Francis Ford, 213, 217n. 4